THE OTTOMAN
SLAVE TRADE AND
ITS SUPPRESSION:
1840-1890

Ehud R Toledano

PRINCETON UNIVERSITY PRESS
PRINCETON, NEW JERSEY

Published by Princeton University Press,
41 William Street, Princeton, New Jersey
In the United Kingdom Princeton University Press,
Guildford, Surrey

LCC 82-47618
ISBN 05369-3

Publication of this book has been aided by the Whitney Darrow Publication
Reserve Fund of Princeton University Press

This book has been composed in Linotron Bembo

Clothbound editions of Princeton University Press books
are printed on acid-free paper, and binding materials are
chosen for strength and durability

Printed in the United States of America by Princeton
University Press, Princeton, New Jersey

CONTENTS

LIST OF MAPS

NOTES

NOTE ON TRANSLITERATION AND PRONUNCIATION

ALL FOREIGN WORDS, excluding foreign names, are italicized. All transliterations follow modern Turkish spelling, even for words which originate in Arabic or Persian. In many cases, however, the origin is indicated in parentheses. There are some exceptions to this rule, when names of persons or places are cited according to the Arabic transliteration, e.g. in the case of the *Şerifs* (Arabic *Sharīfs*) of Mecca. Place names with which the English reader has become familiar by now are cited in their English version (Mecca, and not *Makka* or *Mekke*). For those who are unfamiliar with the pronunciation of modern Turkish spelling, the following very rudimentary rules (according to Geffery Lewis' grammar) may be of some help: *c* is pronounced as *j* in *jam* (thus the name of the Sultan Abdülmecit is pronounced Abdülmejit); *ç* is pronounced as *ch* in *church*; *g* is pronounced as in the word *goat;* *ğ* lengthens the vowel preceding it; *ı* sounds approximately like the *u* in *radium, o* like French *eau, ö* and *ü* as in German *König* and *führer* respectively; and *ş* is pronounced as *sh* in *shall* (thus the title *paşa* is pronounced *pasha*).

NOTE ON DATING

All dates in the text appear in full and only according to the Gregorian style. In the notes, when the dates of documents are cited, the original date is given: Gregorian dates are abbreviated so that 19 January 1872 becomes 19.1.72 (European style), and, unless otherwise stated, all abbreviations refer to the nineteenth century; *Hijrī* and *Mālī* dates of Ottoman documents are cited in full with the corresponding Gregorian date in abbreviated form.

NOTE ON TERMINOLOGY

The following is a list of the relevant terms most frequently occurring in the Ottoman documents from the nineteenth century:

(1) The most common words designating a slave were: *esir* (male), *esire* (female), and *üsera* (plural) from the Arabic *asīr* (though the more common plural in Arabic is *asrā*), originally meaning "captive"; *köle* (male), *cariye* (female, with the plural *cevâri*, also from Arabic *jāriya* and *jawārī*). Other terms were less frequent and in some cases served in legal, religious contexts. They were: *rakik* (used as singular and as plural; if singular, then the plural was *rakikler*) from Arabic *raqīq; abid* (male slave, Arabic *ʿabīd*); *imâ* (female slaves, Arabic *imāʾ*); *memluk* (male slave, Arabic *mamlūk*) and *memluke* (for the female); *gulâm* (male slave, sometime eunuch, Arabic *ghulām*); and *halayık* (plural for female slaves, Arabic *khalāʾiq*). To denote the male and female slaves in a compound, the following expressions occur in the sources: *esir ve esire, abid ve cevâri, memluk ve memluke,* and *cevâri ve gilmân.* To designate color, the adjective *zenci* (Arabic *zanjī*) usually preceded the term used for slave to mean a black slave. Less frequently we encounter the adjective *Arap* (Arabic *ʿArab,* meaning "Arab") as a designation for black slaves (e.g. *Arap cariyesi*); in Turkish usage, as incidentally also in Greek and Russian, *Arap* means "blackamoor." The Persian *siyah* (black) was also in usage (e.g. *siyah köle*). Whites were normally designated by their ethnic origin, e.g. *Çerkes* (Circassian), *Gürcü* (Georgian), *Türk* (Turkish), but also by specific reference to their color, i.e. *beyaz* (white; the Arabic noun *bayāḍ,* whiteness, is used in Turkish as an adjective). Eunuchs were called *tevaşi* (Arabic *ṭawāshī,* plural *ṭawāshiya*) or *gulâm,* but not *khâdim* or *khaṣiyy* as in earlier periods.[1] Since in the period under review most eunuchs belonged to the Imperial Family, or to few other very wealthy families, they were often referred to

---

[1] For a survey of terms used to denote a eunuch, see David Ayalon's recent "On the Eunuchs in Islam," *Jerusalem Studies in Arabic and Islam,* vol. I (1979), pp. 89-92.

by their titles. Thus, the black eunuchs of the Imperial Harem were called *Harem Ağaları*; the Chief Black Eunuch was the *Darüsaâde Ağası*; his deputy, the *Darüsaâde Ağası Vekili*; the Chief Eunuchs of the various Imperial palaces, *Baş Kapı Gulâmı*; the Chief Eunuch in the household of a prince, *Baş Ağa*, etc.

(2) A freed slave was called *azatlı* (from the Persian *âzâd*, free); manumission was *ıtk* (Arabic *ʿitq*); manumission papers or certificates, *azat kâğıdı* and *serbest ve azat kâğıtları*.

(3) For slavery the Ottomans used *esaret* and less frequently *memlukiyet* and *rıkkiyet*.

(4) Masters were usually called *sahip* (Arabic *ṣāḥib*, owner) and *efendi*, but also *mâlik* (Arabic *mālik*), especially in the compound *mâlik ve memluk* (owner and slave), and even *ağa*.

(5) Slave dealers were referred to as *esirci* and less frequently as *esir tüccârı*, or in the plural *celeban* (Arabic *jalab*,[2] already plural, with the Persian plural suffix). If mentioned by name, the title *Ağa* for men, and sometimes *Hatun* for women, usually followed the first name of the dealer (e.g. İsmail Ağa, Ayşe Hatun).

(6) The slave trade was called *esir ticareti* (from Arabic *tijāra*, trade).

(7) The slave market was esir *pazarı* (from the Persian *bâzâr*, market).

(8) Customs duties levied on slaves, *pencik resmi*,[3] or (for blacks) *üsera-ı zenciye resmi*.

(9) The abolition of slavery was termed *sedd-i bâb-ı rıkkiyet* (Arabic *sadd bāb al-riqqiyya* with Persian *Ezâfet*, the closing of the gate of slavery), or *fekk-i rıkkiyet* (Arabic *fakk al-riqqiyya*, the "untying" of slavery).

---

[2] On the *Jallāba*, cf. Walz, pp. 71 ff.
[3] On this term, see below, pp. 69-72.

PREFACE

THE PAST few years have seen a renewed interest in the study of slavery and the slave trade. A host of works on the subject—often using methodological tools of the social sciences—have been published; they cover periods from antiquity to modern times and geographical areas from Southeast Asia to North America. However, no comprehensive study of slavery and the slave trade in the modern Middle East has hitherto been undertaken. A few scholars have examined this or that branch of the Ottoman traffic, but no study has been devoted to the whole network. Nor have the Ottoman archives been used in any of the existing works. As shown by Ottomanists in recent years, these archives contain invaluable material concerning the social, economic, legal, and political history of the Ottoman Empire.

Thus, the present work aims at filling a gap by offering new sources and a somewhat different outlook. While neither ignoring nor belittling the importance of Western sources, this study strives to achieve a synthesis based on both Western and Ottoman sources. Although I have extensively used British, French, and American archives, as well as private papers and travel accounts, my major conclusions are drawn out of the Ottoman material. By a different outlook, I mean the view that all branches of the slave trade to and in the Empire form together a clearly structured network designed to supply the demand of the Ottoman markets. This "system" is best understood in its *Ottoman* socio–economic and cultural framework. What is offered here is a "view from Istanbul" of the Ottoman slave trade and its suppression. The availability of material, the nature of the sources, considerations of space and scope, and my own interest have determined the boundaries of the present book. It deals with the Ottoman slave trade and its suppression, not with Ottoman, nor Islamic, slavery and its abolition; it emphasizes the political, diplomatic, social, and economic aspects, and only marginally addresses the ideational, intellectual, and psychological angles; it focuses on a single system—the Ottoman slave-trading network—and does not espouse a comparative approach. Surely, more and difficult work still lies ahead.

The present book is a revised version of a doctoral thesis prepared at Princeton University under the supervision of Professor Bernard Lewis. I reorganized and partially rewrote the work while in Cairo during 1979-1980. Professor Lewis' immense knowledge of Ottoman and Islamic history, his profound understanding of the Middle East, and his wisdom have guided me throughout my program of graduate studies. For his willingness to share thoughts, to unearth and discuss sources, for his patience, encouragement, and true concern, I am deeply indebted. He is not responsible, however, for views expressed in this book; his ability to admit interpretations which at times conflicted with his own made working with him a unique experience, indeed a privilege.

I am also grateful to Professor Charles Issawi, who carefully read the manuscript, for many important suggestions and for letting me consult his yet unpublished notes on the economic history of Turkey in the nineteenth century. His charming personality made every visit with him in Jones Hall a pleasure.

Professors John R. Willis, Abraham L. Udovitch, Norman Itzkowitz, and Mr. Timothy Mitchell, all of Princeton, Professors Jere Bacharach of the University of Washington in Seattle, ʿAfāf Maḥfūẓ of Ḥilwān University, Egypt, and Gabriel Baer and Etan Kohlberg of the Hebrew University of Jerusalem read the typescript at various stages of its preparation for the press, and I wish to thank them for their helpful comments and suggestions. For both academic and non-academic encourgement, I am indebted to the late and much lamented Professor Rudolf Mach, to Professors Talat Halman, Martin Dickson, and Nehama Bersohn, and to Mrs. Grace Edelman, all of the Near Eastern Studies Department at Princeton.

Financial support for fourteen months of research in Turkey, Britain, and France was provided by the Social Science Research Council, the American Research Institute in Turkey, and the Program in Near Eastern Studies at Princeton. The School of History at Tel-Aviv University and the Shiloah Center for Middle Eastern and African Studies assumed the cost of preparing the maps and kindly defrayed technical expenses. The staffs of the *Başbakanlık Arşivi* in Istanbul, the Public Record Office in London, the archive of the Ministère des Affaires Étrangères in Paris, Rhodes House Library at Oxford, and the Princeton University Library were most helpful and cordial. To Dr. Margaret Case, of Princeton University Press, I am grateful for her wise suggestions, courtesy, and never-failing efficiency. Mrs. Lidya Gareh carefully and diligently typed the manuscript.

Princeton, New Jersey   EHUD R TOLEDANO
August, 1980

THE OTTOMAN SLAVE TRADE
AND ITS SUPPRESSION:
1840–1890

INTRODUCTION

> "Islam, like its two parent monotheisms, Judaism and Christianity, has never preached the abolition of slavery as a doctrine, but it has followed their example (though in a very different fashion) in endeavoring to moderate the institution and mitigate its legal and moral aspects."—R. Brunschvig, "'Abd," *EI²*, vol. I (Leiden, 1960), p. 25

THE DIFFICULTY begins with the title, almost before a discussion can follow. It lies in the use of words, in terminology, which is all the more important when we cross cultural lines, using one language to describe social phenomena belonging to another society which also uses a different language. The term in question is "slavery," certainly a sensitive and "loaded" word to a Western audience. The image it conjures up in our mind is decidedly negative. It connotes exploitation, humiliation, racial discrimination, and a great deal of human suffering. Slavery is the denial of freedom, human dignity, equality before the law, and justice. This concept is informed by Western historical experience and enforced by our process of socialization.

Thus equipped, we come to examine the parallel social institution in another and quite different culture. Reading the nineteenth-century Ottoman sources and putting them in their Ottoman-Islamic context, we find ourselves dealing with a different phenomenon and a different historical experience. Does, then, the extent of the difference between Ottoman-Islamic slavery and, say, slavery in the Antibellum South or in Latin America during the same period of time require the use of a term other than "slavery"? If we retain the term "slavery" also for the parallel Ottoman-Islamic institution, do we then run the risk of "mistranslating" and misrepresenting one culture to another? In short, can we talk about an Ottoman "slave trade"?

My answer is clear and unequivocal: despite important differences which will become apparent in the present study, there can be little doubt that in both legal and social terms we are dealing with the same phenomenon. My task is made even easier, since in this work I do not discuss Ottoman *slavery* and its abolition, but rather the Ottoman *slave trade* and its suppression. True, most of the sources are in agreement that, as a rule, Ottoman-Islamic chattel slavery was milder than its Western counterparts and that slaves were generally well-treated. Domestic slaves were considered as members of the household and a relatively high degree of intimacy existed between them and their masters. Slaves in well-to-do families were often better off than the freemen of the poor classes. But only the strongest among the slaves survived the hardships of the road to reach the relative comfort of city life in the Ottoman Empire. Thus, considering the traffic, we would find on both sides of the cultural borderline great similarity in principle regarding what slave dealers did and what slaves endured.

Rather than dwell any longer on whether or not we can properly talk about an Ottoman-Islamic "slave trade," I shall simply attempt to describe in what the practice actually consisted. I shall examine and analyze its social, economic, and political aspects within its own cultural context. And that with the notion that, as Hugh Trevor-Roper put it,

> ". . . every age has its own social context, its own intellectual climate, and takes it for granted, as we take ours. Because it was taken for granted, it is not explicitly expressed in the documents of the time: it has to be deduced and reconstructed. It also deserves respect. . . . To discern the intellectual climate of the past is one of the most difficult tasks of the historian, but it is also one of the most necessary. To neglect it—to use terms like 'rational,' 'superstitious,' 'progressive,' 'reactionary,' as

if only that was rational which obeyed our rules of reason, only that progressive which pointed to us—is worse than wrong: it is vulgar."[1]

★ ★ ★

As late as the nineteenth century, chattel slavery was still practiced in both the Old and New Worlds. The slave trade, still very active, stretched from West Africa to the Americas and from North and East Africa—as well as from the Caucasus—to the lands of Islam. Though the various branches of the traffic differed from each other in some significant ways, they all had a great deal in common. For one thing, there can be little doubt that there was much brutality in the acquisition and transportation of African slaves Mortality—whether from sickness, fatigue, or ill-usage—was high. The number of slaves imported into the Islamic world was approximately one-third to one-half the number of slaves imported into the New World. For those slaves who survived the ordeal of the journey, slavery in Islam was in many ways different from slavery in the Americas.

Islamic law regulates all aspects of the slave's status [2] It

---

[1] H R Trevor-Roper, *The Past and the Present—History and Sociology* (London, 1969), p 21

[2] A detailed discussion of the legal aspects of slavery is clearly outside the scope of the present study For information beyond that which is provided by Brunschvig (Brunschvig, pp 26-31), the reader may wish to consult the following sources (a) nineteenth-century legal sources The most frequently used authorities were the Hanafi jurist Ibn ʿĀbīdīn (Muhammad Amīn ibn ʿĀbīdīn, *al-Radd al-Muhtār* [Cairo, 1966], vol III, pp 162 ff and 639 ff, vol IV, pp 286 ff, vol VI, pp 97 ff, and other relevant references) and Ibrāhīm al-Halabī (also a Hanafi lawyer, d 1549), whose *Multaqā ʾl-Abhur* was published in the Empire in the nineteenth century in several editions (Ibrāhīm al-Halabī, *Multaqā ʾl-Abhur* [Cairo, 1265], pp 97 ff, 133 ff, 182 ff, and other relevant references, a Turkish translation of this work also exists, Mehmet Mevkûfatî, Istanbul, 1290) (b) *Hadīth* For matters relating to the status of slaves, see A J Wensinck, *A Handbook of Early Muhammadan Tradition* (Leiden, 1971), pp 141-3, 203, 217-8 (c) For modern scholarship, see David Santillana, *Istituzioni di Diritto Musulmano* (Roma, 1925), vol I, pp 141-60, Eduard Sachau, *Muhammedanisches Recht nach Schafiitischer Lehre* (Stuttgart and Berlin, 1897), pp 125-79, Th W Juynboll, *Handbuch des Islamischen Gesetzes* (Leiden, 1910), pp 203-8, 234-6

lays down the obligations of masters and slaves and deter-
mines the relations between them. The law commends manumission but does not require it, though a master can be
compelled by the court to free a slave whom he fails to support or whom he ill-treats. Master and slave can conclude a
contract of manumission, whereby freedom is granted in exchange for payment of an agreed sum. A master can also free
a slave effective after the master's death, or by oath contingent upon the fulfillment of a certain condition. Freedom is
considered the guiding principle in legal matters (*al-aṣl huwa
'l-ḥurriyya*), which meant that jurists were encouraged to rule
in favor of freedom in borderline cases. No distinction is
made between types of slaves—such as according to color,
function, or origin of servile state. However, in reality, a
clear social stratification emerged, with white slaves ranking
at the top in value and esteem, followed by Ethiopian slaves
and, lower still, black slaves.

During the early period of Islam, most of the slaves were
prisoners-of-war captured by the victorious Muslim armies.
With the stabilization of the frontiers, however, this situation
changed and many of the captives were exchanged or ran-
somed. Since the *Şeriat* forbids the enslavement of free-born
Muslims and *Zimmi*s (protected minorities) who do not violate the conditions of their status,[3] and since the various
mechanisms of manumission and the absence of slave-breeding practices limited the ability of the slave population to
reproduce itself, slaves had to be recruited from outside the
Islamic world. The payment of tribute supplied some of the
demand, but, early on, a large number of slaves had to be
purchased in the surrounding lands and imported into the
Abode of Islam.

Acceptance of Islam by a slave did not require his manumission. Since many of the imported slaves did embrace their
masters' religion, we find that the great majority of slaves in
the Islamic lands were in fact Muslim. Military slavery—as

[3] The *Devşirme* system, through which were the Janissaries recruited, was
an aberration. For a discussion of this, see V. L. Ménage, "Devshirme,"
EP, vol. II (Leiden, 1960), pp. 210-13.

in the best-known cases of the Mamluks and the Janissaries—was common in Muslim states between the ninth and seventeenth centuries. Domestic slavery, concubinage, and outdoor menial slavery were also widespread. Where it existed, agricultural slavery was not normally of the plantation type practiced in the West, but rather small-scale cultivation. There were some exceptions to that, the *Zanj* of the Baṣra marches in the ninth century being the most outstanding example. The Ottoman Empire—the last of the great Muslim states—inherited both the legal and social elements of Islamic slavery.

God's *Şeriat* and the Sultan's *Kanun*—the supplementary regulations which, at least nominally, were designed to facilitate the implementation of the *Şeriat*—served as the pillars of law in the Empire. Customary law was also an important component of the legal system; it was mostly incorporated into the *Şeriat* and the *Kanun* and did not officially exist separately. In general, the *Şeriat* was predominant in the areas of personal law, endowments (*vakıf*), and religious-ritual matters, while the *Kanun* regulated the administrative, fiscal, commercial, and criminal laws. Thus, in the Ottoman Empire, the status of slaves—seen as part of personal law—was governed by the principles of the *Şeriat*.

Until the mid-seventeenth century, the Ottomans drew military manpower for their Janissary units from the Christian population of their newly acquired European territories.[4] Black slaves—primarily for domestic use—were imported from the Sudan and sub-Saharan regions via Egypt and the Ottoman provinces in North Africa. Ethiopian slaves came from the *Eyâlet* of Habeş (Ethiopia) via the Hijaz and Egypt, and eastern provinces were supplied from East Africa through the Persian Gulf and Iraq. Many white slaves, for both domestic and military usage, were imported into the Empire from regions bordering on the east and north shores of the Black Sea.

---

[4] *Ibid.*, and H. İnalcik, "Ghūlam," Part IV, *EI²*, vol. II (Leiden, 1960), pp. 1085-91.

Already in the eighteenth century, but more so in the nineteenth, the nature of Ottoman slavery underwent important
changes. Male and female slaves of black, white, and Ethiopian stock were still being imported into the Empire and
employed in a variety of capacities. But the great majority
of imports were now African women intended for domestic
service. Some Circassian and Georgian women were also used
for this purpose, and many of the white and Ethiopian females served as concubines. Circassian women often reached
the harems of the urban upper-class of the Empire, not infrequently attaining positions of prestige and comfort as wives
of middle- and upper-level functionaries. As for male slaves,
blacks and Ethiopians were employed in the Red Sea, Persian
Gulf, and Indian Ocean as pearl-divers, oarsmen and crew
members of sailboats, and—mostly in Arabia—as outdoor
laborers and servants. A minority among the slaves attained
positions of responsibility with their masters and were entrusted with the conduct of their affairs.

Agricultural slavery—a very marginal phenomenon in the
Empire after the fifteenth century—was re-introduced on a
large scale as a result of the forced Circassian migration from
the Caucasus in the early 1860s. The immigrants were allowed to bring their slaves with them to cultivate the lands
which the government gave them for settlement. Military
slavery no longer existed in the Empire at the time, and only
freemen could serve in the Sultan's armies. Nevertheless, on
various occasions, slaves were acquired by the government,
manumitted, and drafted into the army and navy, where they
served in the same conditions as the free-born soldiers. With
the exception of the Egyptian armies of Mehmet Ali Paşa[5]
and his successors, this was not done on a massive scale nor
on a regular basis. During the reign of Sultan Abdülhamit II,
freed slaves were placed in military bands and units where
they acquired naval skills; this was done partly to prevent
their re-enslavement. In the nineteenth century, the black and

[5] See, for example Walz, pp. 226 ff., Baer, pp. 164-5; Lewis, *Race and
Color*, pp. 77-8.

white eunuchs of the Palace no longer possessed their former power. But eunuchs were still being imported into the Empire, though in very small numbers and almost exclusively from Africa.

The growing intensity of abolitionist feelings in Western Europe—primarily in Britain—at the end of the eighteenth and the beginning of the nineteenth centuries had a profound impact on the Atlantic slave trade. Britain outlawed the trade in 1807, and by 1833 abolished the status of slavery in her Caribbean possessions. She then wove a treaty network with other European powers for the suppression of the traffic from Africa.[6] By mid-century, France, Austria, Prussia, Russia, Holland, Portugal, and Spain were persuaded to enter—without much enthusiasm—some form of agreement with Britain toward this end. The treaty network had no noticeable impact on the Ottoman slave trade, which continued to be pursued well into the second half of the nineteenth century. However, with the gradual decline of the Atlantic traffic, public attention shifted to the Ottomans, whose growing dependence on the European Powers made them increasingly susceptible to foreign intervention in the conduct of their domestic affairs. The suppression of the Ottoman slave trade thus became one of the declared goals of Britain's foreign policy in the East.

★ ★ ★

In this work I will try to show how the fact that most of the demand for slaves was created by the major urban centers of the Empire gave the slave trading network cohesiveness and determined the dynamics of its working (see Map A). When political or economic difficulties made it hazardous to transport slaves on one route, other routes were used to ensure adequate supply. The existence of one pricing system—though expressed in different currencies—and the same bureaucratic tradition lent the Ottoman traffic an even greater degree of uniformity. The working of the slave-trading network and the techniques used by the dealers to cope with

[6] For details, see Miers, pp. 9-39.

MAP A: The Ottoman Slave Trading Network in the Nineteenth Century as Seen from Istanbul

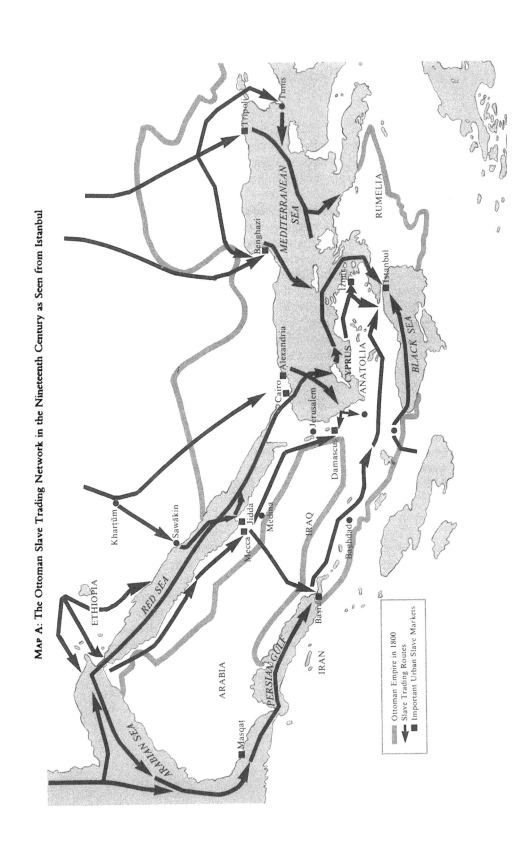

Ottoman Empire in 1800
Slave Trading Routes
Important Urban Slave Markets

mounting difficulties and changing circumstances will be examined in Chapters I and II.

From the late 1840s onward, steps were taken by consecutive British governments to persuade the Porte—at times through direct and indirect pressure—to impose restrictive measures on the slave trade to the Empire. Though the Ottomans made some concessions in 1847, comprehensive action was not taken until the mid-1850s. A *ferman* was issued in 1857 which prohibited the slave trade in Africans (blacks and Ethiopians) throughout the Empire, except in the Hijaz.[7] An Anglo-Ottoman convention for the suppression of the African traffic was concluded in 1880, and in 1890 the Ottoman government joined with other European and non-European powers in signing the Brussels Act against the African slave trade. These developments are the subject of Chapters III, IV, VI, and VII.

A great deal of what was achieved in the suppression of the African traffic to and in the Ottoman Empire was in fact wrung out of the Porte by British pressure. But there can also be little doubt that in many cases, and in the short term perhaps in all, intervention by foreign abolitionists only worsened the slaves' lot. The longer, more difficult routes taken by the slave dealers in order to avoid foreign observers and Ottoman officials increased the suffering of the slaves and raised the death toll. The famous Dutch Orientalist Snouck Hurgronje and others strongly criticized the anti-slavery movement for its attempts to interfere with the Ottoman slave trade.[8] The impact of the anti-slavery "lobby" on British foreign policy and the reaction of the Ottomans to British pressures will be discussed in Chapter VIII.

The suppression of the slave trade in the Empire has to be understood also in its domestic context, that is as part of the reforms introduced during the *Tanzimat* (1839-1876) and post-*Tanzimat* periods. Though some of these reforms were adopted under foreign influence—notably those relating to

[7] The reasons for the exclusion of the Hijâz are discussed below, pp. 129-35.

[8] Snouck Hurgronje, *Mekka*, pp. 17-20; see also Keane, pp. 94-100, Slade, pp. 395-7.

the position of the non-Muslim minorities—many others were evolved independently and out of Ottoman internal needs and considerations. Reforms in law and justice were among those most influenced by Western ideas and notions. However, the area of personal status, to which the laws regarding slavery belonged, remained virtually unaffected by these reforms throughout the period under discussion.

Islam teaches that one should not permit what is forbidden, nor should he *forbid what is permitted*. This and the intimacy of the institution, closely intertwined with family life and the privacy of the home, account for the fierce religious opposition to the attempts to suppress the slave trade. Nevertheless, on their own initiative and without the knowledge of foreign representatives, the Ottomans carefully introduced important reforms which gradually abolished Circassian slavery and slave trade. In spite of their desire to carry their abolitionist zeal into the domain of white slavery, the British were effectively denied any say in these matters. Chapter V is devoted to the discussion of the Ottoman reforms in this area, the difficulties involved in them, and the changes they produced.

Thus, the pattern that emerges is fairly clear. In the early 1840s Britain set out to convince the Ottomans to abolish *slavery*. Soon enough she realistically revised her goal and began to direct her efforts toward the suppression of the Ottoman *slave trade*. Until the late 1850s, this goal included the traffic in both *African* and *Caucasian* slaves. From then onward, there developed two separate modes of dealing with these two quite distinct types of traffic. Britain was permitted to remain an active partner to the suppression of the trade in Africans only; her attempts to interfere with the trade in Circassians and Georgians were rebuffed. The realm of white slavery, then, presented the Ottomans with difficult challenges to which they had to provide their own answers. Eventually, these answers, too, led to the restriction of white slavery and slave trade in the Empire.

The mere fact that this book covers a period of almost a half century indicates that the suppression of the Ottoman slave trade was a gradual, long-drawn out process. Indeed, in their dealings with the Ottoman government, the British proceeded by steps. It was like climbing a ladder whose rungs led from *restriction* to *prohibition* and finally to bilateral *convention*. Each step further narrowed the scope of the traffic. The same path was followed by the Porte with regard to the trade in whites, without, however, the involvement of an outside power.

Government regulation—by promulgation of *fermans* or the issue of more limited instructions—was the vehicle through which the suppression of the slave trade in and to the Empire was to be effected. But social reality clearly lagged behind the explicit intention of the law. Though slave trading had been outlawed in 1857, it continued in varying degrees of intensity into the last quarter of the century.[9] Instructions on the subject had to be repeated every few years, and sometimes every few months. Not surprisingly, compliance with the Porte's orders decreased as distance from the capital increased. In remote provinces, where the control of the Central Government was only nominal, evasion of the prohibition was frequent. In the Empire as a whole, slave owning and slave trading were deeply entrenched; both internal and external efforts to suppress the practice proved long and arduous.

[9] Small numbers of slaves continued to be imported into the Empire until its demise and later into the successor states, particularly in Arabia.

CHAPTER I

From Source to Market—
The Ottoman Slave-Trading Network
in the Nineteenth Century

IN THE NINETEENTH CENTURY, slaveholding among the Ottomans was mostly an urban phenomenon. The large cities of Rumelia, Anatolia, the Balkans, and the Levant were, thus, where the majority of the slaves were bought and sold. In the cities, and in towns, many slaves also found a permanent home. The greatest demand for slaves was generated by Istanbul, where the rich and influential members of the *élite* maintained at least one homestead. Even the less wealthy among the ruling class, as well as the middle classes, could afford to own slaves. Almost all the roads which the slaves trod led to the Gate of Felicity.

This trek *nach* Istanbul and the Ottoman heartland took place in a fairly uniform economy, with its common pricing system, and under relatively unvariegated administrative practices, with common registration and taxation methods. All this produced great similarities within the Ottoman slave trading network, virtually making it a "system." In Chapters I and II, we shall try to identify these similarities and explain the social and economic aspects of the system. This will enable us later to reconstruct the history of the suppression of the Ottoman slave trade on a common basis. No knowledge of events beyond those mentioned in the Introduction will be assumed.

This chapter is devoted to the technical side of the slave trade to and in the Ottoman Empire during the second half of the nineteenth century. We shall follow the slaves and the dealers from the sources of supply to the market and examine the problems involved in each stage of this long journey.

Many aspects of the acquisition, transportation, and sale of slaves in the East have been treated in both popular and scholarly literature. Descriptions of desert caravans and sailboats loaded with slaves are not in short supply. It would be quite superfluous to repeat such accounts here. Instead, our discussion will center on points distinctly Ottoman in an approach to the slave trade which may be termed "a view from Istanbul." We shall also add some noteworthy details that have hitherto been overlooked, or only too briefly treated.

THE ACQUISITION OF SLAVES

The lands which supplied slaves to the Ottoman markets in the nineteenth century lay beyond the borders of the Empire. Central African regions such as Waday, Bagirmi, and Bornu,[1] and the Upper Nile and Western Sudan were the main sources of black slaves; the Galla and Sidama principalities supplied most of the Ethiopian slaves; and Georgia and Circassia gave the Empire its white slaves. There were three ways in which the free inhabitants of these areas were enslaved and fell into the hands of traders who then transported them to Ottoman territory:

(1) *Acquisition through capture in war.* Local wars in all of these regions, but particularly in central Africa and Ethiopia, threw on the market a large number of prisoners of war of both sexes. Among the various African tribes in the interior of the continent, slavery was an accepted institution and the acquisition of slaves through capture in war was widespread; this was the situation long before Africans began reaching the outside world as slaves. The constant warfare in the southern and western principalities of Ethiopia provided many slaves of Galla and Sidama origin. The opening up of these regions to European and Ottoman merchants during the first half of the nineteenth century made slave exporting an important element in the economy of the supplying lands. En-

---

[1] See, for example, the places of origin listed for the slaves caught by the Izmir authorities on board a slaver in 1857 (BA/İrade/Meclis-i Vâlâ/16623, enclosures 28 and 68).

slavement resulting from internal rebellion was rare in the Empire, though in one known case it did occur. During the Kurdish revolt under Bederhan Bey in 1847, Nestorian, Jacobite, and Yazīdī women and children were taken captive and sold into slavery in the Diyarbakır-Mosul area. Some were later freed as a result of British intercession and Porte action. It was ruled in this case that the enslavement of *Zimmis* was contrary to the *Şeriat*.[2]

(2) *Acquisition by raiding and kidnapping.* When war failed to satisfy the demand for slaves, slave-raids were organized to supply the markets. In the late 1850s, raids were still launched from the *Vilâyet* of Tripoli into the areas of Kavar and Aïr in order to produce slaves for the northern markets. Acting as agents for Savana kings, the Touareg and supra-tribal kingdoms "made raiding and capturing of slaves a regular enterprise and fed the victims into a complex trading system." In the Upper Nile, Baḥr al-Ghazāl, and the White Nile areas, the activity of the European and Ottoman ivory traders quickly developed in the 1850s into a massive slave-raiding and slave-trading operation. The nature of the merchant camps, or *zarības*, and their aggressive trading practices soon created a need for slave labor and slave troops, which was satisfied through extensive slave dealing. The raids were led by "northern traders," or Syrian, Egyptian, and north-Sudanese merchants, most of whom were Ottoman subjects.[3]

[2] For central Africa and Ethiopia, see Kopytoff and Miers, "Introduction," p. 13; Abir, p. 54. On Bederhan's captures, see BA/Irade/Meclis-ı Vâlâ/2961, Correspondence—the Grand Vezir, the High Council for Judicial Ordinances, the *Vâli* of Diyarbakır, and the Fetvahane, 31 12 47-28.3 48

[3] On the raids in the *Vilâyet* of Tripoli, see BA/Yıldız/39/2128/129/118, *Layıha* by Muḥammad Bāshāla, 6 Şevval 1311/12 4.94 One of those raids was reportedly organized by the governor of Syrtis in 1859 with a force of 2,000 men (FO 84/1120/156-65, Herman to Russell, 2 7-14.9 60). In 1840, two local shaykhs raided a large slave caravan on its way to Tripoli and escorted by a large force (FO 195/108, Warrington to the Chief Secretary of the government, 22.7.40). For Touareg raids, see Kopytoff and Miers, *loc.cit.* (quoted). For African raids in Bornu—an area which exported slaves to Tripoli—see Roberta Ann Dubar, "Slavery and the Evolution of Nineteenth Century Damagaram," in Kopytoff and Miers, p 160 On the Upper Nile and Sudan, see Holt, *Modern History*, pp 61-3.

In Ethiopia, slave-raiding expeditions were carried out into the southwestern regions and even to the negroid areas surrounding the country. Here, the marauders came from Kaffa and the Galla principalities. The Ottoman governor of Massawa reported in 1860 on slave raids into Ḥubāba, some fifty hours' ride from town. The raids were organized by "five or ten" merchants from Massawa with the cooperation of the tribal shaykhs in the area.[4]

To this mode of acquisition we should add kidnapping, a practice prevalent both at the supply sources and in the Ottoman Empire. Kidnapping differed from raiding in that it was not organized as an aggressive, large-scale operation, but was conducted on a small scale, often on an individual basis. Also, it was aimed at unprotected persons in an isolated position, rather than at whole villages ready to defend themselves against potential marauders. Kidnapping was commonplace in Ethiopia and the regions around Lake Chad. It occurred frequently on the eastern borders of Anatolia among the people of the Caucasus. The Lâz were accused of abducting Georgian women and children while the men were serving in the Sultan's armies. The Ottoman vice-consul in Potide had to intercede with the Russian authorities in 1865 in order to obtain the release of Ottoman subjects who had been kidnapped by Abaza tribesmen and taken to Russian territory. After their migration to the Ottoman Empire in the early 1860s, Circassians were often implicated in the abduction of free-born Muslim children; in Bulgaria they were accused of kidnapping Bulgarian, Greek, and Tatar girls. The Ottoman Penal Code of 1858 imposed a penalty of one year's imprisonment on abductors of children, and the relevant articles were expanded in 1860 and again in 1867.[5]

[4] For Ethiopia see Abir, p 56 The Hubāba raid is described in BA/Irade/Meclis-ı Vâlâ/19711, Pertev Efendi to the Şerif of Mecca, 23 Rebiulevvel 1277/9 10 60

[5] For kidnapping in Ethiopia and the area around Lake Chad, see Abir, pp 54 (note 1), 56, Kopytoff and Miers, *loc cit* (the authors mention here both "casual" and "well organized" kidnapping, see also, Dubar, pp 160-1) On abductions by the Lâz, see BA/Irade/Hariciye/5553, the Grand Vezir

(3) *Acquisition by purchase.* In all the regions from which
slaves were imported into the Empire, periods of hardship
frequently brought about "voluntary" sales of people, that
is, sales without the element of compulsion. In many African
societies, children and adults were bartered for grain in times
of famine, or sold into slavery for default on a debt or if
found guilty of a crime; also, various individuals sometimes
chose slavery for themselves and their children in the hope
of bettering their lot. In Ethiopia, Galla and Sidama rulers
regularly exported their own subjects as slaves to cover part
of the cost of imported goods which were consumed by the
élite in their principalities. Here too, minor offenses and failure to pay taxes often resulted in the sale of the culprits. At
times, children were taken in lieu of taxes, or sold by their
parents during periods of famine. The sale of children was
widespread among the Circassians, mostly among those who
belonged to the slave class. With the consent of master and
parent, girls were sold and taken to the harems of Istanbul
to enjoy the great opportunities believed to be awaiting them
there. In many cases, all parties involved—not least among
them the slave girl herself—were eager to effect the deal. As
put by an upper-class Istanbul lady sold by her widowed
mother at a tender age:

> "One day, however, my mother came to us with joy in
> her face and said to me: 'My children, your father must
> be having in his favor the ear of the Prophet. Here comes
> to us a miraculous help. A rich *Hanoum* wishes to buy
> six or seven little girl slaves. I am going to sell you three
> little girls, and with the money go back to the moun-
> tains to bring up your brothers as true Roumeliotes, not
> like mice in a city.' We were very happy. . . ."

to the Sultan, 28 Zılhıcce 1270/23.9.54. The vıce-consul's ıntercessıon ıs ın
ibid./12344, the Grand Vezır to the Sultan, 28 Zılhıcce 1281/24 5.65, and
other related documents ın thıs fıle. Abductıons by Cırcassıans are men-
tıoned, for example, ın BA/Irade/Meclıs-ı Mahsus/1407, the Grand Vezır to
the Sultan, 24 Zılkâde 1283/30.3.67, and the enclosed documents, Pınson,
p. 79. For the penal code and the relevant amendments, see *Dustûr*, vol. I,
p. 582 (Artıcle 206); Arıstarches, vol II, pp. 254-5, 272

Sometimes, individuals would agree to be reduced to slavery in exchange for a certain amount of money offered by the slave dealers. Such was the case of seven free-born Turkish boys who had been sold to the *Vâli* of Egypt in 1853 and who later demanded their freedom back. During the famine of 1867 in Tripoli, some residents of the border areas reportedly sold themselves into slavery to escape starvation.[6]

Thus, the methods of procurement ranged from the most aggressive warfare and raiding to the voluntary acceptance of slave status. It is asserted that in Africa a supplier's market existed,[7] and much the same can also be said about the nature of the Ottoman market. In other words, captives, abducted persons, and individuals offered for sale in one way or another nearly always found an eager purchaser. But before we get to the Ottoman consumer, we need to look into the network of transportation which delivered the slave from his home country to the market via a complex web of routes.

The Major Routes of the Ottoman Slave Trade[8]

The Ottoman slave-trading system consisted of three elements: sources exporting slaves; major markets importing slaves; land and sea routes—dotted with central and peripheral entrepôts—linking sources to markets. Slaves were being traded throughout the network, so as also to supply local provincial markets on the road. Most of the sources lay outside Ottoman territory, but the other components of the sys-

---

[6] For acquisition by purchase in African societies and in Ethiopia, see Abir, pp. 54 ff. For Circassian practices, see BA/*loc.cit.*; Longworth, vol. I, pp. 278–80; Demetra Brown, *Haremlik*, p. 118 (quoted). On the boys who offered themselves for sale, see BA/İrade/Meclis-i Vâlâ/16542, the Grand Vezir to the Sultan, 7 Muharrem 1274/28.8.57, and the enclosed documents. On the Tripoli famine, see BFASS/Mss. Brit. Emp./S22/G96, De Cosson's report, 16.6.74 (p. 15).

[7] Kopytoff and Miers, p. 14.

[8] In this work I do not deal with the slave trade in the *Vilâyet* of Egypt nor with the Sudanese traffic into Egypt. These subjects form a separate unit and deserve a special study. Here I treat only the Egyptian transit trade, that is, the traffic to Ottoman markets through Egypt.

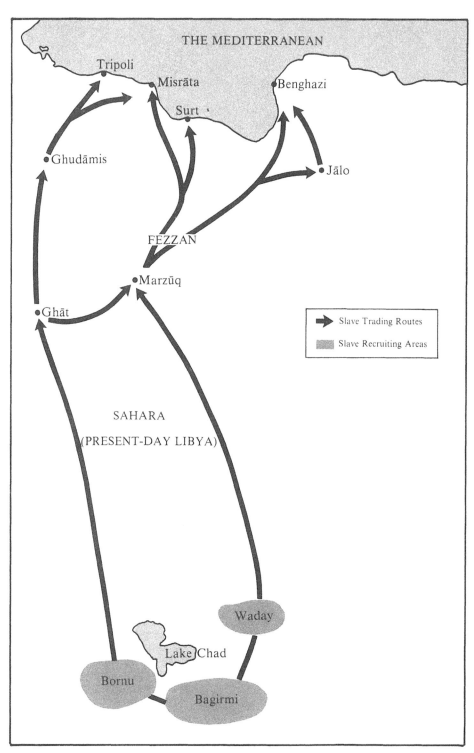

MAP B: Saharan Routes to Tripoli

tem were under the Sultan's jurisdiction. The following list and accompanying maps trace the four main routes from source to market; the kinds of slaves traded along each route are also mentioned.

(a) The North African Traffic (Maps B, C, D)

SOURCES: the regions surrounding Lake Chad, mainly Waday, Bornu, and Bagirmi.

SLAVES: Black.

ROUTES: (1) Overland— (a) to Ghāt—Marzūq—Benghazi
(b) to Ghāt—Ghudāmis—Tripoli
(c) several routes from the *Vilâyet* of Tripoli to Egypt.

(2) By Sea— from Tripoli, Benghazi, and other coastal towns via the Mediterranean islands of Malta, Crete, Rhodes, and Aegean islands to Istanbul, Izmir, Salonica, and other ports in the eastern Mediterranean. Additional routes connected Alexandria, mostly via Cyprus, to Istanbul, Izmir, and ports in southern Anatolia and the eastern Mediterranean.

(b) The Red Sea Traffic (Map E)

SOURCES: Kordofan, Darfur, Blue and White Nile basins in the Sudan; Galla, Sidama, and Gurage principalities in Ethiopia.

SLAVES: Black (Nubians mainly) and Ethiopian.

ROUTES: (1) Overland— (a) from the Upper Nile to Berber and to the Red Sea coast either near Sawākin or near Massawa.
(b) from the White and Blue Nile basins to Qallābāt Qadārif—Kassala—Sawākin or Massawa.

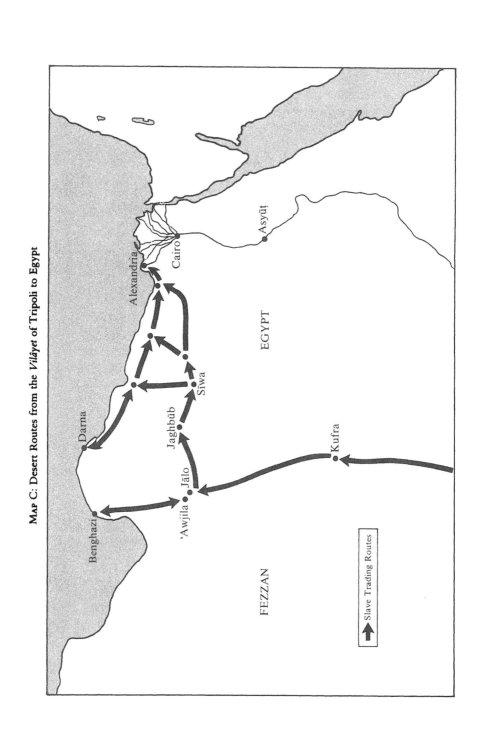

Map C: Desert Routes from the *Vilâyet* of Tripoli to Egypt

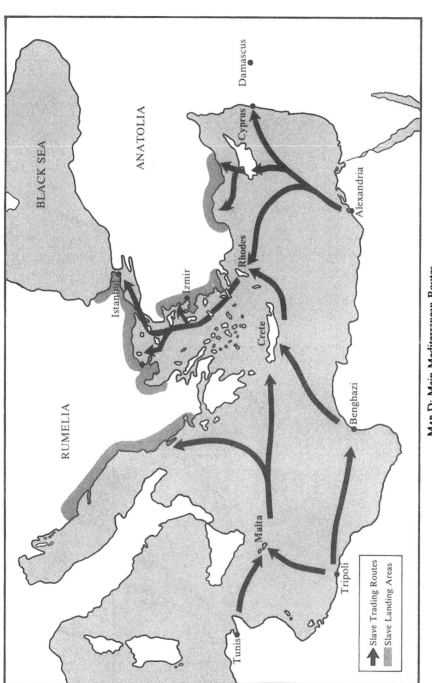

MAP D: Main Mediterranean Routes

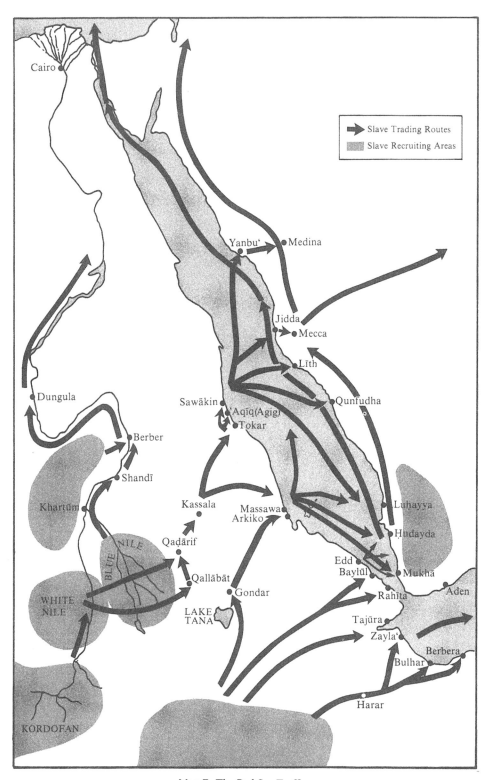

MAP E: The Red Sea Traffic

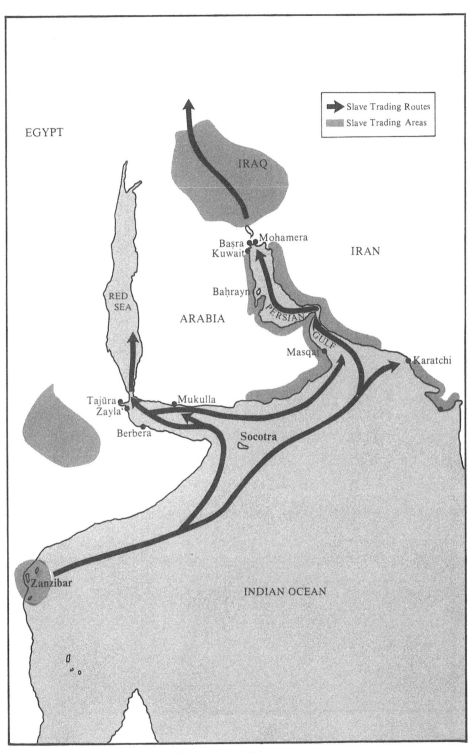

EGYPT

IRAQ

Slave Trading Routes
Slave Trading Areas

Baṣra Mohamera
Kuwait

IRAN

RED
SEA

Baḥrayn

ARABIA

PERSIAN

GULF

Masqaṭ

Karatchi

Tajūra
Zayla'

Mukulla

Socotra

Berbera

Zanzibar

INDIAN OCEAN

MAP F: The Persian Gulf-Iraq Traffic

Map G: The Circassian and Georgian Slave Trade

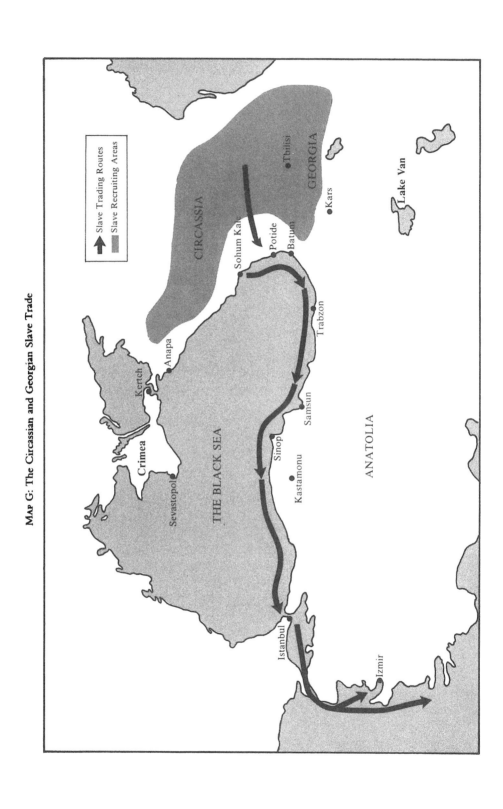

      (c) a partial alternative to (b), up the Blue Nile to Shandī.

      (d) from Galla country through Showa to Rahīta, Tajūra, and Zayla῾.

      (e) from southern Ethiopia to Harar and to Berbera.

      (f) from southern Ethiopia via Showa to Gondar and to the coast around Massawa.

(2) Across the Red Sea: from Sawākin, Agig, Port Mornington, Shaykh Barghūth, Massawa, Baylūl, Tajūra, Zayla῾, and Berbera (and other points along the coast) to Yanbu῾, Jidda, Līth, Qunfudha, Luḥayya, Ḥudayda, and Mukhā (and other points along the coast).

(3) Overland Arabian routes: (a) Ḥudayda—Jidda.

           (b) Jidda—Mecca—Damascus and north (the pilgrimage route).

           (c) Yanbu῾—Medina.

           (d) the Hijaz—Nejd—the Persian Gulf.

(4) The sea route via the Suez Canal to ports in the eastern Mediterranean and Egypt (only after 1869-70).

(c) The Persian Gulf—Iraq Traffic

SOURCES: Zanzibar (to which many slaves came from the areas surrounding Lake Nyasa) and Ethiopia.

SLAVES: Black and Ethiopian.

ROUTES: (1) By sea— (a) Zanzibar—Masqaṭ—Trucial ports—Baṣra/Mohamera.

           (b) Tajūra/Zayla᾽/Berbera—Gulf ports—Baṣra/Mohamera.

(2) Overland— (a) the Hijaz—Nejd—Gulf ports—
Baṣra/Mohamera.
(b) Baṣra—Baghdad—Moṣul—Diyarbakır and eastern Anatolian
destinations.

(d) The Circassian and Georgian Slave Trade (Map G)

SOURCES: Circassia and Georgia.
SLAVES: White.
ROUTES: (1) By sea—from Sohum Kale, Batum, and
smaller ports on the east coast of the Black Sea
via Trabzon, Samsun, Sinop, and other Anatolian cities to Istanbul, Izmir, Salonica, and destinations in the Levant and Egypt.

WAYS AND MEANS OF TRANSPORTATION

(1) The Caravans

The first stage of the slaves' journey from their homes in
Africa was by the overland caravans. It was also the most
difficult part and claimed the highest toll in human lives on
this long road to the Ottoman lands. Most of the distance
traversed by the caravans lay outside Ottoman jurisdiction[9]
and was not affected by the decrees of the Sultan which abolished the slave trade. Nevertheless, the majority of the caravans were headed toward Ottoman territory with the intention of supplying Ottoman markets. Also, the involvement
of Ottoman subjects in the traffic often spread beyond the
boundaries of the Empire, though only rarely do we find
them reaching all the way to the sources of supply. Ottoman
dealers were involved more in the Saharan slave trade than
in the Ethiopian one, but in both branches of the trade the
role of the non-Ottoman transport dealer was very important. It should be noted that throughout the second half of
the nineteenth century little change occurred in the patterns

[9] See map B, p. 20.

of overland slave transportation to the Empire. Let us now turn to examine some of these patterns.

The march from the slaving regions around Lake Chad—mainly Waday, Bornu, and Bagirmi—to the Mediterranean coast took approximately three months. A day-to-day journal of a seventy-day march from Tripoli to Kano is provided by De Cosson, French explorer and teacher, who joined a caravan in 1873. Caravans usually left the *Vilâyet* of Tripoli for the interior in the months of October to March, so as to arrive there before the rainy season, which began in June. Some dealers made their purchases as soon as possible after arrival and departed before the rains, thus reaching Tripoli between July and September. Others left after the rainy season was over, returning to the *Vilâyet* by early spring.[10]

Caravans connecting the interior with the merchant towns on the border of the *Vilâyet* of Tripoli—mainly Ghāt and Marzūq—were conducted mostly by Touareg or Tibboo caravaneers. The Touareg were said to have exacted protection money from all caravans coming from Kano. Caravans crossing the Sahara were either large or very large, for no small caravans would risk the long and arduous journey. One caravan which reached Benghazi in September 1847 was said to have brought one thousand slaves, but this seems to be an exception. The caravan De Cosson joined in Tripoli in 1873 consisted of 245 camels and 85 armed men; such caravans would import a variety of goods, some of the merchandise being carried by the slaves. According to two reports, each male slave would carry a load of twenty pounds.[11]

[10] On the Lake Chad-Tripoli route, see FO 84/1412/47-58, Henderson to Derby, 24.12.75. For De Cosson's journal, and caravan schedules, see BFASS/*loc.cit.* (p. 17); *ibid.*/S18/C54/37-37b, F. L. Carnana (Tripoli) to Allen, 21.6.92; FO/1428/76-9, Henderson to W. H. Wylde, 22.6.74.

[11] On the role played by the Touareg, see, for example, FO 84/919/Herman to Clarendon, 15.1.53; BFASS/Mss. Brit. Emp./S22/G96, De Cosson's report, 16.6.74, pp. 16-8; *ibid.* S22/G22. James F. Church to Louis A. Chamerozowe, n.d. (ca.6.55). For Caravan to Benghazi carrying 1,000 slaves, see FO 84/691/32, Palmerston to Cowley, 20.11.47. On load carried by slaves, see BFASS/Mss. Brit. Emp./S22/G22, Church to Chamerozowe, ca.6.55; FO 84/919/Herman to Clarendon, 15.1.53.

Conditions throughout the desert journey were rough Almost all reports speak of long hours of marching, some of chaining, severe punishments for recalcitrance or simple failure to keep pace with the caravan, and constant fear of reaching a dry well. The British vice-consul in Benghazi listed in a report thirteen well stops during a fifty-day march from Warah, capital of Waday, to Kufra, an important oasis Most of these wells were two to five days apart, but two of the marching intervals spanned fourteen days each! Crossing the Sahara was hard on both dealer and slave, but the latter—unaccustomed to the climate and the road conditions—proved to be considerably more vulnerable. The stories of widespread cruelty on the part of the dealers are probably exaggerated, for the caravaneers knew well that the slaves had more value alive than dead; still, mortality was high by any standards. Estimates vary greatly and range between 7 percent and 40 percent [12]

Most of the caravans went to Ghāt—eighteen days from Tripoli—where slaves were sold and new caravans formed. Sometimes, caravans would continue to Marzūq or Ghudāmis to meet the Ottoman merchants from the coastal towns of the Mediterranean. Marzūq used to supply Benghazi, Ghudāmis supplied Tripoli. In the last quarter of the century, most of the slaves were brought to Jālō—an eight days' ride from Benghazi—sold to dealers, and marched to town in small batches to avoid detection by the authorities.[13] At that point, the trade passed either to the hands of the local market dealers selling for provincial consumption, or to the hands of merchants who exported slaves to the northeastern Mediterranean.

In addition to the trans-Saharan traffic, there were other

---

[12] A concise summary of conditions on the journey is provided in Fisher and Fisher, pp 76-82, and more detailed descriptions appear in the various sources cited in the notes to this section For the Benghazi Vice-Consul's report, see FO 84/1412/47-58, Henderson to Derby, 24 12 75 For some mortality estimates, see FO 84/919/193-5, Herman to Clarendon, 14 3 53, BFASS/Mss Brit Emp /S22/G96, De Cosson's report, 16 6 74, p 19

[13] BFASS/*loc cit* /S18/C37-37b, F L Caranana to Allen, 21 6 92

busy caravan routes also leading to Ottoman markets. Of
equal importance was the overland Ethiopian slave trade to
the Red Sea ports of Massawa, Rahīta, Berbera, Tajūra, and
Zayla'.[14] The first section of this trade was in the hands of
Ethiopian dealers who drove the slaves from the southern
and southwestern Galla, Sidama, and Gurage principalities
to the central Amhara provinces. There the slaves changed
hands and passed into the possession of merchants who took
them to the northern markets of the Kingdom of Showa. In
Showa they were met by caravans from Harar, Tajūra, Aussa,
Rahīta, Wollo, and northern Ethiopia. According to one report, the length of the journey to Tajūra was twenty-one
days, to Rahīta twenty-four days. While the caravans from
the area south of Showa were perhaps as large as those crossing the Sahara, the average Afar caravan consisted of thirty
to fifty merchants and about two hundred slaves. Most Tajūran merchants could afford to buy in Showa only up to
five or six slaves, just enough to support their families.

As a result of the growing demand for Ethiopian slaves in
Arabia during the third quarter of the century—which coin-
cided with the expansion of Showa and the opening of new
trading opportunities—the size of the caravans going in that
direction increased. A British officer sent to observe the traffic
in the Red Sea reported in 1878 that sometimes as many as
forty dealers would have interest in a caravan of four hundred
slaves arriving in Tajūra.[15] On the whole, treatment of slaves
on the road to Showa was not harsh, but the Afar merchants
who conducted the slaves from Showa to the coast were said
to be less gentle with their slaves.

The Ethiopian caravan routes were entirely outside Ottoman jurisdiction and, therefore, were not directly affected by

---

[14] A good account of this trade is provided by Abir, pp. 58-68; for the
following, see also BFASS/Mss. Brit. Emp./S22/G2, report by Charles Gissing
on the Red Sea slave trade, 1.7-31.12.88.

[15] FO 84/1511/132-5, Captain Malcolm's private notes on his visit to the
Red Sea (visited Tajūra on 11-12.2.78), in Vivian to Derby, 22.3.78. Captain
Gissing, who reported on the traffic in 1888, wrote that caravans sometimes
carried as many as 600 slaves (BFASS/*loc.cit.*).

the Porte's instructions regarding the slave trade. Other caravan routes, however, were at least nominally under Ottoman control. These were the desert roads connecting the *Vilâyets* of Tripoli and Egypt, the coastal roads from the Yemen to the Hijaz, and the cross-Arabian and Syrian pilgrimage routes. Through most of the second half of the nineteenth century, slaves were driven along these routes by caravans which mostly engaged in other kinds of commerce. All of these routes served as alternative supply channels to more convenient sea and land routes which ran parallel to them. When difficulties developed on the main routes—such as war or government interference—the traffic was diverted to these secondary overland alternatives. The number of slaves transported on these roads was generally smaller than on the main roads and so were the caravans which transported the slaves.[16]

The overland caravan served as a means of transportation only in the African slave trade; it was not used in the Circassian and Georgian traffic. The majority of the white slaves were imported from the Caucasus to Istanbul by sea, and those taken by land usually accompanied individual dealers who marched them in small groups across Anatolia, from town to town, in hope of effecting a deal. As we shall see, the small sailboat was the main means of transportation in the white slave trade; it also played a crucial role in the African traffic.

(2) The Sailboats

The caravans brought the African slave to the coast. The next step would be a sea voyage, short or long, and in most cases on board a sailboat. The journey of the white slave to the coast was usually a short one, from the mountains of the Caucasus to the Black Sea shore. Though the voyages across the Mediterranean, the Red Sea, the Indian Ocean, the Per-

---

[16] MAE/Corr. Cons./Turquie/Hodeïda/vol. I/pp. 19-20, Lucciana to Tissot, 24.11.80 (Yemen-Hijaz road); FO 84/1450/354-5, Memo by A. B. Wylde (vice-consul, Jidda), 25.11.76 (trans-Arabian road); FO 84/1572/282-9, Count della Sala to Malet, 26.10.80 (Tripoli-Egypt road).

sian Gulf, and the Black Sea had a great deal in common, they differed from each other in a number of technical details.

The determining factor regarding sailboat trading is its total dependence on the direction of the winds. This fact made the East African sea-borne traffic a seasonal trade. Maritime Arab, Iranian, and Indian merchants would sail to Zanzibar for slaves from the beginning of November with the northeast monsoon to return with their cargoes during the summer months with the southwest monsoon. Because of the strength of the southwest monsoon at its height, sailing back in June and July was considered to be unsafe. The traffic from the Persian Gulf to the Ottoman Empire would thus begin in the month of July, at which time groups of slaves who had arrived earlier from Zanzibar to the lower Gulf and Maṣqaṭ ports would start moving up towards Baṣra. Conveniently, this was also the peak of the regular trading season, and the slavers would return down the Gulf with cargoes of dates and other goods from lower Iraq.[17]

There was also the slave trade from East Africa to the Ottoman ports in the Red Sea. However, the direction of the winds here posed a problem to the traders. During the northeast monsoon, when slavers would sail to Zanzibar, winds in the Red Sea blow from south to north. This made it almost impossible for local traders to join their colleagues in East Africa.[18] In summer, when the trade winds blow from the southeast, the Red Sea winds blow from the northwest. This made it virtually impossible to import slaves from Zanzibar to eastern Arabia during the slaving season. To overcome these difficulties, traders from the Red Sea left for Zanzibar in autumn with the south winds, returning to south Arabian ports at the end of the southwest monsoon, so that they could sail up the Red Sea with the change of season.

[17] For details of the above, see Colomb, pp. 24-7, 34 (note 2); Kelly, pp. 413-4; Accounts and Papers, 1870, vol. LXI, pp. 903-5, report addressed to the Earl of Clarendon by the Committee on the East African Slave Trade, 24.1.70 (the full report—pp. 899-915).

[18] Colomb, pp. 53-4; Kelly, p. 413.

But owing to this delicate timing and the ensuing complications, most of the Red Sea traffic did not originate in Zanzibar. Rather, it consisted in importing slaves from Ethiopia
and the Sudan—mainly Darfur, Kordofan, and Sennar—and
running them across the Red Sea to the Arabian markets.

This run would usually take only a few hours and could
be carried out at night.[19] The choice of ports of destination
depended not only on the existence of a market for the slaves,
but also on the direction of the winds. Thus, it could be
expected that most of the trade to Jidda would be carried on
during the winter months with the help of the north wind,
whereas the run from the Sawākin-Massawa coastline to Ḥudayda was likely to be undertaken in the summer with the
south wind. For the same reason, the traffic in Ethiopians
via the Somali coast was probably at its peak during the winter months.

The vessels used in the East African slave trade were called
"dhows" by the British navy, and "buglas" or "buggalows"
(Arabic *baghla*) in documents of the Indian government. The
most-often-used Ottoman terms were *sünbük* (Arabic *sunbuk*,
and sometimes *sunbūk*), meaning a boat, and *sandal* or *kayık*,
meaning a rowboat. "The smallest of these dhows or buglas
are mere boats," writes Captain Colomb, "the largest I have
ever seen, did not appear to be over 350 tons burthen."[20] He
then continues to give the following description:

"If a pear be sharpened at the thin end, and then cut in
half longitudinally, two models will have been made re-
sembling in all essential respects the ordinary slave dhow.
From their form, it is evident the bow must sink deeply
in the water, whilst the stern floats lightly upon it. In
this they differ from the universal practice of European

[19] See, for example BFASS/*loc.cit.*; FO 84/1579/138–43, Annual Report on
the Slave Trade (East Indies Station), by Rear Admiral William Gore-Jones,
24.9.80.

[20] Colomb, p. 35. For terms used for sailboats see *ibid.*, and BA/
İrade/Meclis-ı Vâlâ/10953. On the structure of the dhows, see Hıkoıchı Ya-
jima, *The Arab Dhow in the Indian Ocean* (Studıa Culturae Islamıca, no. 3,
Tokyo, 1976).

ship-building, but it has yet to be proved that they are in principle, wrongly constructed.

"They are seldom wholly decked, and by far the greater number are not decked at all. Cross-beams at intervals strengthen the structure and preserve its shape; and, over these, strips of bamboo in a sort of Venetian blind arrangement afford a footing for the crew, and represent the solid planking of more elaborate specimens of naval architecture. Commonly, especially in the larger class of dhows, a light super-structure occasionally of great size forming a poop is added at the stern, and serves as a dwelling for the captain or owner, perhaps for his wives, family, and personal attendants, the upper class of passengers, if he has any, and sometimes for the whole crew.

"The dhows often carry no more than one mast . . . the sails of these vessels are neither the complete 'lateen,' or triangular sail, of the Mediterranean and India; nor the 'lug' sail of the English Channel, but partake of the nature of both. Their substance is strong soft cotton canvas, of a glittering whiteness, which causes them to shine like a star when first seen above the distant horizon with the sun's rays upon them. . . ."[21]

About the speed of these sailboats the experienced Royal Navy officer comments: "These vessels are enormously swift: they would tax the power of our fastest yachts in light winds: the most speedy man-of-war, under steam and sail, has her hands full when she gives chase to them in a breeze. I have doubted of success, when rushing after them at ten and a half miles an hour. I have missed my quarry when I had not immediate means to go more than ten miles in the hour."[22]

Unlike the vessels used in the Atlantic slave trade—which were especially designed for slaving and were not fit for other kinds of trade—dhows employed in the East African traffic were built to accommodate both slaves and merchandise. Boats

[21] Colomb, pp. 35-6.
[22] *Ibid.*, p. 38.

engaged in the Persian Gulf trade were larger than those used in the Red Sea. They had to endure more difficult conditions for longer periods of time and to carry a larger number of slaves. A British naval officer who conducted a survey of the Gulf traffic in August and September 1840 reported that 100 vessels were engaged in the slave trade, each conveying 50 to 200 slaves. Most of the reports from the Red Sea put the number of slaves per dhow at about 50, with exceptionally large cargoes reaching 100. But most of the vessels employed in the Red Sea ran fewer than 20 slaves each time, crossing back and forth often and carrying slaves in addition to the usual articles of commerce.[23]

Conditions on board dhows coming from Zanzibar were alluded to by the Committee on the East African Slave Trade in the following words: "The slaves, when taken from the slave-dhows, are generally in a filthy state, and ripe for an outbreak of an epidemic disease; it is, therefore, necessary that our cruizers should be relieved from their custody as quickly as possible."[24]

Captain Colomb described his reaction to the conditions of the slaves in a more realistic—if somewhat humorous—way. He wrote:

> "Except that they are more crowded, I have not perceived that the condition of the slave in transit across the Arabian Sea is very different from that of his master.
> . . .
>
> "But, on the other hand, this crowding in so small a space is a crying evil . . . we must not suppose crowding by itself affects the negro, as it does a European, or indeed an Asiatic. We shall meet with at least one cargo of slaves, plump, well-favored, and not unhappy, with the worst of their journey to Arabia over. But if disease, want, and crowding come together, then, God help the wretched items in that crowd! Yet again I have to say

[23] Kelly, pp. 438-9; FO/*loc.cit.*; FO 84/1674/131-5, Jago to Granville, 18.11.84; FO 84/1903/202-4, Wood to Salisbury, 27.10.88.
[24] Accounts and Papers, *loc.cit.*, p. 911.

that I could not choose off hand whether I would rather spend a fortnight in the condition of a slave in an Arab dhow not over-crowded, nor under-provisioned and watered, or in the condition of a peasant in some cabins I have seen in the south of Ireland, whose masters were said to possess a considerable balance at their bankers. I regard both conditions with inexpressible disgust, but if I am to analyze the nature of my sensations, I cannot help noticing that I would rather share a plank with an Irish peasant than with a negro slave, and that therefore, if my disgust be equal, I must regard the condition of the slave in his dhow as better than that of the peasant in his cabin."[25]

As for the Red Sea traffic, the main exporting ports on the African coast were Sawākin, Massawa, and Rahīta; on the Somali coast at the entrance to the Red Sea, the most active slaving ports were Tajūra, Zaylaʿ, and Berbera. The main Arabian ports through which slaves were imported included Yanbuʿ (outlet of Medina), Jidda (outlet of Mecca), Līth, Qunfudha, Luḥayya, Ḥudayda, and Mukhā. The prohibition against the slave trade moved the traffickers away from the main ports and into the creeks and reefs along the coast. Slaves were run at night in small batches to the dealers' houses in town. This practice necessitated a great deal of coordination among carriers and traders on both coasts of the Red Sea, and all actions had to be carried out quickly and accurately. For this purpose, a network of communication was said to have existed among Red Sea traders.[26]

Small inlets on the coast gradually developed into make-shift slaving ports, and their inhabitants totally depended on the dealers for supplies and provisions. Men-of-war could not enter these ports since they were too large and lacked maneuverability, and a circulating Ottoman garrison of five to ten men was ineffective in preventing smuggling. The slave dealers showed great flexibility and were able to move their

[25] Colomb, pp. 41-2.
[26] BFASS/*loc.cit.*

operation to safer outlets when danger seemed to approach. Thus, when the Egyptian authorities tried to suppress the traffic in 1878, one of the active dealers reportedly moved to the southern port of ʿAdd, which lay beyond effective Egyptian control.[27]

The question of who was involved in the sailboat slave traffic to Ottoman territory is indeed a difficult one. The situation is fairly clear with regard to the Persian Gulf trade, for the length of the voyage to and from Zanzibar was conducive to a more organized form of trading and transportation. The vast majority of the transporting vessels here belonged to the Trucial ports on the south Arabian and lower Gulf coasts; some Iranian and Ottoman vessels were also involved. The traders owned their boats and in many cases personally invested in the slaves they brought, not merely acting as agents for merchants on the coast. They often used revenues from pearl fishing to buy slaves in Zanzibar, and with the money received for the slaves they bought dates and other goods in Baṣra which they in turn sold in the Trucial Shaykhdoms or in India.[28]

The situation in the Red Sea was far less clear. The small-scale traffic which was carried on in conjunction with other commerce was probably not in the hands of professional transport dealers, but rather in those of traders who ran slaves on the side if the market was good, the risk minimal, and realizable profits promising. On the other hand, large batches of slaves, say fifty or more, had to leave little, if any, room aboard the dhow for legitimate merchandise. Such boats probably worked for—if they were not owned by—established slave dealers in the coastal towns. The shortness of the

[27] For details, see BFASS/Mss. Brit. Emp./S18/C98/85, A. B. Wylde to Sturge (secretary of the Anti-Slavery Society), 3.5.87; FO 84/1849/154-7, Abdur Razzak (acting consul, Jidda) to White (ambassador, Istanbul), 25.7.87; Accounts and Papers, 1870, vol. LXI, pp. 712-8, Dr. Schimpfer's report, 25.8.68; FO 84/1511/309, Riaz Paşa to Vivian (quoting a report from Gordon), 27.8.78.

[28] Kelly, p. 439; Issawi, *Iran*, pp. 124-8.

run, it seems, was not conducive to the development of a group of transport dealers in the Red Sea.

In the Mediterranean, sailboats transported slaves mainly from the ports of Tripoli, Benghazi, and Alexandria to ports in Anatolia, Rumelia, and the Levant. The most common destinations on these routes were Istanbul, Izmir, and Salonica. Here the trading season was less influenced by the winds at sea and more by the trading cycle of the trans-Saharan caravans and the slave raids in the Sudan. Even the impact of these factors, however, was reduced by the sheer size of the provincial markets of Tripoli and Egypt, which distributed supplies so that demand in Istanbul, Izmir, and other large Ottoman cities could be satisfied all year round.

The limited capacity of the vessels made it necessary for them to call on various ports along the route for water and provisions. The islands of Malta, Crete, Cyprus, and Rhodes often served such purpose. The Aegean islands of Chios, Mytilene, and Lemnos were also frequented by sailboats carrying slaves. Sometimes, slaves were landed there to be transported to Istanbul or Izmir at a later date, that is, after recovering from the voyage, often by another vessel. As the boats moved from one port to another, slaves were disembarked and sold according to demand. An example may perhaps illustrate the practice. Muḥammad Zanṭūṭī, an Ottoman subject born in Tripoli, concluded in October 1848 a deal with a boat owner, whereby the latter would transport him, his son, their five female slaves, and 320 skins of butter from Tripoli to Izmir. Transportation fees were put at 30 *kuruş* per slave, 4 *kuruş* per unit of weight. The slaves were sold on the way as follows: 2 at Chios, 2 at Mytilene, and 1 in Izmir.[29]

This small-scale dealing, mixed with legitimate trade, was

---

[29] For Zanṭūṭī's case, see FO 84/774/157-8, Deposition of Muḥammad Zanṭūṭī (signed before Herman), 31.5.49. On the Aegean traffic see USNA/M46/roll 12, Brown to Buchanan, 4.6.46; FO 84/1428/76-9, Henderson to the Foreign Office, 22.6.74. Until the early 1850s, Mytilene was reportedly the favored entrepôt among slave dealers for the lower duties levied there (FO 84/974/227-8, Newton to Campbell, 22.6.55).

characteristic of the sailboat traffic in the Mediterranean. Much in the same way, slaves were brought to the southern coast of Anatolia, in the vicinity of Antalya, by small Arab and Greek vessels, which took back timber, mainly to Egypt. In a vessel caught near Izmir in 1857, there were 45 slaves divided among 5 slave dealers and a number of Tripoli residents who entrusted their slaves to the dealers for sale. There were, however, dealers who operated on a larger scale. One of the most active of these owned the slaver "Trablusgarp," which sailed regularly between Tripoli and Istanbul and was the subject of a number of British remonstrations to the Porte. Immediately after the promulgation of the *ferman* of 1857, a group of 47 slaves, all belonging to one slave dealer, was detained and manumitted in Crete.[30]

As for specialization among dealers, the situation in the Mediterranean sailboat traffic reflected an admixture of interests. The length of the voyage and the complications which attended to it in the period following the prohibition were such that allowed for the formation of a group of transport dealers who ran slaves from the exporting to the importing ports on a regular basis. But there were also market dealers who either employed agents to purchase and transport slaves for them, or who made trips to North Africa themselves and brought back slaves for sale in the various Ottoman cities.

The vessels used on this route were middle-size dhows, often of 50-100 tons. They were, however, more crowded than the boats employed in the Persian Gulf and Red Sea Traffic. An American report from 1840 mentions two vessels which took slaves on board in Benghazi: one, of 80 tons, took 270 slaves; the other, of 50 tons, took 200 slaves. The report then puts the average space per slave on board the

---

[30] For trade between Anatolia and Egypt, see FO 84/1596/63-4, Colonel Wilson (Antalya) to St. John (Chargé d'Affaires, Istanbul), Secret, 31.12.80. The case of the 45 slaves is in BA/İrade/Meclis-i Vâlâ/16623, enclosures 28 and 68. On "Trablusgarp" see FO 84/1427/310-2, the American consul in Tripoli to Granville, 22.3.73. For the 47 slaves detained in Crete, see BA/İrade/Meclis-i Vâlâ/17636, *Mazbata* of the High Council for Judicial Ordinances, 6 Rebiülevvel 1275/14.10.58, and the enclosed documents.

latter at 4 square feet. Another vessel of 80 tons arrived in Canea in 1855 with 368 slaves. The governor of Crete determined that such crowding of passengers was inhuman and ordered that future loads should not exceed the following quotas: for every 25 tons capacity, 20 passengers; for large vessels, exactly how large is not specified, 10 passengers for every 25 tons.[31]

In the post-1857 period, dealers had to resort to various techniques and tricks to avoid flagrant violations of the prohibition on slave trading. The most common of these was the embarkation and disembarkation of slaves by night outside the main ports, sometimes using small rowing boats to get to and from the transporting vessel, which was anchored off some uninhabited point on the coast. Slaves were landed outside the Dardanelles, or on the shores of the Marmara, and then marched to Istanbul in small batches and quickly distributed among the slave dealers. Again, a network of communication was needed to coordinate the dealers' actions on both ends of the route. Letters which were exchanged between dealers attest to the existence of such networks, which was made more reliable with the establishment of regular steamer lines. Steamers were used for the bi-weekly delivery of mail between Tripoli and Istanbul.[32]

Sailboats played an important role also in the transportation of Circassian slaves from the Caucasus to Trabzon, Samsun, and Istanbul. The difficult conditions of navigation in the eastern part of the Black Sea made passage by sail a

---

[31] For the American report concerning Beghazi, see USNA/M46/roll 7, No. 47, D. Smith McCanley (consul, Tripoli) to John Forsyth (Secretary of State) 3.7.40. For orders of the governor of Crete, see FO 84/974/156-7, Ongley (consul, Canea) to Stratford, 12.5.55.

[32] For examples of the abovementioned techniques, see FO 84/1000/256, Herman to Clarendon, 28.6.56; FO 84/1204/258-60, Herman to Russell, 30.4.63; FO 84/1482/56-61, Layard to Derby, 27.11.77 (a case of landing slaves outside Salonica and marching them to town for sale); FO 84/1428/76-9, Henderson to the Foreign Office, 22.6.74. For letters exchanged among slave dealers, see BA/İrade/Meclis-i Vâlâ/10623, enclosures 9, 20, 21, 22, 30, correspondence—1857; *ibid.*/16856, correspondence between Bayram and Kör İsmâil, 7-8.57.

challenge. The boats were of small to medium size, and slaves were said to have been subjected to excessive crowding. Reports speak of batches consisting of from as few as 30 slaves to as many as 220 slaves per vessel. Some of these boats were no longer than 20 feet. Many were poorly equipped and, with unfavorable winds which prolonged the voyage, passengers often suffered from want of water and provisions. Mortality must have been fairly high, for a special clause was entered into the tariff regulations stipulating that the duties paid for sick slaves who died within fifteen days of disembarkation would be refunded to the dealers.[33]

During most of the first half of the nineteenth century, the Russian blockade of the coasts of Circassia made the transportation of slaves even more hazardous. One of the ways in which captains reportedly tried to evade detection by the Russian authorities was to go to Sohum Kale, perform quarantine, and obtain a permit to load Indian corn or other merchandise on a coast where there was no Russian presence. There they would loan slaves brought down by Abaza dealers and quickly depart for Batum or the slavers' village of Ebu İslak, where they would unload the slaves. If not interfered with by the Russians, they would repeat the trip five or six times, each time bringing slaves and not taking the merchandise specified in their permits. If stopped by a Russian cruiser, they would say that they were going to perform quarantine at Sohum Kale, and when allowed to proceed would go and load the legitimate merchandise. This, of course, could work only if they managed not to be intercepted with the slaves on board.[34]

Like the sailboat traffic in the Mediterranean, the Persian

[33] For conditions on the sailboat traffic of the eastern Black Sea, see MAE/Corr. Cons./Turquie/ Trébizonde et Erzeroum/vol. II, Clairambault (consul, Trabzon) to Guizot (Foreign Minister), 4.11.43; *ibid.*, Clairambault to Guizot, 2.12.44; *ibid.*, Clairambault to Guizot, 20.2.45; USNA/M46/roll 12, Brown to Buchanan, 4.6.46. For refund of duty on dead slaves, see BA/İrade/Meclis-i Vâlâ/1482, the Controller of Customs to the Grand Vezir, 27 Rebiülevvel 1262/25.3.46.

[34] MAE/*loc.cit.*; *ibid.*, Clairambault to Guizot, 2.12.44; FO 84/373/270-3, F. Guarrancino (vice-consul, Batum) to Brant (consul, Erzurum), 10.11.41.

Gulf, and the Red Sea, the slave trade in the Black Sea too was intertwined with regular commerce. It appears that, owing to the difficulties of the voyage, transportation was in the hands of boat owners rather than of market or provincial dealers. During the forced Circassian emigration in the early 1860s, many of the emigrants were transported by sailboats. In the chaotic conditions of the time, captains were said to have taken up a slave trade of their own by exacting from the passengers a transportation fee of one child per thirty persons; victims were chosen by drawing lots. This practice was prohibited later by the Immigration Commission.[35]

The sailboat continued to play a role in the slave trade throughout the period under discussion. Generally, however, the dealers learned how to avail themselves of the latest technological progress in sea-borne transportation—the steamer. By the late 1860s and early 1870s, a large part of the slave trade to the Ottoman Empire was carried by steamers.

(3) The Steamers

From the viewpoint of the slave dealers, the advantages of the steamer over the sailboat were quite obvious. The voyage was shorter, less hazardous, and less trying, all of which meant that mortality was lower and profits higher. However, the disadvantages were also obvious. Virtually all steamers were owned and operated either by the Ottoman government or by foreign companies. Thus, they were more liable to inspection and supervision by officials and foreign consuls. The risks of being caught and of losing the slaves in the process were, therefore, considerably greater on board a steamer than on a privately owned sailboat. Nevertheless, the ingenuity of the slave dealers combined with government apathy and difficulties inherent to steamer transportation to

[35] ASR, 3rd series, vol. XII (1864), p. 198, quoting the *Levant Herald* of 17.8.64; on the slave trade during the Circassian immigration see below, pp. 149-52; on the Immigration Commission, see below, pp. 152-7.

make active trafficking aboard steamers an undeniable reality during most of the last third of the century.

The opening of the Suez Canal in 1869 and the establishment of regular steamer lines between the Yemen and the northeastern Mediterranean ports via the Hijaz offered great opportunities for slave trading The major companies operating on this route were the government-controlled Ottoman Mahsuse, the Khedive's Aziziye, and the Austrian Lloyd's. The Aziziye and Lloyd's were under contract with the Porte to transport soldiers and supplies to and from the Arabian provinces. Military and civilian personnel stationed in the Hijaz and Yemen were reported to be regularly carrying on small-scale, private traffic in slaves to Istanbul and Izmir.[36] The abundance of slaves in southwestern Arabia and their cheap prices created sufficient incentive for exportation Some slaves were purchased for domestic use by the buyer himself; others were bought as gifts to superiors in the capital or for resale upon arrival at the home market

The slaves were invariably presented to the authorities and to unfamiliar inquirers as servants or domestic slaves of the passengers and often carried certificates of manumission Many slaves accompanied their masters out of their own free will, hoping to enjoy the amenities of life in a large Ottoman metropolis. In such circumstances, the companies found it hard and embarrassing to interfere with "family affairs," which were fiercely protected by the traditional Near Eastern and Islamic milieu. The head office of the Austrian Lloyd's Company in Trieste reportedly instructed its agents in Hudayda to admit all suspected slaves as servants of the returning passengers.[37] No inspection of passengers was reported to have

---

[36] For an example of a transportation contract, see BA/Irade/Mechs-ı Mahsus/1945, enclosures 12 and 14, the Azızıye Company to the Council for Military Affairs, 22 Muharrem 1290/22 3 73 For examples of small-scale slave trading aboard steamers, see FO 84/1427/235-7, Francis to Elliot, 7 11 72, ibid /88, Cuming to West, 16 9 72, FO/1429/40-1, Beyts to Derby, 7 8 75, FO 84/1571/94-102, Burrel to Goschen, 25 9 80, FO 84/1849/271-4, Jago to the Foreign Secretary, 4 4 87

[37] FO 84/1482/231-6, Beyts to Derby, 29 5 77

taken place on board the Mahsuse and Aziziye steamers. Owing to the sensitive nature of the issue, officials could hardly be expected to take any strong action.

The crews of the Ottoman steamers also partook of the trade in the hope of realizing small profits in the northern cities. In September 1872, for example, the British consul in Suez inspected an Ottoman steamer en route from the Yemen to Istanbul. He found 14 persons whom he suspected of being freshly imported slaves. They were 12 Ethiopians and 2 blacks, 12 females and 2 males. The ship's clerk owned 3 girls, the coffee server (*kahveci*) 3 girls, the second officer 1 girl, a physician in the Ottoman service 1 girl, an Ottoman official returning from a mission to Jidda 2 girls, an Iranian woman passenger 2 girls, a doorkeeper (*kavas*) from Jidda 2 boys. This was reported to the consul by the British captain of the vessel, who asserted that such was the situation aboard every steamer coming from the Yemen.[38]

Small-scale, rather private traffic was carried on also by returning pilgrims. The above-mentioned companies shared the north-bound transportation market, but most of the Persian Gulf transport business belonged to British steamers. During the peak of the pilgrimage season, all liners were extremely crowded, and company agents, captains, and port officials in both Jidda and Yanbu' were under a great deal of pressure. Passenger lists did not exist and tickets were issued without the bearer's name, often in the passenger's absence. In short, smuggling slaves even on board British vessels was an easy task. Here, too, freshly run and bought slaves were presented as domestic slaves and servants who had accompanied their master from the outset. Certificates of manumission were often submitted to foreign consuls, including the British, for authentication, though there was no guarantee that they would not be destroyed after disembarkation. British and Ottoman attempts to remedy the situation proved to be ineffective. Again, the reluctance to impinge upon the

[38] FO 84/1427/85-6, West to Stanton, 26.9.72; *ibid.*/88, Cuming to West, 16.9.72.

privacy of the family—for example, by asking women to
unveil and identify themselves—was as strong as ever. To
this we should add the alleged participation in the traffic of
the captains and crews of Ottoman steamers, who reportedly
accepted payment of full or partial fare in slaves.[39]

The slave trade from Tripoli, Benghazi, and Alexandria
on board the Aziziye, Mahsuse, and often the Austrian Lloyd's
companies differed in some aspects from the Red Sea steamer
traffic. In many cases, it was carried on not only by pilgrims
or officers who hoped for small personal profits, but also by
professional slave dealers. These transport dealers made frequent trips to the province, during which they purchased
slaves and brought them back to Istanbul and Izmir. Since
the usual method was to present the slaves as members of
the dealer's household, the number of slaves imported on
each trip had to be reasonably small. To avoid interference
by the Maltese authorities, dealers instructed slaves to present the certificates of manumission with which they had been
furnished and to deny being slaves. Later, the tactics changed
and slaves were told to admit their status, but to insist that
they were accompanying their masters out of their own free
will. In either case the result was the same—the authorities
could not prevent the passage of the slaves through Maltese
territory. Some dealers even taught the slaves basic Turkish
to create the impression that they were not new imports and
to prepare them for the market.[40]

[39] On trafficking by pilgrims, see FO 84/1482/223-8, Foreign Office Consultation—Wylde, Derby et al., 4-12.7.77; British steamers also took part in
transporting pilgrims to the Mediterranean (FO 84/1370/171-2, Cumberbatch to Granville, 13.3.73); FO 541/3439/4, Commander Francis S. Clayton to Vice-Admiral Sir R. Macdonald, 21.3.77. For the alleged role of
captains and crews, see FO 84/1412/130-1, Cumberbatch to Elliot, 19.2.75.

[40] For examples of slave dealers' tactics, see: two women dealers who had
been caught four times in the past were detected again with six female slaves
(FO 84/1428/74, Silley to Francis, 21.5.74); three dealers brought seven female slaves from Alexandria to Mytilene (*ibid.*, Roboly to Cumberbatch,
3.11.71); FO 84/1427/116/31, Van Stanbenzee (governor of Malta) to Lord
Kimberly (Colonial Secretary), 8.11.72; FO 84/1482/292-3, Major General
C. Elmhurst (Malta) to Lord Carnarvon (Colonial Secretary), 19.1.75.

It was reported in 1869 that all slaves transported from Alexandria to Izmir on board the Aziziye steamers carried manumission papers. However, it was impossible to ascertain that the documents would not be taken from them after landing, for the slaves could not read them or understand what they meant or how they might be used. Thus, in what probably was a typical example, a high-ranking official from Tripoli was said to have had manumission papers issued for his slaves and even authenticated by the British consul. But the papers were taken from the slaves following embarkation in Tripoli, then returned to them before disembarkation in Canea, only to be collected again upon leaving the port. Following inspection by the port authorities in Salonica, the manumission papers were collected for the last time and destroyed by an aide to the said official. Other reports speak of attaching slaves to passengers to be later re-possessed by an agent or dealer waiting at the port of destination; of sales effected on board during the voyage; and even of slaves being transported by the official Ottoman mail steamers.[41] Like other reports, these too are hard to substantiate, for no Ottoman source can be expected to corroborate them. They are cited here only to convey an impression of the possibilities which existed for slave trading aboard steamers and of the enormous problems involved in trying to suppress this traffic.

Steamers also played an important role in the Circassian and Georgian slave trade. Once carried by sailboats from Russian territory to Ottoman ports, slaves were regularly transported to Istanbul and other cities by Ottoman, British, French, and Austrian steamers. Three British steamers reportedly made two trips per month each between Trabzon and Istanbul; on each trip they carried some 50 Circassian passengers, of whom about a third were believed to be slaves.

[41] FO 84/1305/335-7, Cumberbatch to Clarendon, 8.6.69; FO 84/1090/73-8, Brunt (vice-consul, Üscüp) to Longworth (consul, Monastir), 15.3.59; FO 84/1305/385-7, Cumberbatch to Clarendon, 21.8.69; FO 84/1354/234-5, Cumberbatch to Clarendon, 23.5.72; FO 541/25/67-9, Wood to Granville, 10.6.83; FO 84/1849/249-50, Billioti (consul, Crete) to the Foreign Secretary, 22.4.87.

Following action by the Embassy, the British company refused to transport a group of 70 Circassians, thereby fore-
going a payment of £100. The company then complained
that the French journalists of Pera always and unjustly accused its vessels of slave trading. But the French Messageries
itself was said to have transported slaves from Trabzon, as
were Ottoman vessels, including an Imperial navy frigate.
However, the American chargé d'affaires in Istanbul reported that British steamers were preferred by the dealers for
their large size and better deck conditions.[42]

All routes, whether in desert or sea, ultimately led to markets. Small or large, they all offered the surviving—and often
weary—slaves a chance to find a buyer and a home. A certain
number of them were indeed sold in provincial markets, but
for many the final destinations were the large Ottoman cities
of Rumelia, Anatolia, and the Levant. Wherever they were,
slave markets signaled the end of long suffering and the hope
of beginning a new and better life.

THE SLAVE MARKETS

Slaves changed hands and transactions were effected in market towns situated in various places along the routes to the
Ottoman heartland. Such places were usually the meeting
points of provincial dealers, transport dealers, and market
dealers. It is important to note that slaves were sold all along
the route to supply the demand of provincial markets, a
practice which thus cut into the share of Istanbul and of the
other large Ottoman cities. As will be shown, the size of this
cut was determined by market forces which affected the ever-
fluctuating prices along the route and in the capital.

The first kind of market which the African slaves reached

---

[42] For the role of steamers in the Circassian traffic, see USNA/M46/roll
12, Brown to Buchanan, 4.6 46; Mac Farlane, vol II, p. 411; FO 84/1-
29/60-7, Stevens (acting consul, Trabzon) to Clarendon, 31.12.57; FO
84/857/35-45, Correspondence—Canning, Palmerston, Brant, Stevens, 19-
27.5.51. The French "Messageries" was implicated also in the Mediterranean traffic and was said to be transporting slaves between Mytilene and
Istanbul.

after setting out on their agonizing journey were the great entrepôts of the overland trade. In those towns, mostly located on the desert caravan routes, slaves and other export items from the areas surrounding Lake Chad were exchanged for European and Ottoman goods, often including salt, arms, and liquor. More often than not, trading was by barter, and slaves were the "currency."[43] The most frequently mentioned entrepôts in the North African slave trade to the Ottoman Empire were the Saharan towns of Marzūq, Ghāt, Ghudāmis, and Jālō (all in present-day Libya). The importance of Qallābāt (Matamma) in the Red Sea and Nile traffic was paramount. Owing to the different nature of the trade in Circassians and Georgians—it was carried mainly by boat and not by caravan—no such entrepôts were to be found on the eastern route.

In 1859, seventeen Ottoman slave dealers from Ghudāmis and Fezzan petitioned the *Vâli* of Tripoli, complaining that the 1857 prohibition against the traffic in Africans excluded them from any commercial activity in Ghāt, for slaves were the only barter accepted there. With the application of stricter measures in Tripoli, the traffic reverted to Benghazi. This made Jālō the most important North African entrepôt in the 1870s and 1880s. In this town of about 8,000 inhabitants, the caravans would stay for a month or two so that the slaves could recover from the journey and learn a little about their captors' language, religion, and customs. Benghazi dealers would then buy them and bring them to town in small batches of 8 to 10. The British consul in Benghazi, who visited Jālō in 1883, listed the names of 70 dealers who had imported from Waday to Jālō a total of 680 slaves during the preceding season. In a letter to the editor of the *Times*, published on 9 October 1874, the experienced traveller De Cosson stated that he had counted in Qallābāt 500 slaves offered for sale and he claimed knowledge of 300 more who had been on their way to town.[44]

---

[43] Fisher and Fisher, pp. 156-9.

[44] For effect of prohibition on Ghāt, see Accounts and Papers, 1859 (session 2), vol. XXXIV, p. 516; on the position of Jālō, see FO 84/1412/47-58, Vice-Consul Henderson's report on his visit to Jālō, 24.12.75, and FO

Another phenomenon found on the road were a few small villages, usually located on the coast, which served as resting points and slaving entrepôts. Four of these villages are mentioned in our sources. The British vice-consul in Batum, on the eastern coast of the Black Sea, asserted in 1841 that the chief pursuit of the inhabitants of the village Ebu İslak was slave trading. The village lay some eight hours' ride south of Batum. In order to avoid detection by the Russian and Ottoman authorities, small sailboats were employed to run the slaves to Ebu İslak. From there, slaves were conducted to the markets of Rumelia and western Anatolia. In 1869 it was reported that the Aegean islands of Cos and Laros were being used as recuperation places for slaves imported by sailboat from Egypt and North Africa. Slaves were landed on these islands and kept there until the dealers determined that they were physically fit to proceed to Istanbul for sale. The Yemeni village of Marawa, about twelve miles from Ḥudayda, was inhabited by holy men, and regarded as a holy place; it was frequented by many pilgrims every year. Reports said that in the 1880s slaves transported from Zaylaʿ were landed on the Yemeni coast and marched to Marawa, where they were sold to the pilgrims. Another village, named ʿAdda and located a few miles north of Jidda, was inhabited by freed slaves, whose business it was to feed and lodge the caravans going from Lidd to Jidda. Slaves brought by these caravans were usually run from the port of Sawākin.[45]

Slaves were also bought and sold in large annual fairs, which attracted traders from various parts of the East. They were, however, only one of the "commodities" traded at these fairs—and not necessarily the most important. The great fair of Berbera on the Somali coast offered the best opportunity for

---

84/1641/81-93, Wood to Granville (Confidential), 14.3.83. For Qallābāt, see ASR, vol. XIX (1874-5), pp. 1-2 (citing the full text of De Cosson's letter).

[45] For the village Ebu İslak, see FO 84/373/270/3, F. Guarracino to Brant (consul, Erzunum), 10.11.41; on Cos and Laros, see FO 84/1305/391-3, Cumberbatch to Clarendon, 26.8.69; on Marawa, see FO 84/1597/343-8, Report by Yūsuf Qudsī (Dragoman, Jidda Consulate), 25.2.81; on ʿAdda, see Accounts and Papers, 1870, vol. LXI, pp. 712-8, Memo by Dr. W. Schimpfer, 25.8.68.

trading in slaves, especially in Ethiopians. Each year between September and April a large number of merchants attended the fair. They would come from India, Iran, the Persian Gulf, Ḥaḍramawt, the Yemen, Somali, Ethiopia, and the interior of Africa. To give an idea of the variety of goods traded in Berbera, we should perhaps list the most common items: coffee, gum arabic, ghee, hides, sheep skins, tallow, ostrich feathers, bullocks, goats, sheep, dried fish, honey, myrrh, henna, ivory, sugar, rice, durra, corn, flour, tobacco, salt, balls of cotton, earthern ware, iron products, boards, lead, brass wire, glass beads, buttons, carpets, and slaves. Trading was mainly, but not solely, by barter. Attendance depended on political and economic conditions such as the safety of the roads, government taxation and regulation, and the success or failure of crops. A smaller fair took place in Bulhar, a town inhabited only during the trading months. At the central Rumelian fair of Pristina during the month of September, slaves were said to have been traded as late as 1869. They were reportedly imported to Pristina by land from Salonica.[46]

The slave markets in the provincial cities of the Empire were usually located on or close to the major slave routes. By far the most active cities in this respect were Jidda, Mecca, Medina, Ḥudayda, Baṣra, Tripoli, Benghazi, and Izmir. As for Egypt, one should mention the Khartum-Cairo trade, with exports through Alexandria. All of these cities had slave markets which operated openly until the promulgation of the *ferman* of 1857. The *ferman* of 1857 did not apply to the Hijâs, so slave markets in that province continued to operate as usual. With the exception of some interruptions caused by pressure from the Porte, the slave market of Jidda was active until 1874.[47]

The largest and busiest slave market in the Empire was the

---

[46] For the Berbera and Bulhar fairs, see Kelly, p. 418; FO 84/1511/136-51. Captain Malcolm's notes on the slave trade in the Red Sea (Berbera was visited by him between 2-7.2.78). For the fair in Pristina, see FO 84/1305/304-5, Reade (consul, Scutari) to Clarendon, 12.10.69. Cf. Baer, p. 176 (the Ṭanṭa fair).

[47] FO 84/1412/162-4, Beyts to Derby, 15.1.75.

one in Istanbul. It was located near the chicken market (*tavuk
pazarı*), northwest of the Nuruosmaniye Gate to the Covered
Bazar. The market served as a major attraction for European
travellers, who visited the city and then described the market
in their travel books in picturesque terms.[48] The best and
probably the most accurate description is provided by Charles
White. The following is an excerpt from his account

"[The market] is entered by a large wooden gate, open
during business hours, that is, from eight a.m. to mid-
day, excepting upon Fridays, when it is closed to purchasers. . . . The interior consists of an irregular quad-
rangle. . . . In the center is a detached building, the
upper portion serving as lodgings for (*yessirjee*) slave
dealers, and underneath are cells for *ajamee* (slaves newly
imported). To this is attached a coffee-house, and near
to it is a half ruined mosque. Around the three habitable
sides of the court runs an open colonnade, supported by
wooden columns, and approached by steps at the angles. Under the colonnade are platforms, separated from
each other by low railings and benches. Upon these dealer
and customers may be seen seated during business hours
smoking and discussing prices

"Behind these platforms are ranges of small chambers, divided into two compartments by a trellice-work
The habitable part is raised about three feet from the
ground; the remainder serves as passage and cooking-
place. The front portion is generally tenanted by black,
and the back by white, slaves These chambers are exclusively devoted to females. Those to the north and

---

[48] For the location of the slave market in Istanbul, see map in White, vol
II, at end, see also, Pakalın, vol I, p 553 (*Esir Pazarı*) For examples of
some travel accounts of the market, see Edmund Spencer, *Travels in Crimea,
Krim Tartary*, etc (London, 1837), pp 149-52, Earl of Albemarle (Major
George Keppel), *Narrative of a Journey Across the Balcans* (London, 1831), pp
79-80, Charles Mac Farlane, *Turkey and its Destiny* (London, 1850), vol II,
pp 416-7, Albert Smith, *Customs and Habits of the Turks* (Boston, 1857), p
111

west are destined for second-hand negresses (Arab),[49] or white women (*beiaz*)—that is, for slaves who have been previously purchased and instructed, and are sent to be resold, perhaps a second or third time. Some are known to have been resold many times. . . .

"The platforms are divided from the chambers by a narrow alley, on the wall side of which are benches, where black women are exposed for sale. This alley serves as a passage of communication and walk of the *dellal* (brokers or criers), who sell slaves by auction and on commission. In this case, the brokers walk round, followed by the slaves, and announce the price offered. Purchasers, seated upon platforms, then examine, question, and bid, as suits their fancy, until at length the woman is sold or withdrawn. . . .

"Underneath the above-mentioned galleries are ranges of cells, or rather vaults, infectiously filthy and dark. Those on the right are reserved for second-hand males; the furthest and worst of these dens being destined for those who, from bad conduct, are condemned by the kihaya to wear chains. . . ."[50]

The Istanbul slave market was abolished in 1847. But slave trading did not stop; it merely reverted to the back alley. That is, it was carried on in private houses belonging to the dealers, away from the inquisitive eyes of foreign, mostly English, representatives. Black slaves were reportedly sold in Fatih, white slaves in Tophane and Karabaş. Still, in September 1854, the Grand Vezir and the Council of Ministers ordered the police to prevent public trading, which they said was being carried on in most of the streets of Istanbul, as well as in Galata and Bey Oğlu. In January 1877 the Council of State ordered the immediate cessation of all public slave trading, which cropped up anew in Fatih and in other parts of the capital.[51]

[49] See "Note on Terminology," pp. xiv-xv, above.
[50] White, vol. II, pp. 281-3.
[51] For the abolition of the Istanbul market, see below, pp. 107-8. On the

Movement from open market trading to discreet in-house dealing took place not only in Istanbul but also in the provincial cities which had active slave markets In most cases it occurred after the 1857 prohibition had come into effect Slave trading was carried on also in public khans in the cities and in *kervan sarays* on the main trading routes. It was estimated that in Ḥudayda there were in 1880 approximately two hundred slave dealers who operated at home, often holding no more than two or three slaves each. If the police inquired, slaves were presented as domestics. Though dealers were generally known to the authorities, they were rarely interfered with. Sir Henry Elliot's earlier observation on the attitude of police seems relevant here. "The slave dealers are probably as well-known as the pickpockets and burglars are to the London police, and like them carry on their business till detected in some overt breach of the law. . . ."[52]

---

continued trade in the city and recurring instructions, see Pakalın, vol 1, p 554 (*Esir Pazarı*), BA/Irade/Hariciye/5553, the Grand Vezir to the Sultan, 28 Zilhicce 1270/23 9 54, *ibid* /Şura-yı Devlet/1602, enclosure 1, *Mazbata* of the Council of State, 2 Muharrem 1294/17 1 77 Even when the market still operated, newly imported white slaves were rarely sold in it, they were brought directly to Tophane and handled by merchants who resided in that part of the city (White, vol II, p 384, Kırbrıslı, pp 175-7, Mac Farlane, vol II, p 416)

[52] FO 84/1305/102-4, Elliot to Clarendon, 27 10 69 (quoted) For trade in Khans and in Hudayda, respectively, see FO 84/1324/293-5, Cumberbatch to Elliot, 4 8 70, FO 84/1571/117-24, Burrell to Granville, 15 10 80 For slave-trading practices in Egypt, cf Baer, pp 174-6, and Walz, pp 185-93

CHAPTER II

The Economics and Volume
of the Ottoman Traffic

AT THE END of the road, often but not always in markets, waited the buyers. They came from almost all walks of life, but were mostly city dwellers. More slaves were owned by the upper and middle classes than by the lower classes. Fairly large segments of the population could afford to and did own a black domestic slave for menial work, but white harem slavery was practiced almost exclusively by the well-to-do. In regions lying closer to the sources of African slaves—such as Tripoli, Egypt, Arabia, and the Persian Gulf—slave holding was common even among the lower classes. Slaves there were cheaper.

Slave owners and slaves were joined through the services of slave dealers, the men and women who laid down the system and put it to work. For them, the incentive to engage in the traffic was the profit they realized on sales. Who were they? How many slaves did they move within the network? How did they make their money and how large was their share? This chapter attempts to provide at least partial answers to these questions.

THE SLAVE DEALERS

The slave trade in the Ottoman Empire was by no means the monopoly of the professional slave dealers. A large part of the traffic was carried on by private individuals who availed themselves of the opportunity to make a small profit while travelling through areas where slaves could easily be acquired. Pilgrims to Mecca and Medina, army officers returning from duty in the Hijaz and Yemen, and officials of the provincial administration of Tripoli accounted for much of

the small-scale traffic in slaves. Many such deals were used
to defray travel costs, and it was said that vacations in Istanbul were not infrequently financed by the importation and
sale of a few slaves.[1] The involvement of slave dealers in
transactions of this sort was usually limited to the place of
purchase and, if sale was not effected through personal contacts, also to the travellers' place of destination. In this section, however, we shall deal only with the professional slave
dealers.

Owing to the distance of the sources of supply from the
market and the ensuing complexity of the traffic, there existed a tendency among slave dealers to specialize in one of
a number of types of slave trading. In other words, one rarely
reads about a slave dealer who set out from, say, Istanbul to
a sub-Saharan market town, purchased slaves, and returned
to Istanbul to dispose of them. Such ventures required intimate knowledge of many factors bearing on the trade in each
and every section of the route, as well as the investment of
substantial resources. To be profitable, such an expedition
would have to bring back a large number of slaves, which
was virtually impossible in the Ottoman Empire in the post-
1857 period. Even before the prohibition, such expeditions
were too complicated to launch, and there is no evidence of
their actually being undertaken. Instead, a slave trading network evolved to suit the needs and limits of the Ottoman
market. In it, a clear distinction emerged between provincial
and market dealers, that is, between those dealers who operated in the slave trading provinces and those who operated
in major Ottoman cities and who sold directly to users. To
these two categories might be added a third and somewhat
overlapping one—that of the transport dealers, or those dealers who specialized in conducting slaves, by sea or by land,
from the province to the market.

Another way of classifying slave dealers is according to
the scale of their operation. A small number of dealers op-

---

[1] FO 541/25/72–4, Wood to Granville, 20.9.83 and 2.10.83 This practice
was also common among African pilgrims; it is what Bernard Lewis called
slaves used as "traveler's checks" (Lewis, *Race and Color*)

erated on a large scale involving, in some cases, thousands of slaves annually. On the other hand, the great majority of dealers handled only a small number of slaves each, probably not more than a few dozen a year. Provincial dealers, especially in remote parts of the Empire, where the control of the Central Government was weak, normally handled many slaves; it is only among them that we find the very large-scale operators. In Istanbul and other Ottoman cities, where dealers had to evade government and foreign inspection, small-scale trading proved to be more efficient.

Though rare, large-scale slave trading did exist in the southern parts of the Red Sea. The example of al-Zubayr in the Sudan—where slave dealers commanded armies and controlled vast territories—was not matched here; the closest to that, however, was the governor of Zayla', Abū Bakr Paşa.[2] Zayla', a town of 4,000 to 5,000 inhabitants in 1878, was an important exporting point for Ethiopian, and to a lesser degree black, slaves to the Persian Gulf and the Hijaz. It has been estimated that during the first two-thirds of the nineteenth century, approximately 6,000 slaves were annually exported from Zayla' and Tajūra. In 1869, the British consul in Jidda put the number of slaves exported from Zayla' to Hudayda alone at 3,500 to 4,000 a year. Abū Bakr and his family were said to have been the chief dealers in the area, often trading openly in defiance of the prohibition of 1857. They had close connections with the local rulers in the Sudan and Ethiopia, and until 1875 paid tribute to the Ottoman Sultan through the governor of the Yemen. As a result of an Ottoman-Egyptian accord in 1875, Zayla' came under Egyptian rule. But the Khedive was reluctant to act against Abū Bakr, for fear of losing his cooperation. This cooperation enabled the Egyptian forces in Ethiopia and the Sudan

---

[2] On al-Zubayr, see Holt, *The Mahdist State*, index, s.v. For estimates of Zayla' exports, see: Richard Pankhurst, "The Ethiopian Slave Trade in the Nineteenth and Early Twentieth Centuries: a Statistical Inquiry," *Journal of Semitic Studies*, vol. IX (1964), p. 227; FO 84/1305/271-82, Raby (consul, Jidda) to Clarendon, 10.12.69.

to maintain communications and flow of supplies through the port of Zayla'.

Across the waters, in Ḥudayda, it was reported in 1880 that the slave trade was dominated by Sayyıd 'Alī b Hārūn, the president of the Administrative Council (*Meclıs-ı Idare*) He was said to have used his position to facilitate the passage of slaves into town and to release slave dealers jailed for violation of the prohibition. At various times during the second half of the nineteenth century, a number of high-ranking Ottoman officials in Tripoli and Jidda were accused by British consuls of engaging in the slave trade However, even if true—and this is difficult to ascertain—these cases never reached the proportions of Abū Bakr's trade, nor were they as overt and extensive as 'Alī b Hārūn's dealings At an earlier period, the Circassian traffic was said to be controlled by four families, each possessing 300 to 400 slaves for sale, but in the period under review this monopoly no longer existed.[3] Throughout the Empire, professional slave trading was clearly dominated by the small-scale dealer We shall examine his or her mode of operation later in this chapter

The ethnic background of the dealers was as diverse as that of the general population. Natives of the Arabian Peninsula dominated the slave trade by sea from East Africa, and the Dunqulāwīs controlled the overland traffic to the coasts of Somali and Eritrea. Turks, Albanians, and Arabs had the Mediterranean trade; North African Arabs and Tiboo and Touareg tribesmen shared most of the trans-Saharan traffic. Circassians, Georgians, Lâz, and Turks traded in white slaves. Ḥaḍramī dealers were often mentioned in connection with the Red Sea slave trade. They numbered 2,000 in Jidda alone in the 1850s, were heavily armed and deeply resentful of British efforts to interfere with their activities. And in the port towns of East Africa, Arabia, and the Gulf, Gujerati Indian traders—better known as Banyans—were involved in the finan-

[3] On 'Alī b Hārūn, see FO 84/1571/117-24, Burrell to Granville, 15 10 80, on the four Circassian families, see FO 84/1596/93-9, Lt Herbert Chermside to Col Wilson (consul-general, Anatolia), 15 3 81

cial side of the trade. Iranian slave dealers were said to be active in Egypt in the early 1870s. A Maltese British subject was tried in 1849 for slave dealing in Benghazi, and other Maltese merchants were later implicated in the Tripoli traffic. I found no evidence indicating that the non-Muslim minorities—Armenians, Greeks, Jews—participated in the trade; indeed, Pakalın asserts that slave trading in the Empire was confined to Muslims.[4] However, since information on the background of the slave dealers is limited, a decisive conclusion regarding this question is perhaps premature at this point.

Most of the slave dealers were men, though among market and transport dealers women were also active. Women are mentioned as accompanying slaves from Tripoli to Istanbul and as small-scale dealers in the capital itself, where, according to one source, they constituted the majority of the slave dealers. In fact, it was said that the police refrained from harassing female dealers in Istanbul in the 1880s, while keeping a close watch on male dealers. Out of the 42 Istanbul dealers named by the Second Dragoman of the British Embassy between 1881 and 1884, 14 were women. Women of the upper-class were also involved privately in the lucrative and highly selective trade in white females. Girls of tender age, mainly Circassian, were purchased by the ladies of the large harems of Istanbul, carefully reared and trained in upper-class etiquette, and a few years later sold to the Imperial Harem or to other large harems. The eunuchs of these harems also participated in this type of trade.[5]

[4] De Cosson claims that the majority of the dealers in Istanbul were Armenian and Greek, and that some of them were located at Fener (BFASS/Mss. Brit. Emp./S22/G96/p. 1). However, no other source supports this view. Cf. Pakalın, vol. 1, p. 553 (*Esirci*), and Baer, p. 173.

[5] Source on women being majority of Istanbul slave dealers is Pakalın p. 554 (*Esir Pazarı*); for police and female dealers and for lists of dealers in Istanbul, see FO 84/1674/43-62, Memo by Hugo Marinitch, 30.7.84, and *ibid.*, Table A; for trade in young Circassian girls by upper-class women, see FO 84/1324/94-105, Correspondence—Elliot, Francis, Cumberbatch, 8-14.8.70; Blunt, Part I, p. 252; ASR, vol. XXI (1878-9), pp. 69-72, 96; a vivid account of the practice is given in Demetra Brown, *Haremlik*, pp 116-25; Longworth, vol. I, p. 281; Pakalın, vol. I, p. 554 (*Esir Pazarı*).

In many cases the slave trade was linked to other trades and many slave dealers devoted only part of their time to this occupation. Transport dealers in particular were often engaged in other business as well. A group of Circassian slave dealers used to bring slaves to the Empire and take back linen cloth to Circassia. The caravans and sailboats which carried slaves by land and sea usually engaged in regular commerce, slaves being but one of the items in which they traded. In Başra, the slave trade was closely linked to the date season, and boats which brought slaves took back dates. But even market dealers sometimes had other occupations besides slave trading. One of the active dealers of Istanbul, for example, was also the warden of the shoemakers' guild. Another dealer was at times a maker of pipe bowls (*lüleci*), and another a treasurer to a Paşa.[6] This phenomenon may suggest that profits of market dealers did not suffice for maintenance, at least in some cases of small-scale traders. Or, it could reflect the seasonal nature of the slave trade and the instability brought upon it by political actions like the prohibition and by economic developments like the increase in legitimate commerce. The uncertainty of continuous supply in the post-1857 period must have made the dealers' lives more difficult and led them, perhaps, to diversify their sources of income.

Like members of other trades in the Empire, the slave dealers were organized in each city as a special guild headed by a Shaykh and a *Kethüdâ* (warden). Mid-nineteenth century Ottoman sources mention such associations in Istanbul, Tripoli, and Egypt, but they must have existed in every city in which there was a slave market. According to Charles White—whose account of life in Istanbul in the early 1840s is usually most detailed and reliable—the slave dealers' guild in the capital

---

[6] For Circassians and linen cloth, see BA/İrade/Meclis-i Vâlâ/1482, Petition of Circassian slave dealers, 17 Rebiülevvel 1262/15.3.46. On Başra date and slave trade, see Kelly, p. 414. For warden of shoemakers' guild and maker of pipe bowls, respectively, see BA/*loc.cit.*/16856, *Mazbata* of the High Council of Judicial Ordinances, 5 Cemaziyulevvel 1274/22.12.57, and *ibid.*/16542, Protocol of the court's hearings in Egypt, pp. 1,4 (the events took place in the year 1269/1852-3). Cf. Baer, pp. 172-4.

was strictly organized and regulated and had its headquarters in the slave market.[7] During the second half of the nineteenth century, the guilds were considered as abolished throughout the Empire, but they continued to exist nevertheless.

Ottoman sources contain a number of references to slave dealers' guilds, indicating that they continued to function despite the ban.[8] Early in 1862 the Minister of Police himself asked the *Kethüdâ* of the guild in Istanbul to estimate the value of a female slave whose freedom the government had decided to purchase out of humanitarian considerations. In 1864 the existence of the guild was mentioned again in the course of an investigation into a case of ill-treatment of a female slave by one of the guild's members in the capital. In the early 1870s a number of reports reached the Central Government containing allegations that slave dealers in Sivas, Konya, Kastamonu, Trabzon, and Sinop were secretly organizing illegal associations. Although no further details are provided, this could be an indication of the guilds' clandestine activities following the government's attempt to control the Circassian and Georgian traffic to the above-mentioned areas. The sources do not enable us to determine whether separate guilds existed for dealers in African slaves and dealers in white slaves. In Istanbul, however, as we have seen, dealers in different types of slaves congregated and traded in different places.

[7] For the guild in Istanbul, Tripoli, and Egypt, respectively, see BA/İrade/İngiltere mesalihine dair/831, the *Vâli* of Tripoli, Mehmet Ragıp Paşa, to the Grand Vezir, 21 Muharrem 1264/29.12.47. BA/İrade/Meclis-ı Vâlâ/16542, *loc.cit.* For Whites' description, see White, vol. II, 287, Lûtfi, vol. VIII, p 134. For the guild in Cairo, cf Walz, pp 131 ff. and Baer, *Guilds*, pp. 30, 35, 148.

[8] For the following, see BA/İrade/Meclis-ı Vâlâ/21316, the Minister of Police to the Grand Vezir, 8 Muharrem 1279/6 7 62; *ibid* /23102, *Mazbata* of the Council of Police, 17 Zilhicce 1280/24.5 64; BA/Ayniyat/1136, nos 211, 215, the Porte to the Immigration Commission, 28 Şevval 1288/10.1.72; *ibid.*, no. 224, the Porte to the Immigration Commission, 12 Zilkâde 1288/23 1 72; *ibid.*, no. 127, the Porte to the Immigration Commission, 24 Rebiülâhır 1289/1.7.72.

MARKET PRICES OF SLAVES

First, a note about currencies and rates of exchange in the Ottoman Empire in the nineteenth century. For the sake of simplicity, prices in this work are quoted in Ottoman *Kuruş* (piastre). However, a number of European currencies were also in circulation, and many of the figures appear in our sources in Maria Theresa thalers ($M.T.), French francs (ff), or pounds sterling (£). The $M.T. widely circulated in Arabia and East Africa and was commonly used in the Red Sea slave trade. Francs and sterling were often used in North Africa; in Tripoli and Egypt, most prices of slaves were cited in these two currencies and in Ottoman money. In Rumelia and Anatolia, prices of slaves were usually given in *kuruş*. All figures in Ottoman sources were quoted in Ottoman currencies.

The question of rates of exchange during the period under discussion is relatively simple. The main European currencies reached stability in the first quarter of the nineteenth century and the rapid depreciation of the Ottoman currency was considerably slowed down by mid-century. Thus, the rates of exchange remained much the same throughout the second half of the century. In 1848 the pound was worth in Istanbul 109 *kuruş*, and the franc 4.325 *kuruş*; in 1893 the pound fetched 112 *kuruş*, and the franc 4.347 *kuruş*. If we calculate the $M.T. at approximately 4 for the sterling, its value in 1848 and 1893 would be 27.25 and 28 *kuruş* respectively. The debasement of the Ottoman currency, which resulted in part from the post-1860 decline in the value of silver, was expressed in the latter part of the century in rates of 19 *kuruş*, instead of 20, to the silver *mecidiye*, and 105.26 *kuruş*, instead of 100, to the Ottoman gold *lira*.[9]

There are various reasons why it is difficult to provide accurate answers to questions about prices of slaves and other

[9] For details and rates of exchange, see Issawi, *Economic History*, pp. 520–2; William Tate, *The Modern Cambist* (London, 1849), p. 54; Hermann Schmidt, *Tate's Modern Cambist* (London, 1893), pp. 98–9; Kelly, p. 423.

economic aspects of the Ottoman slave trade. These include the paucity of available documented information; the lack of systematic registration of market prices; the method of taxation, which was based on an average, pre-determined valuation rather than on an individually assessed price; the instability of market prices; and the crucial importance of the personal qualities of the slaves in determining his or her price. All these make it virtually impossible to write about prices with any claim to precision. Therefore, the conclusions presented in this section are no more than relative and tentative.

Slaves were evaluated according to their physical attributes and, as far as could be judged, their temperament. The former could be assessed by the buyer at the dealer's house or in the market; the latter depended in large measure on the dealer's word and could be verified only by experience. Therefore, a trial period of a few days was granted by the dealers, after which the purchase was considered as final.[10] Potential buyers looked for qualities in slaves according to the intended usage. Thus beauty was important for prospective concubines, household skills for domestic slaves, strength for male slaves, intelligence for male slaves intended for positions of responsibility and trust. But prices depended also on supply.

Through most of the second half of the nineteenth century, the demand for slaves in Ottoman markets remained constant. The social norms which made female domestic slavery an essential part of medium-sized and large Muslim households outweighed the fact that free labor was both available and more economical. Thus, with demand at a stable level, prices would fall; on the other hand, scarcity would drive prices up. Political difficulties in the countries from which slaves were imported, climate problems on the road, local famines, and even unfavorable winds had their impact on the prices of slaves. In the post-1857 period, the degree to which the government enforced the prohibition against

---

[10] White, vol. II, pp. 292-3.

the slave trade also became a factor in the price system through the effect it had on the flow of slaves from source to market. Owing to the relative stability of rates of exchange and the prices of staples, we do not witness great fluctuations in the prices of slaves beyond those determined by the supply situation. Also, there is no evidence to suggest that the prohibition of 1857 had any long-term, noticeable impact on the prices of African slaves. The prices of Africans begin to show a steady increase only in the middle and late 1880s, when a powerful combination of factors brought about a sharp decrease in the Red Sea traffic. We shall now examine the actual prices paid for slaves in the Ottoman Empire during the period under discussion.

African Slaves

In mid-century the average price of an African slave of either sex was estimated by the government for calculation of customs duties at 2,000 *kuruş*. This was a realistic and fair assessment of the Istanbul price level, where most of the African slaves were sold for 1,500 to 2,500 *kuruş*. According to both the Ottoman and foreign sources which I have consulted, the lowest price paid for a black slave in Istanbul was 900 *kuruş*; the woman in question was sold as a "second-hand" slave for the said amount in 1864. Immediately after the prohibition of 1857, it was rumored in Tripoli that prices in the capital had gone up sharply and that black female slaves fetched as much as 4,000 to 5,000 *kuruş*. Even if true, this situation did not last long and probably resulted from the psychological impact of the *ferman* and the steps taken in Istanbul and Izmir to put it into effect. These measures were relaxed after a while and prices returned almost to their previous level. The highest amount quoted in my sources for an African slave was paid in Istanbul in 1874 for a woman, 3,600 *kuruş*. On two occasions, in 1852 and 1858, the government paid 3,000 *kuruş* to purchase the freedom of a black female slave. Charles White asserts that "second-hand slaves, clean, healthy, and well-instructed" fetched higher prices than freshly imported ones; they averaged, according to him 2,500 to 3,000 *kuruş* but never sold for more than 5,000 *kuruş*.[11]

Prices in Istanbul were somewhat higher than in Tripoli and Arabia, thereby making it profitable to export slaves to the capital. Male slaves fetched slightly lower prices than female slaves. Ethiopian slaves of both sexes, but especially women, sold for higher prices than blacks. In 1889 the average price of a black female in Jidda was said to have reached more than 3,600 *kuruş* and that of a black male more than 2,200 *kuruş*. In 1892 Ethiopian female slaves were reportedly selling in Jidda for as much as 7,000 *kuruş*.[12]

White Slaves

Here we have to distinguish between two different categories of female slaves: those intended for menial work and those intended for concubinage and possible marriage. The gap in prices between these categories was quite significant. Furthermore, within the latter category, beauty and training created a broad spectrum of prices, which did not necessarily depend on market forces. In the second half of the nineteenth century, white male slaves were rare in Ottoman cities. They were mainly to be found in villages as cultivators with the

[11] The sources for prices quoted above are: for customs calculations, see below, pp. 67 ff; for lowest price, see BA/İrade/Meclis-ı Vâlâ/23102, *Mazbata* of the Council of Police, 17 Zılhıcce 1280/24 5 64, for Tripoli prices, see, *ibid.*/16623, enclosure 9, Binbaşı Âlı ağa's mother to him, 15 Cemazı-yülâhır 1273/10.2.57 (a rise in prices in Tripoli following the prohibition was also reported in *ibid.*/16856, the slave dealer Bayram to his partner İsmâil Ağa, 5 Zılhıcce 1273/27.7.57); for highest price, see BFASS/Mss Brit. Emp./S22/G96, De Cosson's report, 16.6 74, p 1, for freedom purchased by government, see BA/İrade/Dahılıye/27039, the Grand Vezır to the Sultan 16 Zılhıcce 1274/28 7.58, and enclosures, and *ibid* /Harıcıye/4530, the *Baş Kâtıp* to the Grand Vezır, 26 Sefer 1269/9.12.52; for White's figures, see White, vol II, p. 285. For comparison, see prices in Egypt in Walz, pp 207-12

[12] For prices of Ethiopians, see Kelly, pp. 417-8, Abir, p. 68; average Jidda prices are in BFASS/Mss. Brit Emp /S22/G2, Captain Gissing's report, 1.1 89; prices of Ethiopians in Jidda are in *ibid.*/S18/C64/83, Osborne to Allen, 4 11 92

status of serfs/slaves; their families shared their work and their status.[13]

White women for menial service were somewhat more expensive than African women intended for the same occupation. The lowest price for a white female slave, according to the records, was paid in Istanbul in 1860—1,500 *kuruş*—but the average price was probably close to 3,000. Five white boys were sold in Istanbul in 1864 for an average price of a little over 3,000 *kuruş* each. Other boys, however, fetched considerably higher prices in Egypt in 1863: 4 were bought in Istanbul for 11,000, 5,000, 5,500, and 4,500 *kuruş*, to be sold later in Egypt for a total of 46,000 *kuruş* (16,000 for the first, 30,000 for the rest); two other boys who belonged to this group fetched 10,000 *kuruş* each. The government's estimated average for white slaves of both sexes was fixed at 8,000 *kuruş* in 1840, and then reduced to 6,500 in 1846 following a petition by a group of Circassian slave dealers. In response to this petition the government stated, nevertheless, that even in 1846 the 8,000 *kuruş* valuation was justified, for many white slaves sold at the time for 5,000, 8,000, 10,000, 15,000 *kuruş*, and more. The reduction was made on humanitarian grounds.[14]

White women intended for concubinage or future marriage sold in Istanbul for higher prices. Charles White wrote in 1843 that beautiful, young, and trained girls fetched in the capital 20,000 or 30,000 *kuruş*, and some of them were sold for as much as 60,000 and 70,000 *kuruş*. The wife of the Grand Vezir Kıbrıslı Mehmet Emin Paşa put the highest price paid for such girls at approximately 88,000 *kuruş* (£800). But the Ottoman records appear to be much more conservative. In 1892, the Deputy Minister of the Interior paid for a Cir-

[13] See below pp. 148 n. 1, 151, 182-3.

[14] Sources of prices mentioned above are: lowest price for white female is in FO 84/1120/121-3, Abott (acting consul, Dardanelles) to Russell, 18.9.60; average price of 5 boys is from BA/İrade/Meclis-i Mahsus/1407, enclosure 9, price list, ca. 1866; prices of boys in Egypt are in BA/İrade/Meclis-i Vâlâ/16542, the Grand Vezir to the Sultan, 7 Muharrem 1274/28.8.57, and enclosures; for government-estimated averages, see below pp. 68-9.

cassian female slave 8,400 *kuruş* (80 Ottoman *liras*); in 1893, the same person paid 6,300 *kuruş* (60 Ottoman *liras*) for another Circassian girl. During the year 1891, the palace purchased 11 girls for the Imperial Harem for the total amount of 1,540 Ottoman *liras*, or an average of approximately 14,700 *kuruş* per slave girl.[15]

Eunuchs

By the second half of the nineteenth century, the power of the Chief Black Eunuch (*Darüssaâde Ağası* or *Kızlar Ağası*) and his corps had declined, and only few eunuchs were still being imported into the Ottoman Empire. The Imperial Family and the wealthiest households alone could afford to buy them. They were usually given as gifts and not purchased on the market. When they were, however, their prices were very high. Almost all eunuchs in the second half of the century were African. The register of the eunuchs held by the Imperial Family shows their number in 1903 to be 194.[16] Many of these eunuchs had been manumitted by that time, but continued to serve their mistresses and masters in their previous capacities.

CUSTOM DUTIES PAID FOR SLAVES IN THE EMPIRE

Before the enactment of the prohibition of 1857, customshouses in the Empire officially exacted duties for slaves. The

[15] For figures by White, see White, vol II, p 288, for prices cited by the wife of Kıbrıslı, see Kıbrıslı, pp 175-7. Some of the Ottoman records on prices of Circassian slaves are BA/Yıldız/18/480/141/123/53, private papers of Ahmet Refik Paşa, Deputy minister of the Interior, receipt of 27 Şaban 1310/16 3.93; *ibid* /18/480/136/123/53, receipt of 19 Tişrın-ı evvel 1308/7.10 92. For Palace purchases, see *ibid.*/35/2027/44/109, enclosure 7, price list of slaves purchased during 1891. We should mention, however, that according to a report of the British consul in Trabzon, a Circassian girl from the area had been sold in 1870 to the Imperial harem for 400 Ottoman *liras*, or approximately 40,000 *kuruş* (FO 84/1324/319, Palgrave to Clarendon, 6 7.70).

[16] BA/*loc cit* 36/140/11/140/XXI, register of the biographies of the black eunuchs of the Imperial family, 7 Sefer 1321/5 5 1903.

calculation of duties was based on an estimate of the average price of a slave taxed at 9 percent, plus 10 percent of the duty added as expenses (*harç*). Thus, the price of a white slave was reckoned by the government in 1840 to be 8,000 *kuruş*, and the amount assessed as duties was therefore put at 792 *kuruş* (720 [9 percent] + 72 [10 percent of 720]). Duties charged for sick slaves who died within fifteen days of disembarkation were returned to the dealers. With regard to duties, no distinction was made between male and female slaves. Although no primary evidence could be found on the calculation of duties imposed on black slaves, it is likely that the same method applied to them too. Charles White states that 800 *kuruş* were paid for each white slave—which he probably rounded up from 792 *kuruş*—and 200 *kuruş* for each black slave. This would mean that the government assessed the average value of a black slave at 2,000 *kuruş*, and levied customs duties of 198 *kuruş*, which White rounded up to 200.[17]

These estimates could be revised by the government to suit price and currency fluctuations. In March 1846 a group of Circassian slave dealers petitioned the government to reduce the duties, claiming that they could not make any profits under current regulations.[18] They asserted that the system was inflexible, for the same amount was being charged for all slaves, though values actually varied between 1,000, 2,000, and 5,000 *kuruş* per white slave. Responding to the petition, the Controller of Customs wrote to the Grand Vezir that the estimate of 8,000 *kuruş* had been fixed in 1840 on the basis of known market prices of 5,000, 8,000, 10,000, 15,000, and more per white slave. However, out of consideration for the Circassian dealers, who had to travel a long way, he sug-

[17] For details, see: BA/İrade/Meclis-i Vâlâ/1432, the Controller of Customs to the Grand Vezir, 27 Rebiülevvel 1262/25.3.46; White, vol. II, p. 286.

[18] BA/*loc.cit.*, petition of Circassian slave dealers, 17 Rebiülevvel 1262/15.3.46; *ibid.*, the Controller of Customs to the Grand Vezir, 27 Rebiülevvel 1262/25.3.46; *ibid.*, *Mazbata* of the High Council for Judicial Ordinances, 11 Rebiülâhir 1262/8.4.46; *ibid.*, the Grand Vezir to the Sultan, 18 Rebiülâhir 1262/15.4.46, and the *İrade*, Rebiülâhir 1262/18.4.46.

gested that the valuation might be reduced to 5,000 *kuruş*, thereby cutting the duties by 297 *kuruş*, to 495 per slave. Alternatively, the Controller added, the tax could remain the same and dealers could be allowed to accumulate a debt to the government, which would be payable at a later date. The High Council for Judicial Ordinances decided to revise the estimate and put it between the previous rate of 8,000 *kuruş* and the 5,000 *kuruş* proposed by the Controller of Customs. Thus, beginning in April 1846, the valuation was lowered to 6,500 *kuruş*, and the customs duties put at 654.5 *kuruş* per white slave, that is, a reduction of approximately 17.3 percent. Though no specific evidence regarding similar changes in the valuation of African slaves can be adduced at present, regulations regarding them were probably as flexible.

Some sources suggest that duties on slaves were calculated differently in some of the provinces.[19] In Benghazi in 1841, for example, $M.T. 5 were levied on each slave imported to the province, plus $M.T. 2 upon entering the town—that is, $M.T. 7 per slave, or roughly 150 *kuruş*. This was lower than the Istanbul rate of 200 *kuruş* per African slave. In Tripoli in 1851, the import duty levied upon arrival in town was said to be 200 *kuruş*; but regulations changed in 1854 so that, if sale was effected in Tripoli, 80 to 100 *kuruş* were exacted, and if exported to Istanbul, 150 *kuruş* were paid in the capital. In Prevesa in 1853, reported duties were close to the Istanbul rates, but the way they were calculated was quite different. The tariff valuation of white slaves was cited as 6,500 *kuruş*, that of African slaves as 1,784 *kuruş*. Then 16 percent of the valuation was deducted and on the resulting amount 12 percent (9 percent internal duty + 3 percent export duty) was levied as duty. Thus, importers were assessed 655.2 *kuruş* per white slave (or 1.2 *kuruş* above the Istanbul rate), and 180 *kuruş* per African slave (or 18 *kuruş* below the Istanbul rate).

The duty paid on slaves was called *pencik resmi, pencik* being

[19] FO 84/373/390-2. Wood to Warrington, 22.6.41; Accounts and Papers, 1854, vol. LXXIII, pp. 810-11. Report for the year 1853; *ibid.*, p. 816, Saunders (consul, Prevesa) to Clarendon, 5.8.53.

the title deed given to the owner by the customshouse upon payment of the duty. Literally it means "tax of a fifth" and has its origin in the Qur'ānic decree which allotted to the Prophet one-fifth of all prisoners-of-war. As we have seen, the Ottomans exacted less than half of one-fifth of the slave's value. As with most other taxes, the collection of the *pencik resmi* was farmed out (*iltizam*) to individuals who undertook to pay the Treasury a fixed amount of money each year and levy the taxes by their own means After the 1857 prohibition on slave trading, the duties on slaves were deleted from the tariff, and tax-farmers (*multezims*) were released from their obligation to the Treasury. In the *Kaza* of Fezzan, for example, the bulk of the revenue of the customshouse consisted of the tax on black slaves (*userâ-i zenciye resmi*), and the *multezim* was released from his contract in the year following the issue of the prohibition A *multezim* from Trabzon complained in December 1858 that the tariff was not clear enough, for it still listed *pencik resmi*, while the dealers had actually been told not to pay it in Trabzon any more, but in Istanbul. This ambiguity was settled throughout the Empire by omission of the tax on slaves from the official registers.[20] In many cases, however, unofficial payment in various forms continued to be levied.

Following the promulgation of the 1857 *ferman*, the Treasury instructed the Instanbul customshouse to cease levying the duty on slaves, and a special duty-collector (*pencikçi*) was reportedly appointed to detect infractions of the *ferman*[21] Under the watchful eyes of British representatives and close to the seat of government, payment of the duty in Istanbul

[20] A detailed discussion of the question of booty, including slaves, can be found in al-Qurtubī's commentary on the Qur'ānic verse which deals with *Khums*, or fifth (*al-Jāmi' li-Ahkām al-Qur'ān*, vol VIII, Cairo, 1967, pp 1-30, but especially pp 4-5) For the release of the Fezzan *multezim*, see BA/Irade/Meclis-i Vâlâ/16624, *Mazbata* of the High Council for Judicial Ordinances, 3 Sefer 1274/23 9 57 The complaint of the Trabzon *multezim* is in *ibid* /18167, a tax farmer to the governor of Trabzon, 12 Kanun-i sânı 1274/31 12 58, and the Grand Vezir to the Sultan, 3 Ramazan 1275/6 4 59

[21] FO 84/1060/44-6, Phillip Sarell (Dragoman, Istanbul Embassy) to Alison (Chargé d'Affaires, Istanbul), 25 1 58

and Izmır stopped, and ıts conversıon ınto brıbes to cover up vıolatıons was more dıfficult than ın remote provınces. Although, of course, no records exıst whıch can prove whether brıbes were ındeed paıd, persıstent reports by both foreıgn and local observers assert that ın many cases, the *pencık resmı*—wholly or ın part—was converted ınto hush-money of sorts. Most of these reports come from Hudayda, Jıdda, and for a later perıod Benghazı They speak of regular payments ın varıous ways, both ın cash and ın "kınd," ı.e., ın slaves

Alleged recıpıents of brıbes ranged from governors to po-lıce commandants, to quarantıne and customshouse offi-cıals [22] Amounts saıd to have been paıd varıed from as low as 10 *kuruş* per slave ın Jıdda ın 1876 to as hıgh as £10 per adult slave ın the same year. Assessment was reportedly eıther at a fixed amount for each slave, regardless of value, or by percentage rates. The abolıtıon of the officıal duty on slaves ıncreased the abılıty of the dealers to pay more and larger brıbes, and the prohıbıtıon made ıt easıer for officıals to de-mand brıbes, for they could claım to be rıskıng theır posıtıon by allowıng dealers to vıolate the *ferman*. In remote areas such as Jıdda and Hudayda, where the Porte had weak and sometımes ıneffectıve control, temptatıon and opportunıty could have often been too strong to resıst for an underpaıd Ottoman functıonary It should be stressed agaın, however,

[22] For reports regardıng governors, see MAE/Corr Pol /Turquıe/ Trébızonde et Erzeroum/vol I (1841-3), Outrey (consul, Trabzon) to the Foreıgn Mınıster, 14 11 43, Accounts and Papers, 1870, vol LXI, pp 772-8, memo by Dr W Schımpfer, 25 8 68, FO 84/1427/63-6, Ellıot to Gran-vılle, 28 9 72, FO 84/1572/274-6, Count Louıs Penazzı (Guadarıff, the Su-dan), to Dr Dutrıeux (extract), 30 8 80, FO 541/25/91-2, Captaın Garforth to the Secretary of the Admıralty, 28 6 83 For reports regardıng polıce commandants, see FO 84/1481/238-40, Henderson to Derby, 27 4 77, FO 84/1571/159-61, Zohrab (consul, Jıdda) to Granvılle, 30 12 80 For reports regardıng quarantıne officıals, see FO 84/1597/343-8, report by Yūsuf Qudsī, 25 2 81, MAE/Corr Cons /Turquıe/Hodeıda/I/p 65, the vıce-consul to the Foreıgn Mınıster, 15 9 81 On customs-house officıals see FO/1450/162-3, Ellıot to Safvet Paşa, 22 7 76 For further detaıls see also ASR, 3rd serıes, vol XX (1876-1877), p 40, MAE/Corr Cons /Turquıe/Hodeıda/vol I/pp 19-20, Alex Luccıana (vıce-consul), to Tıssot (ambassador, Istanbul), 24 11 80, *ıbıd* /pp 115-7, vıce-consul to the Foreıgn Mınıster, 8-29 7 83

that no unequivocal evidence could be found of the actual culpability of Ottoman officials in regard to the slave trade; nor, for that matter, should we expect the official records, and rarely the private papers, to supply such evidence.

PROFITS IN THE OTTOMAN SLAVE TRADE

It is difficult to gauge the profits involved in the Ottoman slave trade. The few European reports that exist on the subject tend to exaggerate the margin of profit and do not seem to rely on accurate calculations but rather on second-hand impression or sheer imagination. At the present stage of our knowledge, it is virtually impossible to estimate profitability over the whole network from source to market. For that we would need to know much more about prices and pricing systems in the various African markets, such as those of Waday, Bornu, Bagirmi, and Ethiopia. We would also need much better data regarding mortality rates along the different sections of the route, to be able to calculate the loss suffered by dealers on their initial investment. I shall therefore limit my enquiry to the question of profits within the Ottoman Empire, that is, profits made on exports from provincial markets to the major importing centers.

Here, too, we are faced with paucity of information and difficulty in assessing the meaning of the available data. Clearly, the important elements to be considered in regard to the profitability of the slave trade are the initial investment made in the slaving province, the amount of money spent on clothing, feeding, and transporting the slave to market, the duties or perhaps bribes paid on the way, and the price of the slave in the market. Professor Issawi estimates that an average of 1 *kuruş* per day could provide adequate food for one adult in the Empire during the period under discussion. This figure is reasonably close to the amount assessed by the Ottoman government for daily maintenance of slaves. A woman whose slave had been imprisoned for murder in 1846 was asked to pay for the slave's maintenance in prison 2 *kuruş* per day, but when she petitioned the government, the High

Council for Judicial Ordinances found the amount too high. Maintenance of manumitted slaves in the city of Benghazi in 1890 was cited in official sources as 1.5 *kuruş* per slave. Owners who wished to place their slaves in the Istanbul slave market for sale were required to pay to the dealers 1.25 to 1.50 *kuruş* per day for maintenance.[23] The relative stability in the prices of foodstuffs in the Ottoman Empire during most of the second half of the century makes it feasible to use one figure for maintenance expenses, say 1.25 *kuruş*, for the whole period.

The cost of transportation poses considerable difficulties and will have to be discussed separately for each route. A few figures may give a general idea about the most important routes.

(1) The Mediterranean

In 1848, a slave dealer was said to have paid the owner of a sailboat 30 *kuruş* for each of the 5 slaves he transported from Benghazi to Izmir together with 329 skins of butter. This seems to be a very low fare, especially if we consider that in the same year it cost approximately 60 *kuruş* to convey one slave from the Dardanelles to Istanbul on a British carrier. In 1853 an Ottoman frigate was reportedly prepared to take slaves from Tripoli to Istanbul for approximately 100 *kuruş* per slave. A fourth-class ticket on a French vessel from Istanbul to Alexandria in 1855 cost 335 *kuruş*. In 1857 a slave dealer paid 940 *kuruş* for the transportation of 5 slaves from Tripoli to Izmir on board an Ottoman vessel, that is, an individual fare of 188 *kuruş*. The man entrusted these slaves to his personal servant, also a slave, whose fare—presumably in better quarters—was 400 *kuruş*. A cheap ticket on a British

---

[23] For Issawi's estimate, see Issawi, *Economic History* (in the press). I am indebted to Professor Issawi for making this yet unpublished material available to me. For maintenance of the female slave in prison, see *ibid./* Dahiliye/62927, *Mazbata* of the Interior Department of the Council of State, 28 Rebiülevvel 1308/11.11.90. For maintenance charged in the Istanbul slave market, see Pakalın, vol. I, pp. 553–4. Cf. for Egypt, Walz, pp. 203–4.

steamer going from Malta to Istanbul in 1876 cost approximately 450 kuruş.[24]

As we have seen, slaves were regularly presented as domestic servants and transported as passengers on this line, not infrequently on board British steamers. A slave dealer was said to have paid in 1887 approximately 14,300 kuruş (165 Napoleons) for his own transportation and that of his 17 female slaves from Benghazi to Salonica on board a two-masted schooner.[25] Allowing for a higher fare for the dealer, a sum of 700 kuruş per slave appears as a likely average fare paid in this case. This is indeed a very high fare and, if correct, might have been a remuneration for risks undertaken by the boat owner, which in this case proved to be real and caused the detention of the vessel. Considering the general decline in passenger and freight rates after 1870, due to improvement in steamers and greater competition, we should perhaps put the Mediterranean fare at 200 to 300 kuruş per slave.

(2) The Red Sea

The cost of running slaves from the African coast to Arabia must have been very low. The run was short, with relatively few risks and almost no cost for maintenance during the journey. The transportation of slaves from Ḥudayda and Jidda to Istanbul and Izmir was, however, quite expensive. Ac-

---

[24] For the above-mentioned data, see the following documents: 5 slaves from Benghazi in FO 84/774/157-8, deposition of Muḥammad Zanṭūṭī (signed before Herman), 31.5.49; cost per slave from Dardanelles to Istanbul is based on the fact that the British company charged £125 for transporting 250 slaves on that route (Mac Farlane, vol II, p. 411), charge by Ottoman frigate is from FO 84/919/181, 197-200, Herman to Clarendon, 22 5-26 7.53; cost on French vessel is in BA/İrade/Hariciye/6047, bill of the French Company attached to the Grand Vezir's report to the Sultan, 16 Şevval 1271/2 7.55; 5 slaves on Ottoman vessel from Tripoli to Izmir is from *ibid* /Meclis-i Vâlâ/16623, enclosure 18, Ibn al-Bāqī Khalīl to al-Ḥājj Ahmad al-'Isawī, 12 Cemaziülâhır 1273/7 2.57; cost of ticket on British steamer is in FO 84/1450/158, Elliot to Derby, 8.76, the amount quoted is £4-0-8.

[25] FO 84/1849/350-3, deposition of Mehmet, a sailor aboard the Mahruse, 3.6.87.

cording to the records of the Council for Military Affairs, which contracted Ottoman and foreign companies to transport soldiers, supplies, and equipment on this route, the lowest fare from Ḥudayda to Istanbul was paid by enlisted men and deck passengers.[26] In 1873 that fare was 600 *kuruş* (6 Ottoman *liras*). Since slaves were taken as regular passengers, it is reasonable to assume that this amount was actually paid per slave transported on this line.

(3) The Black Sea

It is impossible to provide more than a very general estimate for this route. A British company complained in 1848 that it lost £100 for refusing—under pressure from the British ambassador in Istanbul—to transport 70 Circassians, many of them slaves, from Trabzon to the capital. This meant an average fare of approximately 160 *kuruş* per passenger, freemen and slaves. During the mass Circassian migration in the early 1860s, captains of various vessels were said to have exacted a "fare" of one person per 30 passengers; they would then sell these people as slaves.[27] If we reckon the average price of a Circassian slave at the time—with supply exceeding demand and driving prices down, perhaps to the level of prices paid for African slaves—as being 2,000 to 2,500 *kuruş*, we would reach a 66 to 83 *kuruş* transport fare per slave. At any rate, an average fare during the period under review was likely to have been about 100 *kuruş* per slave on the Trabzon-Istanbul route.

(4) The Persian Gulf

I have no figures regarding the cost of transportation from Zanzibar to Baṣra. Most dealers here were essentially what I called transport dealers, that is, they were mainly engaged in

---

[26] BA/İrade/Meclis-i Mahsus/1945, enclosure 14, list of estimated costs of operating the line Istanbul-Izmir-Red Sea ports, attached to a letter from the Aziziye to the Council for Military Affairs, 22 Muharrem 1290/22.3.73.

[27] For the complaint of the British Company, see Mac Farlane, vol. II, p. 411. On slaves as "fare," see ASR, 3rd Series, vol. XII (1864), pp. 198.

conveying slaves from market to market. In many cases, they owned the boats they operated. Their main expenditure was, then, for their own maintenance and that of their slaves. Maintenance will have to be calculated for the period of the journey as well as for the time spent in Zanzibar, Masqaṭ, and other entrepôts. It would still not amount to much money, and certainly would not exceed 75 to 100 *kuruş* per slave.

At this point we should perhaps look at one example of a deal involving 5 slaves from Tripoli who were sent to Izmir in 1857.[28] The following is an itemized list of expenses incurred by the Tripolitan dealer and forwarded to his partner in Izmir:

3 black female slaves at 2,000 *kuruş* each	6,000	*kuruş*
1 black female slave	2,200	
1 black male slave	1,100	
Transportation for all	940	
Clothing for all	404.5	
Maintenance in Tripoli for all	200	
Certificates of passage for all	18	
Amount paid to 4 officers (cavalrymen? *süvarı*) 15 *kuruş* each	60	
Miscellaneous	184	*kuruş*
Total	11,106.5	*kuruş*

If we assume that equal amounts were spent on all 5 slaves, each of them cost the dealer 373.3 *kuruş* in addition to the sum paid for them. In order to make any profit on these slaves, the dealer had to collect the following amounts: 2,373 *kuruş* for each of the first 3 females, 2,573.3 *kuruş* for the fourth woman, and 1,413 *kuruş* for the male slave. At the time, i.e., immediately following the promulgation of the *ferman* of 1857, prices in Instanbul were higher than usual, which could probably result in a modest gain for the dealer.

[28] BA/İrade/Meclis-i Vâlâ/16623, enclosure 18, Khalīl to al-'Isawī, 12 Cemaziyülâhir, 1273/7.2.57.

However, it is quite clear that we are not dealing with large profits.

Prices in the North African towns of Ghāt, Marzūq, or Ghudāmis were said to be lower than in Tripoli by as much as 50 percent, but then the dealer had additional expense resulting from the march to the coast, which cut into his margin of profit. These expenses included fees paid to scouts, or caravan guides, and maintenance for approximately 20 days.[29] In addition, there was the very real risk of losing some of the slaves on the march. Thus, profits on Mediterranean routes must not be exaggerated; they should not be assumed to have greatly exceeded 20 percent.

The margin was perhaps somewhat higher in the Persian Gulf, mainly because of the low prices of slaves in Zanzibar. Profits were estimated at 20 percent in Masqaṭ and 50 percent in Baṣra. As a result of the low prices of slaves in the Kingdom of Showa, dealing in Ethiopian slaves was more profitable. But here, too, the length of the journey from the coast to the interior and back and the expenses incurred for maintenance reduced the profits, which would have otherwise exceeded 100 percent. As mentioned above, most of the Tajūran slave dealers could afford to buy only very few slaves each and their profits were quite modest.[30]

The Circassian traffic was highly lucrative for those who dealt in young girls intended for high harem positions. It was less so with regard to women destined to share the burden of menial work with the African women slaves. As we have seen, however, the close to 800 *kuruş* levied by the customshouse on white slaves was a major grievance of the Circassian slave dealers, who claimed they were unable to make

---

[29] For difference in price levels between Tripoli and the desert entrepôts, see BFASS/Mss. Brit. Emp./S22/G96, De Cosson's report, 16.6.74, p. 20. The fees paid to scouts and guides were said to amount to $M.T. 60-100 (about 1,650-2,750 *kuruş*) for the difficult 8-day march from Kufra to Jālō (FO 84/1412/47-58, Henderson's report, 24.12.75), and to ff 20 (about 100 *kuruş*) per slave for the march between Jālō and the coast (FO 84/1641/81-93, Wood to Granville, 14.3.83, and enclosures).

[30] For Baṣra and Masqaṭ margins of profit, see Kelly, p. 417; and Issawi, *Iran*, pp. 127-8. On Tājūra, see Abir, pp. 65, 68.

any profit.[31] After examining the problem in detail, the government acceded to the dealers' demand and reduced the duties by 17 percent.

Financing in the slave trade from East Africa to the Ottoman Empire was often provided by Banyans who resided in the Red Sea and Persian Gulf ports. There and in the Mediterranean traffic, purchases were frequently made on order, with or without an advance payment. In many cases, slaves were entrusted by an owner or a dealer to a broker, or to another dealer, for exportation and sale, with various financial arrangements binding the parties involved in the deal. To coordinate such transactions, slave dealers carried on regular correspondence among themselves and abided by an unwritten code of conduct in business which ensured both secrecy and trust.[32] Like other professions, slave dealing too had its ethics.

As indicated above, demand for slaves in the Ottoman Empire remained almost constant during the third quarter of the nineteenth century; it gradually declined in the last quarter. The main reason for the constant demand was social, not economic, i.e., the reluctance to allow into the intimacy of the Ottoman home persons who were not members of either the family or the household. Whereas a slave was considered a member of the household, a free servant was not. A female slave could appear unveiled before the male members of the family, a free Muslim female servant could not. Thus, though free domestic servants could be recruited from among the women of the non-Muslim minorities, the clear tendency was to prefer a Muslim slave. Even if poor, free Muslims were reluctant to allow a female member of their family to take

---

[31] See above, pp. 68-9.

[32] On financial arrangements and communication, see Kelly, p. 417; FO 84/1305/165-74, Rogers to Clarendon, 24.11.69; *ibid.*/285-6, Moore to Clarendon, 28.10.69; BA/İrade/Meclis-i Vâlâ/16623, enclosure 69, Petition of 5 slave dealers, 4 Zilhicce 1273/26.7.57; *ibid.*, enclosures 2, 9, 20, 21, 22, 30; *ibid.*/16856, Correspondence between the slave dealers Bayram and Ismâil, 7-8.57.

up a job outside the home. These social norms changed gradually. When they did, they were often replaced by a practice similar in many ways to domestic slavery. That is, free parents would place a young daughter as a servant with a wealthier family, in exchange for a promise to take care of her needs, educate or train her, and, ultimately, after years of service, marry her off. Thus, patronage was maintained, but without the bond of legal slavery.

Still, it is interesting to examine the economic aspects of domestic slavery. It is possible to estimate—albeit very generally—the average wages paid to free domestic servants in the major cities of the Empire in the period under review. In 1857 the Ottoman government detained a group of slaves freshly imported from Tripoli to Izmir. The slaves were manumitted and placed as servants with local families in Izmir. The monthly wages of the 28 women in the group averaged 42 *kuruş* per woman. During the same year, a kadi in Istanbul ordered the manumission of 2 female slaves, placed them as domestic servants, and fixed their wages at 50 *kuruş* per month for the older and 20 *kuruş* for the younger. In 1860 the mental hospital of Süleymaniye was allowed to hire 4 additional servants, owing to the increase in the number of patients. The servants were to be given 100 *kuruş* per month for what admittedly was going to be a difficult job. A servant in the hospital attached to the hostel for immigrants received in 1865 monthly wages of 75 *kuruş*. Another servant was reportedly paid in 1874 the sum of 50 *kuruş* per month.[33] Though wages obviously varied according to the qualifications of the individual, it seems feasible to assume that the

[33] Monthly wages for slaves manumitted in 1857 are in *ibid.*/16623, enclosures 28 and 68. Wages decided by a Kadi in Istanbul are mentioned in FO 84/1028/166-74, Stratford to Clarendon, 22.2.57. Wages of mental hospital work mentioned in BA/İrade/Meclis-i Vâlâ/19337, the Grand Vezir to the Sultan, 11 Rebiülevvel 1277/27.9.60, and enclosures. (They were also given 1 *kuruş* per day for maintenance.) Wages of hotel servant are in BA/BEO/758, no. 109 (for the year 1282/1865-6), ca. 10-11.65. Servant earning 50 *kuruş* is mentioned in FO 84/1428/74, enclosed in Silley to Francis, 9.5.74.

average monthly pay of a free domestic servant was approximately 40 *kuruş*. If we add to that maintenance at 1.25 *kuruş* per day, we may reach an annual figure of 480 *kuruş* wages plus 450 *kuruş* maintenance, or 930 *kuruş* total.

Thus, a slave bought for the average 2,000 *kuruş*, for blacks, would begin to justify the investment after a service of 6 years and 3 months. This calculation is based on a rate of interest of 8 percent on the initial investment and maintenance expenses of 1.25 *kuruş* per day for both free domestics and slaves.[34] It is perhaps no accident that we rarely read of slaves being manumitted before this initial period of service. Though many slaves remained long years in servitude, sometimes 20 and 30 years, the period most often referred to in the sources as the normal length of service is 7 years. White female slaves bought into the Ottoman upper-class harems justified the large investment made in them when they were married, within the household or outside it, thereby either saving the high expenses of a dower, or bringing in dower from the groom's family.

Male slaves in Arabia had more tangible economic value as pearl-divers, oarsmen, and sailboat crew members, agricultural workers in the Yemen and northern Hijaz, and as hired laborers who brought their wages home to their masters. Circassian agricultural slave families had a very clear economic value as cultivators. The fact that grass-cutters and reapers in the Adana area were paid in the 1870s 1.5 to 12 *kuruş* per day during the harvest season may serve to illustrate this point. In the late 1830s in Circassia, if the land changed hands and the agricultural slave remained on it, the buyer had to compensate the seller at a rate of approximately 1,650 to 2,200 *kuruş* per person.[35]

---

[34] According to the same calculation, a slave bought for 2,500 *kuruş* justified the investment after 8 years and 11 months, and a slave bought for 3,000 *kuruş*, after 12 years and 6 months.

[35] For use of male slaves in Arabia, see Colomb, pp. 59-61, and FO 84/1570/171-2, Zohrab to Layard, 13.3.80. Wages of agricultural workers in Adana are from Davis, p. 171. Rate of compensation for agricultural slaves is from Bell, vol. I, pp. 179-81.

THE VOLUME OF THE SLAVE TRADE
TO THE OTTOMAN EMPIRE

Only a very general estimate of the volume of the trade can be offered at this stage, for the official Ottoman records which can throw light on this question, if they indeed survived, have not yet been made available at the Istanbul archives. Thus, we have to make do with the material which is available at present, namely a limited number of Ottoman documents; British, American, and French consular reports; and a few travel accounts which have generally proved to be reliable. The main problem is obviously that of credibility. Even if a particular observer is believed to have had no interest in giving false information, we have to make allowances for possible mistakes in judgment, for the human eye is by no means an absolute and objectively accurate measuring device. I say the human eye, because in many cases no systematic counting methods were applied by the observers, nor did they record figures over a sufficiently long period of time. Therefore, we should use the available figures with utmost caution. Still, if we leave out those sources, and they are indeed few, which provide much higher or much lower estimates than most other sources, we can come up with a general idea of the scope and volume of the slave trade.

In a vast territory such as that of the Ottoman Empire, and during a period of over fifty years, fluctuations did occur and, therefore, figures are valid only when they refer to specific places at specific periods of time. The number of slaves traded depended on both local and general factors, political as well as economic, which influenced supply and demand. Both the availability of slaves and the ability to pay for them were gradually waning, but even in this trend we can notice temporary reversals. Rather than engage in generalities which at present can hardly be subtantiated, it seems more useful simply to list the most reliable data that the sources consulted for this study provide. The following table offers information which is either directly stated in the listed source, or has been extrapolated from the data supplied by the source.

Some Estimates Regarding the Slave Trade to the Ottoman Empire in the Nineteenth Century

(All figures are annual estimates unless otherwise stated)

Year	The Vilâyet of Tripoli	The Red Sea	The Persian Gulf	Istanbul	Other
1839	2,000–2,500 passed through Tripoli to Bengazhi[36]				
1840	3,000 traded in Tripoli; increase noted[37]	2,000 arrive from Tajūra[38] 5,000 to the Red Sea, mainly to Jidda[39]	4,000–5,000 sold in the Gulf, most of them in Başra, Kuwait, Bahrayn and Bushire[40]		
1841	2,000 entered Tripoli from January to June[41]	200–300 arrive in Mukhā every month[42]			
1842		800–1,000 arrive from Massawa;[43] in the 1840s— 2,000–3,000 go to the Red Sea and Hadramawt[44]		1,400 Circassians (800 male + 600 female) enter Turkey,[45] 2,800 Africans were imported to Istanbul, 500 Circassians[46]	
1843	approximately 900 arrive on average[47]			about 40 passed through customs in January[48]	
1844	only 300 reached Tripoli as a result of an insurrection in the Fezzan[50]			about 240 passed through customs in June[49]	
1846				4,000–5,000 Africans and 3,000–4,000 Circassians imported to Istanbul[51]	

| 1847 | 2,000 exported from the Vilâye*t*[52] | 5,000 imported to Başra and Bushire[53] |

36 USNA/T40/roll 7, D. Smith McCanley (consul, Tripoli) to John Forsyth (Secretary of State), 3.10.39.

37 FO/195/108, Warrington (consul, Tripoli) to Palmerston, 1.8.40, 10.8.40.

38 Kelly, p. 418.

39 *Ibid.*, pp. 416-7.

40 *Ibid.*, pp. 438-9; Issawi, *Iran*, pp. 127-8.

41 FO 84/373/390-2, Wood (vice-consul, Benghazi) to Warrington, 22.6.41.

42 Kelly, p. 418.

43 *Ibid.*

44 *Ibid.*, pp. 416-7.

45 MEA/Corr. Pol./Turquie/Trébizonde et Erzuroum/vol. I, Outrey (consul, Trabzon) to the Foreign Minister, 2.3.42.

46 White, vol. II, p. 286.

47 USNA/M46/roll 12, Brown to John C. Calhoun (Secretary of State), 10.4.45.

48 BA/Kepeci/5263/pp. 1-2, Register of the revenues of the Istanbul customs-house (*icmal*), Kanun-ı Sâni 1259/January 1843

49 *Ibid.*/pp. 3-4, Register of the revenues of the Istanbul customs-house (*icmal*), Haziran 1260/June 1844.

50 USNA/*loc.cit.*

51 *Ibid.*, Brown to Buchanan (Secretary of State), 4.6.46.

52 *Ibid.*/T40/roll 8, M. J. Gaines (consul, Tripoli) to Daniel Webster (Secretary of State), 31.3.52.

53 FO 84/691/85, Rawlinson (consul, Bagdad) to Wellesley (Istanbul), 3.3.47.

Some Estimates Regarding the Slave Trade to the Ottoman Empire in the Nineteenth Century (cont.)

Year	The Vilâyet of Tripoli	The Red Sea	The Persian Gulf	Istanbul	Other
1848	2,462 arrived in Tripoli and Benghazi, more than 2,000 were exported from the Vilâyet[54]	in 1840s about 2,000 exported from Massawa, in 2nd quarter of the 19th century 6,000 exported from Matamma, Tajūra, Zayla', Massawa and Berbera (1,000–2,000 sold at the Berbera fair, a few hundred go to the Red Sea, about 1,000 to the Gulf, 1,500–3,000 exported from Tajūra alone)[55]			
1842	1,602 reached Tripoli and Benghazi, 1,424 were exported from the Vilâyet, 2,384 passed through Murzūq[56]				
1850	2,733 exported from the Vilâyet (1,474 from Benghazi, 1,259 from Tripoli)[57]				
1851	only 450 exported from the Vilâyet[58]				

1852   2,008 exported from the
      Viláyet (1,007 from Benghazi,
      1,001 from Tripoli); 2,458
      arrived at Marzūq (some sent
      to Egypt[59]

1853   1,158 exported from the
      Viláyet (858 from Tripoli,
      300 from Benghazi); 2,609
      arrived at Marzūq[60]

1854   1,408 exported from the
      Viláyet (526 from Benghazi,
      472 from Tripoli, 410 from
      Misrāta); 2,900 arrived at
      Marzūq[61]

during 1st 2/3 of the
19th century (annually):
1,750 exported from Massawa,
1,500 from Baylul, 6,000 from
Tajūra and Zaylaʿ, 17,000
from the Sudanese frontier,
350 from other ports, total
of 26,700 Ethiopian slaves[62]

[54] FO 84/774/118, Crowe (consul, Tripoli) to Palmerston, 1.3.49.

[55] Abir, pp. 66-9.

[56] FO 84/815/313-20, Crowe to Palmerston, 20.1.50. The British reports from the *Viláyet* of Tripoli were based on the receipts of the local customs-house. It is possible that not all slaves passed through customs.

[57] FO 84/857/9, Palmerston to Canning, 21.3.51.

[58] USNA/M46/roll 12. *loc.cit.*

[59] FO 84/919/185-8, Herman (consul, Tripoli) to Malmesbury (Foreign Secretary). 15.1.53.

[60] Accounts and Papers, 1854, vol. LXXIII, pp. 810-1, Returns from Tripoli, 20.1.54.

[61] *Ibid*, 1854-5, vol. LVI, pp. 807-9, Herman to Clarendon, 22.1.55.

[62] Richard Pankhurst, "The Ethiopian Slave Trade in the Nineteenth and Early Twentieth Centuries: a Statistical Inquiry," *Journal of Semitic Studies*, vol. IX (1964), p. 227. The figure for the Sudan is certainly too high.

Some Estimates Regarding the Slave Trade to the Ottoman Empire in the Nineteenth Century (cont.)

Year	The Vilâyet of Tripoli	The Red Sea	The Persian Gulf	Istanbul	Other
1855	2,262 exported from the Vilâyet (1,330 from Tripoli, 812 from Benghazi, 120 from Misrāta)[63]				
1860		200 imported into Jidda every month; average for 1859-86— 2,000 slaves per annum[64]			
1861		200 imported into Jidda all year (sharp decline noted by observer)[65]			
1869		2,000-2,500 arrive in Jidda (500-600 from Sawākın and Massawa, rest from Hudayda); 3,500-4,000 from Zayla' to Hudayda (2,000 remain for Yemeni markets)[66]			
1870			10,000-11,000 exported from Zanzibar to Arabia, the shores of the Red Sea, and the ports of the Persian Gulf[67]		

1874	about 1,330 sold in Tripoli and Ghāt,[68] and more than 2,000 went to Egypt through the Vilâyet[69]	no less than 5,000 land in the Hijaz[70], 11,000 on average exported on the Showa–Tajūra route[71]
1875		25,000–30,000 imported into the Hijaz and Yemen (increase noted by the observer)[72]
1876	no exports from the Vilâyet, about 110 brought and sold locally[73]	30,000 imported into Arabia, many continue to Turkey and Syria[74]

[63] FO 84/1000/236–41, Herman to Clarendon, 26 1 56

[64] FO 84/1144/209–12, Stanley (consul, Jidda) to Colquhoun (consul-general, Egypt), 21 1 61, average suggested on basis of 9 years by Ochsenwald, p 122

[65] Ibid

[66] FO 84/1305/271–82, Raby (consul, Jidda) to Clarendon, 10 12 69

[67] Accounts and Papers, 1870, vol LXI, pp 903–5, report addressed to the Earl of Clarendon by the Committee on the East African Slave Trade, 24 1 70

[68] BFASS/Mss Brit Emp /S22/G96, De Cosson's report, 16 6 74 (pp 20–1) The author states that the value of the slaves sold in Tripoli and Ghāt was ff 498,980 My calculation is based on an average price of ff 375 per slave

[69] FO 84/1428/76–9, Henderson (vice-consul, Benghazi) to the Foreign Office, 22 6 74

[70] BFASS/Mss Brit Emp /S18/C43/16–16a, E B Evans (Jidda) to Rev B Millard, 12 8 74

[71] ASR, vol XIX (1874–5), p 146, "Slave Trade in Galla Countries," a letter to the Anti-Slavery Society, 10 12 74

[72] FO 84/1412/169–74, Beyts (consul, Jidda) to Derby (Foreign Secretary), 10 6 75

[73] FO 84/1450/64–7, Drummond-Hay (consul-general, Tripoli), to Derby, 22 2 76

[74] Ibid /354–5, Beyts to Derby, 25 11 76

Some Estimates Regarding the Slave Trade to the Ottoman Empire
in the Nineteenth Century (cont.)

Year	The Vilâyet of Tripoli	The Red Sea	The Persian Gulf	Istanbul	Other
1877					600 imported to Damascus by the pilgrims (overland), 150 arrive in Beirut from Egypt (by sea)[75]
1878		1,500–1,700 into Arabia, 727 captured by HMS "Wild Fawn" in one month[76]			
1879		3,000 sold in Hudayda from June to September[77]			200 imported to Syria by the pilgrims' caravan[78]
1880		3,000 landed in the Hijaz and more than that number are landed in the Yemen and marched to the Hijaz[79]			about 40 imported to Syria by the pilgrims[80] over 100 land on the south coast of Anatolia[81]
1882	about 1,000 arrive at Jālō (on their way to Benghazi)[82]				

1883   300 landed in Hudayda over the 6 weeks preceding the report[83]

1884   600–700 run within 3 weeks in November from Zayla' to the Hijaz[84]

1887   42 imported into Syria[85]

[75] BFASS/Mss Brit Emp /S18/C92/98a-99a, Rev Waldmeier (Mount Lebanon) to Joseph Cooper, 29 1 77, and Rev Waldmeier's memo "Slavery in Syria," 25 1 77

[76] FO 84/1511/132-5, Vivian (consul-general, Egypt) to Derby, 22 3 78, FO 84/1510/303-4, Extract from Beyts's annual report of 31 3 78

[77] FO 84/1579/138-43, Annual Report on the Slave Trade (East Indies Station), by Rear Admiral William Gore-Jones, 24 9 80

[78] FO 195/1262, Jago (vice-consul, Damascus) to the Foreign Office, 15 2 79

[79] FO 84/1571/94-102, W P Burrell (acting consul, Jidda) to Goschen (ambassador, Istanbul), 25 9 80

[80] Ibid /218-21, Jago to Layard (ambassador, Istanbul), 10 2 80

[81] FO 84/1596/63-4 Colonel Wilson (Antalya) to St John (Chargé d'Affaires, Istanbul), Secret, 31 12 80

[82] FO 84/1641/81-93, Cecil G Wood (consul, Benghazi) to Granville (Foreign Secretary), 14 3 83

[83] FO 541/25/91-2, Captain Garforth to the Secretary of the Admiralty, 28 6 83

[84] FO 84/1674/13105, Jago (consul, Jidda), to Granville, 18 11 84

[85] FO 84/1849/255-8, John Dickson (consul, Damascus) to Iddesleigh (Foreign Secretary), 26 1 87

Some Estimates Regarding the Slave Trade to the Ottoman Empire in the Nineteenth Century (cont.)

Year	The Vilâyet of Tripoli	The Red Sea	The Persian Gulf	Istanbul	Other
1889		2,000 exported from Baylūl to the Hijaz, 1,600 from Tajūra, 1,000 from Rahita[86]			

If we center on the third quarter of the nineteenth century as the period during which the slave trade to the Ottoman Empire was at its peak, we may venture to suggest the following, very tentative conclusions exports from the *Vilâyet* of Tripoli were probably around the level of 2,000 slaves per annum, imports into the Ottoman ports of the Red Sea and the Persian Gulf were approximately 7,000 slaves a year, with 4,000–5,000 going to the Hijaz and Yemen and the rest to the Gulf, exports from Egypt could have amounted to about 1,000–2,000 slaves per annum, the Circassian traffic might have accounted for another 1,000–2,000 slaves a year, though it increased during the migration of the 1860s Thus, the volume of the Ottoman slave trade, excluding Egypt's internal traffic, was probably around 11,000 a year and is unlikely to have exceeded 13,000

For the sake of comparison, we may add that the traffic into Egypt was estimated to have been in the 1850s less than 5,000 slaves per annum, in the 1860s it rose temporarily to over 25,000 slaves every year [87] Circassian and Georgian slaves, too, were being sent to Egypt via Istanbul and Izmir, but only in small numbers Recent figures indicate that between the years 1811 and 1870, an average of 31,000 slaves were being imported each year from Africa into North, Central, and South America [88] The present work, however, cannot address the vast and complicated comparative aspects, which deserve special treatment

[86] BFASS/Mss Brit Emp /S22/G2, Report on the Slave Trade in the Red Sea, by Charles Gissing, Commander of H M S "Osprey" and Senior Officer of the Aden Division, 1 7-31 12 88
[87] Baer, pp 171-2
[88] Curtin, Table 67, p 234

CHAPTER III

The Road to Prohibition—
Anglo-Ottoman Contacts Regarding
the Suppression of the Slave Trade,
1840-1855

THE SOCIAL—and to an extent economic—importance of Ottoman slavery, the Islamic sanction which attached to it, and its relatively mild nature account for the fact that the Ottomans expressed no desire to abolish the institution. The suffering and high mortality that accompanied the slave trade from the sources of supply to the Empire—if at all known to the majority of slave-holders—were vague and removed notions; they happened in distant and unfamiliar countries and did not seem very real in Instanbul and the other Ottoman cities. Slavery was taken for granted and abolitionism—fairly new even in the West—was an alien idea; it came from Britain, was little understood, and won few or no converts. But this very fact makes it convenient for us to follow the history of the suppression of the slave trade in and to the Ottoman Empire from the very beginning, that is, from the early British attempts to induce the Porte to act against the traffic and the institution.

This chapter deals with the mounting British pressure and the Ottoman reaction to it in the years 1840-1855, or from the first contacts between the two governments to the prohibition of the Circassian and Georgian slave trade. Those years saw Britain relinquish her ambitious goal of abolishing Ottoman slavery altogether. She would then settle for the more modest but realistic effort to suppress the slave trade in and to the Empire. Also in this period, a distinction was beginning to emerge in the policies applied to the two different types of traffic: the African versus the Circassian and

Georgian. But let us turn first to the earliest British attempts to convey to the Ottoman government what Britain regarded as the message of enlightenment.

Although the first Anglo-Ottoman contacts concerning the slave trade had taken place as early as 1812,[1] a serious effort to induce the Porte to suppress the traffic and abolish slavery was not made until 1840. As normally in matters of abolition, the lead was provided by the powerful British and Foreign Anti-Slavery Society. With significant achievements already to its credit—such as the Emancipation Acts of 1833 and 1838 and the measures, British and international, against the Atlantic slave trade—the Society now extended its activities to include also the Islamic countries in the East, with special emphasis on the Ottoman Empire. In view of the Sultan's virtual dependence on British support against his rebellious governor, Mehmet Ali Paşa of Egypt, the moment seemed opportune to exact concessions from the Ottoman government.[2]

Not losing sight of these political circumstances, the General Convention organized by the Society in London in mid-June 1840 unanimously adopted a resolution urging Foreign Secretary Palmerston to assist "in obtaining such declarations from the Sultan, as are likely to lead to the entire suppression of Slavery in the Countries subjected to the Sultan's Govern-

---

[1] At the time, the British asked the governor of Baghdad to check the importation of Indian women into the province. The governor issued a decree prohibiting such importations (Kelly, p. 419).

[2] For the history of the anti-slavery movement in Britain, see Frank Klingberg, *The Anti-Slavery Movement in England* (New Haven, 1926); Sir Reginald Coupland, *The British Anti-Slavery Movement* (London, 1833); Howard Temperley, *British Antislavery 1833-1870* (London, 1972); Edith Hurwitz, *Politics and the Public Conscience* (New York, 1973). For a general discussion of the political situation at the time, see F. Rodkey, *The Turco-Egyptian Question in the Relations of England, France and Russia* (Urbana, 1921); C. K. Webster, *The Foreign Policy of Palmerston, 1830-1841*, 2 vols. (London, 1951); P. E. Mosely, *Russian Diplomacy and the Opening of the Eastern Question, 1838-1839* (Cambridge, Mass., 1934); M. Sabry, *l'Empire Egyptien sous Mohamed Ali et la question d'Orient, 1811-1849* (Paris, 1930); Şinasi Altındağ, *Kavalalı Mehmet Ali Paşa isyanı: Mısır meselesi, 1831-1841*, vol. I (Ankara, 1945).

ment." Lord Palmerston was quite receptive to the Society's requests, and in the following months communicated them to Lord Ponsonby, the British ambassador in Istanbul. Continuation of British support of the Empire, Palmerston wrote to Ponsonby in November 1840, was contingent upon the favorable disposition of public opinion in Britain toward the Porte, which in turn was tied to some Ottoman action against slavery and the slave trade.[3] Lord Ponsonby, who took the matter to the Ottoman government, reported his impressions at the end of December:

"I have mentioned the subject and I have been heard with extreme astonishment accompanied with a smile at a proposition for destroying an institution closely interwoven with the frame of society in this country, and intimately connected with the law and with the habits and even the religion of all classes, from the Sultan himself down to the lowest peasant. . . . I think that all attempts to effect your Lordship's purpose will fail, and I fear they might give offence if urged forward with importunity. The Turks may believe us to be their superiors in the Sciences, in Arts, and in Arms, but they are far from thinking our wisdom or our morality greater than their own."[4]

This discouraging assessment stifled any further attempts on the part of British governments for the next six years. True, in May 1841, the Foreign Office circulated to British consulates the memorial of the General Anti-Slavery Convention, and there were also some independent actions taken by the Anti-Slavery Society with regard to Ottoman slavery, but nothing more was done. In October 1842 the Secretary of the Anglo-Maltese Anti-Slavery Association accused the

---

[3] BFASS/Mss. Brit. Emp./S20/E2/18/39–40, protocol of the session held on 17.6.40; and FO 195/108, Thomas Clarkson to Palmerston, 20.6.40; FO 195/108, Palmerston to Ponsonby, 22.8.40 and 8.10.40; *ibid.*, Palmerston to Ponsonby, 9.11.40; and Kelly, p. 586 (part of the text cited).

[4] FO 193/108, Ponsonby to Palmerston, 27.12.40, and Kelly, *ibid.* (full text cited).

British ambassador in Istanbul, Sir Stratford Canning, of being "afraid to disturb the matter."[5] The experienced ambassador—not known for his unwillingness to meddle in Ottoman domestic affairs—had declined to assist the Association in obtaining signatures for an anti-slavery petition addressed to the Queen. He wrote in his reply:

> "Greatly as I desire to see the abolition of slavery throughout the civilized world and happy as I should be to assist in the accomplishment of so benevolent an object, I cannot overlook the considerations belonging to my official position at a court where slavery is recognized and practised invariably under the sanction of established law. . . . With respect to my own opinions upon the subject of slavery as it exists in this country, they will not fail to come under the notice of Her Majesty when necessary, in the regular course of my official correspondence."[6]

In mid-1846 Sir Stratford still thought that Ottoman slavery was mild and anyway could not be interfered with. This restraint might be attributed, in part at least, to the constant exhortations of the Earl of Aberdeen, Palmerston's successor as Foreign Secretary, to refrain from intervention in the domestic affairs of the Ottoman Empire. These were privately communicated to the ambassador by Aberdeen, who was concerned to maintain unity of action among the European powers with regard to the Empire and to check Canning's desire to push the Porte toward internal reform.[7] While negotiations were in progress with Arab rulers in the Persian

[5] FO Circular 5/41 (Print Series); address of the Anti-Slavery Society to "those who love justice and mercy among the Mohammadans" 11.43 (BFASS/Mss. Brit. Emp./S20/E2/20/4-7); *ibid.*/S18/C/21/34, J. Richardson (Malta) to John Scoble, 22.10.42.

[6] BFASS/*loc.cit.*, citing in full Canning's letter of 27.9.42.

[7] USNA/M46/roll 12, John P. Brown (Dragoman and Chargé d'Affaires *ad interim*, U.S. Embassy, Istanbul), to James Buchanan (Secretary of State), 4.6.46; Aberdeen Papers, vol. C, BM/Add. Ms. 43138/290-1, Aberdeen to Stratford, Private, 20.11.44; *ibid.*/319-21, Stratford to Aberdeen, Private, 1.3.44; *ibid.*/323, Aberdeen to Stratford, Private, 5.3.44.

Gulf for the suppression of the slave trade—as we shall see later in this chapter—Aberdeen showed no interest in moving on the same path with the Ottoman Empire. This, however, was to change with Palmerston's return to the Foreign Office in mid-1846, though with a significant difference: the more ambitious goal of the *abolition of Ottoman slavery* was abandoned; instead, efforts would thenceforward center on the *suppression of the slave trade* in and to the Empire.

SUPPRESSION OF THE SLAVE TRADE
IN THE PERSIAN GULF—THE *Ferman* OF 1847

In seeking to suppress the slave trade from East Africa to the Persian Gulf, the British government had to negotiate with the four parties most involved in it: the Imām of Masqaṭ and the rulers of Berbera, Zaylaʿ, and Tajūra, whose ports served as the main outlets for the slave trade on the African coast; the Trucial Shaykhs, whose subjects transported the slaves in their vessels and operated the slave depôts on the route; and the two monarchs into whose territories the slaves were being imported—the Shah of Iran and the Ottoman Sultan. Without the cooperation of all, the slave trade could not be effectively suppressed. It was only gradually, and much through "trial and error," that the British government came to realize this fact. In August 1846 Lord Palmerston issued the first instructions to the British ambassador in Istanbul to approach the Porte on the matter. By that time, Britain had already concluded treaties concerning the slave trade with both the Imām of Masqaṭ and the Trucial Shaykhs of the Gulf.[8]

Saʿīd, the Imām of Masqaṭ, was committed by a treaty signed on 17 December 1839 not to engage in slave trading south and east of the modified "Morseby Line." This was a line drawn on the map from Cape Delgado on the African coast, via a point 2° east of Socotra, to Pasmi on the Maqrān coast (see Map H). The original line ended at Diu Head on

---

[8] For details, see Kelly, pp. 424–45, 580–9.

the coast of Kathiawar and was named after Captain Fairfax Morseby, who signed the first slave trade treaty with Saʿīd on 4 September 1822. On Saʿīd's demand, the modified "Morseby Line" was drawn specifically to exclude his Maqrān possessions. The Royal and Indian navies were given the right to search suspected vessels of the Imām, and to seize those found to have slaves on board. The treaty also prohibited the enslavement and importation of Somalis.

Similar treaties were signed between Britain and the Trucial Shaykhs of Abū Ḍabī, Umm al-Qaywayn, and Sharja on 1-3 July 1839. The dividing line in these treaties, however, ended at Cape Guadel on the Maqrān coast. All treaties excluded the Red Sea and Persian Gulf areas, and were meant to suppress the slave trade to Western India only. In June 1841 Palmerston redefined the British policy to include the suppression of the slave trade in these areas as well. This change had to result in a confrontation with Saʿīd and the Trucial Shaykhs, for it concerned their most lucrative slave routes. In order to succeed in her efforts, it was essential for Britain to obtain from the Ottoman and Iranian governments a commitment to prohibit the use of their flags and ports by slave dealers.

There was a negative reaction to the first attempt to carry out Palmerston's instructions when in January 1842 they were read to Saʿīd. However, on 2 October 1845, after protracted negotiations, he signed a treaty forbidding all slave exportations from his African possessions. It was to come into effect on 1 January 1847. The man who negotiated the treaty with Saʿīd, the political agent and consul in Masqaṭ, Captain Hamerton, asserted in May 1846 that the cooperation of the Ottoman and Iranian governments was necessary if the slave trade in the Persian Gulf was to be effectively controlled. Britain should seek to obtain by treaty the right to enforce a prohibition of the trade in vessels and ports belonging to these two powers. This, Hamerton maintained, would prevent the Trucial Shaykhs from switching to Ottoman and Iranian colors after signing treaties with Britain which would forbid the pursuit of the slave trade under their own colors.

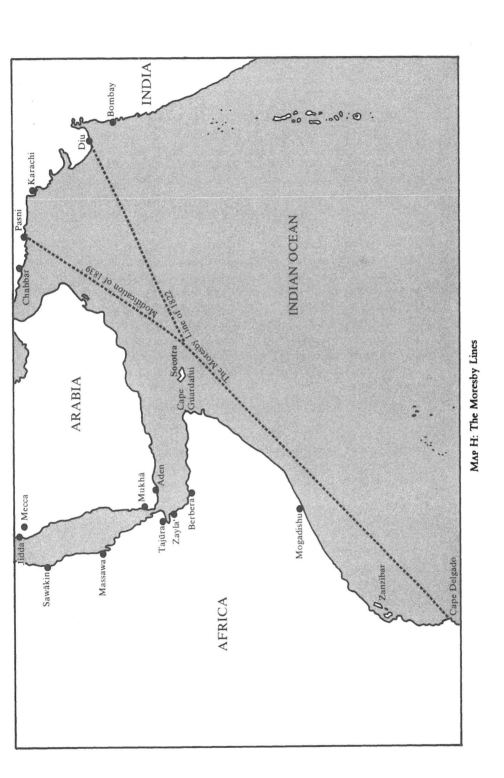

Map H: The Moresby Lines

Palmerston acted in accordance with Hamerton's recommendation and on 31 August 1846 instructed the British ambassador in Istanbul, Richard C. Wellesley, to secure from the Porte a *ferman*, or Imperial decree to this effect.[9] The Ottomans were told that a similar *ferman* was being sought from the Shah of Iran; they were asked to prohibit the slave trade from Africa to the Persian Gulf and to grant Britain the right to enforce it.

Almost two months later, Wellesley replied that he had talked with the Grand Vezir Mustafa Reşit Paşa, Foreign Minister Âli Efendi, and other ministers about the slave trade in the Persian Gulf.[10] There was more willingness, he noted, to comply with Palmerston's request than he had expected. The ambassador sensed, however, a concern among the ministers that Britain might later press for a general abolition of slavery in the Ottoman Empire. Indeed, this was but one of the possibilities which worried the ministers and came up in their deliberations.

The Council of Ministers (*Meclis-i Hâss*) met on 27 November 1846 to discuss the British request.[11] The ambassador's draft agreement consisting of four clauses was presented to the ministers and reviewed by them. The abolition of slavery and the slave trade by the Bey of Tunis, announced in 1841, was mentioned in the meeting as a step

---

[9] FO 195/108, Palmerston to Wellesley, 31 8 46

[10] FO 84/647/14-5, Wellesley to Palmerston, 17 10 46

[11] The *Meclis-i Hâss* or *Meclis-i Vukelâ*, established by Sultan Mahmut II, should not be mistaken for a European cabinet At the beginning it was more of a privy council composed of a few heads of newly formed ministries under the presidency of the Grand Vezir It had no corporate existence or responsibility and its members were appointed directly by the Sultan However, as more ministries were created in the late 1830s and early 1840s, their heads joining the council with the title of minister, it becomes appropriate to translate *Meclis-i Hâss* and *Meclis-i Vukelâ* as Council of Ministers, bearing in mind, of course, the differences which still existed between these two European and Ottoman bodies (cf Lewis, *Emergence*, pp 98-9, 376-8, Shaw, *History*, vol II, pp 36-7), for information concerning the Council's meeting of 27 11 46, see BA/Mesâil-ı Muhimme/Ingiltere Mesalihine Dair/822, the Grand Vezir to the Sultan, 8 Zilhicce 1262/27 11 46 (hereafter—BA/Mes Muh /Ingiltere/   )

taken merely to placate the British government; it could serve as a warning of what might come out of the proposed agreement. But the opinion that there was no room for comparison between the two cases prevailed among the ministers. There was nothing in the draft, certainly not from a religious aspect (*mezheben*),[12] that could bring about a general abolition of slavery (*sedd-i bâb-ı rıkkiyet*), the Grand Vezir wrote to the Sultan. He added: "This agreement is aimed only at preventing the entrance of slaves brought by Ottoman and Iranian slave dealers to the ports of the Persian Gulf in order to enable the complete application of the treaties concluded on this matter (by Britain) with the Imām of Masqaṭ and the independent rulers in that area." The Council did not lose sight of other problems either, such as the effect the agreement might have on the supply of slaves to the Ottoman Empire.

The Council noted that the supply of black slaves to Istanbul, Rumelia, and Anatolia did not come from the Persian Gulf but from Tripoli and Egypt. To further allay the suspicions of critics, a curious explanation was put forward—the prohibition was aimed at preventing a slave trade from the Hijaz to America(!) Out of concern for continued supply, this time of white slaves, the ministers recommended a precautionary measure. The Russians, they observed, were constantly throwing obstacles in the way of the Circassian slave trade from the Caucasus. If they learned of the proposed agreement, they would immediately demand similar privileges in the Black Sea. This could involve also questions of sovereignty and should be avoided, the Council asserted.

As for the right of search and seizure, the Council decided at first that it should remain the privilege of the Imperial Ottoman Navy. For this purpose, the ministers recommended that a number of vessels be sent to the Gulf to assist in enforcing the prohibition. Further contacts with the British Embassy failed to convince the ministers of the need to

---

[12] On the religious aspect, see above, pp. 3, 5 note, 6-7, 12, and below, pp. 104, 118, 129-35, 158-67, 276-8.

grant Britain the right of search and seizure. It is hard to infer how much might have been promised to Wellesley orally, but neither the Grand Vezir's report to the Sultan nor the latter's *İrade* bear any specific mention of such a right being given. It is, however, quite clear from the Grand Vezir's report that the ministers were not enthusiastic about complying with the British demands. They would have gladly refused to cooperate, but their desire to keep on good terms with England prevailed. They especially mentioned the positive impact that such cooperation would have not only on the British government but also on British subjects as individuals. Still, the Council remained firm in refusing to sign a *treaty* (*muahede*) or enter any *public* engagement to suppress the slave trade in the Persian Gulf.

Instead, the ministers recommended that the Sultan issue confidential instructions to the *Vâli* of Baghdad, prohibiting slave trade in the Persian Gulf. These orders would be written along the line of previous ones sent to the *Vâli*s of Trabzon and Samsun, on the Black Sea coast, to check the Circassian slave trade. Appearing in the same document which earlier demanded secrecy to avoid further interference with the Circassian slave trade, the reference to previous orders on the matter raises questions about the motives behind the Council's move. Did they intend the *Vâli* of Baghdad to ignore the new orders in the same way the governors of Trabzon and Samsun were expected to ignore orders regarding the Circassian slave trade? Were the new orders to serve the same purpose as the old ones, i.e., to satisfy the demands of a foreign power (Russia in the Circassian case) without actually changing the situation which had given rise to the demands?

It seems that both questions can be answered in the negative. The Ottoman government honestly wanted to meet Britain's wishes, in part because they were convinced that doing so would not diminish the supply of either African or, if secrecy maintained, Circassian slaves into the Empire. But there appears to have been also a sincere desire to keep and improve the friendly relations with Britain, something perhaps lacking with regard to Russia. In any event, the Circassian slave trade was not at all mentioned in the British request addressed to the Porte; rather, it was brought up by the ministers on their own initiative. This clearly points out that, despite the difference between the African and Circassian branches of the traffic, in Ottoman eyes they still belonged in one and the same context.

The Sultan accepted the Council's recommendations on 11 December 1846,[13] and ordered that instructions be issued to the *Vâli* of Baghdad to prohibit slave trade into Ottoman ports in the Persian Gulf. The Kapudan Paşa, commander of the navy, was ordered to send some vessels to the area to enforce the prohibition; the Foreign Minister was told to "try to appease and satisfy" (*iskât ve irzalarına çalışılması*) the British Embassy. The latter task proved to be more difficult.

Although only briefly reported home by Wellesley, some hard negotiations must have taken place in Istanbul after the Council's decision had been communicated to the Embassy.[14] Wellesley found the instructions proposed by the Porte to be insufficient and demanded—"persistently" (*musırâne*), as the Grand Vezir informed the Sultan—that a *ferman* be issued and the right of search and seizure granted. The technical problem of issuing a secret *ferman* was solved in confidential negotiations with the Embassy, the British undertaking to give it no publicity. There was no mention of search

---

[13] *Ibid.*, the *Baş Kâtip* to the Grand Vezir, 22 Zilhicce 1262/11.12.46.

[14] FO 84/691/50-3, Wellesley to Palmerston, 1.2.47; Wellesley wrote that at first the Porte was reluctant to enter a meaningful agreement and that the matter was further pursued in negotiations with Ali. The ambassador's reports do not give a full picture of these negotiations; a much better account is provided by the Ottoman records. It cannot be said, however, that Wellesley tried to conceal information from his superiors or to mislead them. Rather, it seems that he thought he could handle the situation himself without involving the Foreign Office in the details of his contacts with the Porte; BA/Mes. Müh./İngiltere/823, the Grand Vezir to the Sultan, 2 Sefer 1263/20.1.47; text of *ferman* in *ibid., Bağdat Vâlisine Hüküm*, and in *Mühimme-i Mektume*, vol. 9, p. 162. It is dated Evâil-i Sefer 1263, or the beginning of Sefer 1263 (1 Sefer 1263 is 19.1.47, but the *ferman* was probably issued on 23.1.47).

and seizure in the Grand Vezir's report to the Sultan, submitted on 20 January 1847, but the attached *ferman* contained a timid reference to it.

The *ferman*, addressed to the *Vâli* of Baghdad Hacı Mehmet Necip Paşa, is important because it is the first to prohibit in any measure the slave trade in Africans to an Ottoman province. It is issued, the Sultan states, in order to facilitate the application of treaties signed by Britain with African rulers for the prevention of the slave trade to America! Violations of these treaties occur when slaves are *stolen (üsera sirkatiyle)* from the African coast and taken elsewhere. This trade in stolen slaves is quite different from that which supplies Istanbul, Rumelia, and Anatolia. Out of compassion and humanitarian considerations, it is henceforth forbidden. No slave trade shall be allowed under the Ottoman flag, and the Imperial Navy will send ships to the Bay of Başra to enforce this prohibition. Vessels engaged in the slave trade will be subject to seizure by the Ottoman Navy—or by British warships cruising in the area—and will be handed to the Ottoman port authorities. The *ferman* goes on to say that captains of slavers will be punished, but there are no instructions on what to do with the captured slaves.[15] Care is taken not to condemn, even by implication, other branches of the slave trade or the practice itself. Wellesley, however, saw it in a different light.

Reporting on the issue of the *ferman*, the ambassador asked Palmerston to accept the Ottoman demand for secrecy, and added: "Nothing but a sincere desire on the part of the Sultan and his government to prove their friendship to Great Britain could have induced them to consent to a proposition, which they cannot but feel is the first blow struck at slavery in this country." Whereas he was probably right in judging the motivation behind the Porte's compliance with his request, he was soon to be proved quite wrong about the ef-

[15] From a later document it appears that instructions concerning captured slaves were communicated to the governor of Baghdad separately (BA/Mes. Müh/İngiltere/828, Mehmet Necip Paşa, *Vâli* of Baghdad, to the Grand Vezir, 27 Cemaziyülevvel 1263/13.5.47).

fects of the *ferman* on slavery, or even on the slave trade, in the Ottoman Empire. For his part, Palmerston was pleased; he praised the Ottoman government, and agreed to observe the secrecy of the Sultan's policy in the Persian Gulf.[16]

Needless to say, the precise implications of the *ferman* required further clarifications before full application by the *Vâli* of Baghdad was possible. The *Vâli*, Necip Paşa, and the British consul in Baghdad reached an understanding which prevented a likely clash between the Arab principalities of the Gulf, under whose flags most slavers sailed, and the Ottoman authorities. Such a clash could have ensued from strict application of the *ferman*. Amendments were needed and the matter was again referred to London and Istanbul.[17] Another issue which still had to be considered was the future of slaves who would be seized as a result of the promulgation of the *ferman*.

For more than four months after the first *ferman* had been issued, in January 1847, the Foreign Office, the British Embassy in Istanbul, the Porte, and the governor of Baghdad were all engaged in attempts to settle the question of how to handle captured slaves.[18] From a letter written by Necip Paşa to the Grand Vezir Mustafa Reşit Paşa in May 1847, it appears that orders had actually been given by the Porte to manumit such slaves and return them to their countries of origin. In two separate instructions sent to Istanbul in March

[16] FO 84/691/50, Wellesley to Palmerston, 1.2.47; *ibid.*/4–7, Palmerston to Wellesley, 12.3.47.

[17] For details see, *ibid.*/85–7, Rawlinson to Wellesley, 3.3.47; *ibid.*/79–81, memo by Palmerston, 2.4.47; *ibid.*/104–11, Rawlinson to Wellesley, 16.3.47; *ibid.*/116–7, Wellesley to Palmerston, 6.4.47.

[18] Our account of these attempts is based on the following documentation: BA/Mes. Müh./İngiltere/828, Mehmet Necip Paşa, *Vâli* of Baghdad, to the Grand Vezir, 27 Cemaziyülevvel 1263/13.5.47; FO 84/691/9–17, Palmerston to Wellesley, 12 and 22.3.47; *ibid.*/100–2, Wellesley to Palmerston, 18.4.47; see also, *ibid.*/124–5, Cowley to Palmerston, 15.6.47; *ibid.*/19–21, Palmerston to Cowley, 24.5.47; BA/Mes. Müh./İngiltere/828, the Grand Vezir to the Sultan, 24 Cemziyülevvel 1263/9.6.47 and the enclosed order to the *Vâli* of Baghdad, n.d.; FO 84/691/124–5, Cowley to Palmerston, 15.6.47.

1847, Palmerston urged Wellesley to obtain from the Porte a modification of the orders so that slaves could be taken by British vessels to Mauritius. This was the best way, Palmerston maintained, to ensure that the liberated slaves would not be re-enslaved either on the African coast or even on Ottoman soil. Under British protection in Mauritius, he asserted, they could earn their living as free men and women.

Wellesley brought up the idea in a conversation with Âli Efendi, the Ottoman Foreign Minister, who thought that the Council of Ministers would object to it on religious grounds. They might see that, Âli told the ambassador, as an attempt to encourage these newly converted Muslim slaves to embrace Christianity. In response, Palmerston instructed Wellesley (now Lord Cowley) to forgo the specific mention of Mauritius as the destination of captured slaves. Simply state that British vessels will carry the slaves overseas to be set free, he suggested.

In his above-mentioned letter to the Grand Vezir, the *Vâli* of Baghdad asked for a clarification of earlier instructions on the matter. From the moment of manumission, Necip Paşa wrote, slaves were regarded as free persons and their will had to be respected. They should be allowed to stay in Ottoman territory if they so wished to do, or be given help to return home if they preferred that. However, he continued, the distance to those countries from Başra was great and transportation expensive. Further instructions were needed, the *Vâli* concluded.

Responding to this request and to British presentations, the Grand Vezir drafted a new order to the governor of Baghdad, which he submitted to the Sultan on 9 June 1847. In order that freed slaves would not be re-enslaved when they returned to their countries of origin, wrote Mustafa Reşit Paşa, those who wished to stay in Ottoman territory should be allowed to settle wherever they chose. Each of them would be given a certificate of manumission to ensure that they remained free. As for those liberated slaves who preferred to return to their countries, they should be helped to do so safely. For that purpose, and based on humanitarian considerations, they would be handed over to British officials in order to be taken on board British ships. The Sultan gave his assent to these instructions on 12 June 1847, Lord Cowley wrote to Palmerston that the modification was an important concession on the part of the Ottoman ministers.

In the following months, the British consul in Baghdad reported that the Ottoman authorities fully cooperated with him in carrying out the Porte's instructions The immediate effect was a considerable reduction in the slave trade to Başra. Having achieved satisfactory results with the Ottomans, Britain then turned to deal with the other parties involved in the slave trade in the Persian Gulf During April and May 1847, Britain concluded treaties with the Shaykhs of Sharja, Dubbay, ʿAjmān, Umm al-Qaywayn, Abū Ḍabī, and Baḥrayn; these agreements prohibited slave exportation from Africa in vessels belonging to these principalities. Britain was given the right to search and seizure, and the treaties were to go into effect on 9 December 1847.[19] The Shah of Iran was the only sovereign in the Gulf without an agreement with Britain on slave trade, dealing with him turned out to be more difficult

The Shah was approached about the slave trade in August 1846, at the same time that the Ottomans were asked to prohibit the trade in their Persian Gulf ports. He refused to comply with the British demand and was unwilling to change his mind even after the Ottomans had issued their *ferman* of prohibition. Shah Mohammed asserted that slavery was lawful in Islam and promoted conversion. The British consul in Baghdad tried to obtain a *fatwa* against the trade from Shaykh Muḥammad Ḥasan of Najaf, the highest Shīʿī authority, hoping that it might induce the Shah to relent. He failed.[20]

---

[19] FO 84/691/216, Rawlinson to Palmerston, 28 10 47, FO 84/737/21-3, Rawlinson to Cowley, 5 1 48, see also FO 84/691/162-8, Kemball (acting consul, Baghdad) to Cowley, 28 7 47 For treaties with the shaykhs, see Kelly, pp 588-9

[20] Kelly, pp 593-600, FO 84/737/38-40, Rawlinson (consul, Baghdad), to Sheil (ambassador, Teheran), 8 11 47, *ibid* /42-3, Rawlinson to Farrant (Teheran), 15 1 48

In the meantime, the slave trade was diverted from Baṣra to the Persian port of Mohamera, taking with it legitimate trade as well, thereby rewarding the Iranians for their refusal to yield to British demands.[21] To prevent that, Palmerston renewed the pressure on the Shah and for a while considered ordering search and seizure of Iranian vessels even without an agreement. The Shah gave in and on 12 June 1848 issued a *ferman* prohibiting the importation of slaves into Iran by sea. He tacitly agreed to an order of the governor of Fars which gave Britain the right of search and seizure of Iranian vessels. Palmerston, however, was not satisfied and continued to press for a more formal commitment.

After further negotiations with the Iranian government in later years, the right of search and seizure was officially granted to Britain in 1 January 1852.[22] A year later, an Iranian commissioner was appointed to enforce, in cooperation with the British squadron in the Gulf, the prohibition of the slave trade. This arrangement was most successful during the first stage of its operation; it became less effective when later the central government had difficulties imposing its will on the coastal tribes.

Thus, by the early 1850s, all parties involved in the Persian Gulf slave trade—except for the Shaykhs of Berbera, Zayla', and Tajūra—were brought into agreements with Britain, committing them to coordinate action against the traffic. The rulers of Berbera, Zayla', and Tajūra found it increasingly difficult to export slaves to the Persian Gulf and reverted almost exclusively to the Red Sea route. Owing to various problems—such as the lack of cruisers, legal difficulties arising from delays in parliamentary action, ineffective control of the Ottoman and Iranian governments over their provincial governors in the area, and the existence of conditions favorable to smuggling—some slave trade continued to be carried on in the Persian Gulf in later years. However, it was

[21] FO 84/691/162-8, Kemball to Cowley, 24.11.47; FO 84/774/82-6, Kemball to Palmerston, 15.1.49.
[22] Kelly, pp. 606-13.

dealt a severe blow and never assumed again its earlier proportions.

As pointed out earlier,[23] the Persian Gulf slave trade was not an important source of supply to the principal markets of the Ottoman Empire in Istanbul, Anatolia, Rumelia, and the Levant. Most of the slaves who entered the Empire via this route were disposed of within the *Vilâyet* of Baghdad and some occasionally reached markets in Diyarbakır and other eastern Anatolian provinces. Ottoman cooperation with the British anti-slave trade policy in the Gulf was nonetheless important. It denied the slave dealers an outlet for their human cargo and prevented them from using Ottoman colors when the Trucial and Iranian ones no longer offered them immunity from search and seizure by British cruisers. Moreover, a precedent was thus established, and successive Ottoman governments thereafter accepted British intercession in regard to the African slave trade. Nevertheless, the right of search and seizure, as granted by the *ferman* of 1847, was not extended to British cruisers in other areas before 1880, and in no other case were British cruisers allowed comparable freedom of action in transporting captured slaves.

ABOLITION OF THE ISTANBUL SLAVE MARKET, 1847

In keeping with tradition, the Ottoman Sultan used to pay a ceremonial visit to the Porte, the seat of the Grand Vezir, at the beginning of the new Muslim year. During such a visit, in December 1846 (Muharrem 1263), Sultan Abdülmecit participated in a meeting of the *Meclis-i Umumi* (General Council), which was convened to discuss the introduction of important reforms. The General Council was composed of senior ministers, retired officials, and all the members of the High Council for Judicial Ordinances; its task was to review proposed legislation and recommend it to the Sultan for ratification. In the course of the session, the Sultan brought up the question of the Istanbul slave market, for he had heard

[23] See above, p. 91.

that slaves traded there were being mistreated and humiliated. This situation being contrary to Şerî and humanitarian principles—wrote the Imperial Historiographer Ahmet Lûtfi—the Sultan immediately ordered the abolition of the slave market in the capital.[24] However, private trading continued to be legal during most of the nineteenth century.

The abolition of the slave market in Istanbul was undertaken completely on Ottoman initiative and can be regarded as part of the reforms introduced within the framework of the *Tanzimat*. Mustafa Reşit Paşa, who was appointed Grand Vezir in September 1846, embarked at the time on new reforms in education, penal and commercial law and justice, and in the provincial administration, in what is seen as the second phase of the *Tanzimat*. Thus, in addition to the explanation given by Lûtfi, open slave trading in the midst of a "Westernizing" capital was probably also regarded as no longer conforming to the ideas of the time. Indeed, the abolition of the Istanbul slave market was hailed by the British government,[25] but in fact did little to reduce the slave traffic to the imperial city. One of the main attractions for European travellers in Istanbul became a thing of the past; with it were gone the lively descriptions that helped to shape so much of the negative image of "the Turk" in the eyes of Europe.

FIRST RESTRICTIONS ON THE AFRICAN SLAVE TRADE IN THE MEDITERRANEAN

During the decade following the promulgation of the 1847 *ferman* against the slave trade in the Persian Gulf, Britain increased her efforts to induce the Ottoman government to suppress the slave trade altogether in the Empire. Attention was focused on the important supply routes bringing in black

[24] Lûtfi, *Tarih*, vol VIII, pp 133-4, Shaw, *History*, vol II, p 77, text of edict of abolition in BA/Cevdet, Maliye/3177 (1847), Wellesley's report on abolition, FO 84/691/41, Wellesley to Palmerston, 18 1 47

[25] Palmerston praised the step taken by the Porte and instructed Wellesley to express to the Ottomans the appreciation of the British government (FO 84/691/2, Palmerston to Wellesley, 8 2 47)

slaves from Tripoli and Benghazi and white slaves from the Caucasus. As we shall see, the Hijaz and Red Sea slave trade was not interfered with during that period.

In late 1847, the attention of the British government was drawn to the slave trade from Waday and Bornu to the Ottoman *Vilâyet* of Tripoli. Reports reached the Foreign Office of a large caravan which came to Benghazi from Waday with more than 1,000 slaves, mostly women. The British vice-consul in Beghazi wrote:

"The journey from Waday has occupied exactly five months. The mortality among both the slaves and the camels has been very great, but it is difficult to ascertain the real number of casualties. I have been informed for certain that between Angola and Benghazi (a journey of eight days) 32 slaves died, or rather were abandoned to their fate. . . . I have been told that the chief reason of so many being abandoned on the journey is not so much the scarcity of food and water, but that from the swelling of their feet in traversing the hot sands, they are unable to keep up with the others and there being no spare camels to carry them, they are left to die in the Desert."

On instructions from the Foreign Secretary, the British ambassador in Istanbul, Lord Cowley, made a representation to the Porte demanding that measures be taken to put an end to such practices.[26]

On 4 November 1847, Grand Vezir Mustafa Reşit Paşa issued an order to the governor of Tripoli enjoining him to ensure that no similar incidents would occur in the future. He wrote:

"It is superfluous to say, that our holy law in permitting the holding of slaves, enjoins us to treat them with paternal kindness; God prohibits ill-usage towards them. And this precept is so well known, that those who have

[26] FO 84/691/224, T. H. Gilbert (vice-consul, Benghazi) to Crowe (consul-general, Tripoli), 10.9.47; *ibid.*/32, Palmerston to Cowley, 20.11.47.

brought the slaves above-mentioned have, in treating them in so cruel a manner, lost all right to be called human beings. . . . It is consequently the duty of the authorities to prevent such iniquitous acts toward slaves. Therefore, Your Excellency will cause to come into your presence the merchants who have bought the slaves in question, and you will give them to understand well, that if once more they dare commit similar excesses with regard to slaves, they will be punished for it with the greatest rigor. . . . You will exercise an active and un-interrupted inspection over matters of this kind, and you will deliver over to justice to be tried and punished those who shall dare to contravene your orders in this re-spect."[27]

The Grand Vezir's order, however, did not prohibit slave importation into the province, nor the exportation of slaves from Tripoli, nor did it condemn the slave trade as such. It was on humanitarian grounds alone that Mustafa Reşit Paşa based his objection to the excesses reported from Benghazi; he saw this reasoning as both compatible with and emanating from the *Şeriat*. Accordingly, if proper measures were taken by the slave dealers, the slave trade could be carried on in a "humane" manner.

Lord Cowley was impressed by the Grand Vezir's prompt reaction to his remonstrance and wrote to Palmerston: "I must do justice to the Turkish Ministers in adding that they have evinced the utmost abhorrence of any such practices, and the enclosed instructions [i.e., Mustafa Reşit Paşa's or-ders to the *Vâli* of Tripoli] are an unequivocal proof of the sincerity of their feelings."[28]

The "practice" of which "abhorrence" was expressed was no more than the ill-usage of slaves. However, Cowley— eager to detect change in the Ottoman position regarding the slave trade—might have been tempted to interpret this in-

---

[27] For a French translation, see *ibid.*/36, Cowley to Palmerston, 17.11.47.
[28] *Ibid.*

struction as a general disapprobation of the traffic. If so, he was wrong, as later events would show. Mustafa Reşit Paşa's instruction to the governor of Tripoli, though strongly worded, did not signal any change, as yet, in the Porte's position concerning the slave trade in Africans.

Away from the watchful eyes of British officials, the wheels of the Ottoman bureaucracy slowly rolled on. In December 1947 the *Vâli* of Tripoli, Mehmet Râgıp Paşa, reported to the Grand Vezir on the steps he had taken in compliance with the latter's instructions on the slave trade. The *Vâli* stated his sincere intention to carry out to the letter the Grand Vezir's orders "without wasting a minute" (*dakika fevt etmeksizin tenfiz ve icrası*), and added that he had already assembled all the slave dealers in Tripoli and explained to them the government stance. He warned them, Mehmet Râgıp Paşa wrote, that offenders would be severely punished. Also, he had the instruction translated into Arabic and sent to the *Kaymakams* of Fezzan and Benghazi. The report was presented to the Sultan and was endorsed by him on 19 February 1848.[29]

On paper, everything appeared settled, but the British were soon to find out that the slave dealers did little to improve their treatment of the slaves, as required by the Porte. Before long, new reports would reach the Foreign Office, indicating that the suffering of slaves on the desert road to Tripoli and the resulting high mortality continued to attend the North African slave trade. A policy agreed upon with the Ottoman government and communicated to local authorities, the British would learn, was not readily translated into a new reality in the province. Indeed, this gap between policy and practice became endemic to most Anglo-Ottoman dealings concerning the suppression of the slave trade.

In October 1849 news reached Palmerston of the tragic fate of a large caravan on its way from Bornu to Marzūq, a major slaving and commercial entrepôt in the *Vilâyet* of

---

[29] BA/Mes. Müh./İngiltere/831, Mehmet Râgıp Paşa to the Grand Vezir, 21 Muharrem 1264/29.12.47; *ibid.*, the Grand Vezir to the Sultan, 3 Rebi-ülevvel 1264/13.2.48.

Tripoli.[30] The caravan was said to have carried 1,600 slaves, in addition to a considerable amount of goods and animals intended for the coastal towns of North Africa, as well as for the European and Ottoman markets. When the caravan reached an oasis and found the wells dry, an attempt was made to return to the oasis which the caravan had left several days before. But the water supplies the people carried did not last and they all, slaves and dealers, perished

Palmerston instructed Sir Stratford Canning, back in the position of ambassador to Turkey, to make a strong representation to the Porte and to demand action to prevent such horrors in the future. On 28 November 1849 the Grand Vezir issued another instruction to the *Vâli* of Tripoli on the slave trade.[31] Mustafa Reşit Paşa reminded the *Vâli* of orders sent to his predecessor in 1847 concerning the maltreatment of slaves on the desert route, reiterating that although Islam allowed slavery, it clearly commanded that slaves be treated with kindness and compassion. The slave dealers were obliged, he continued, to carry ample food and water supplies for the slaves and to minimize their suffering on the road as much as possible. If they failed to do so, thereby acting contrary to the will of the Sultan, they would be severely punished

Despite his strong condemnation of the slave dealers' conduct, Mustafa Reşit Paşa was as yet unwilling, or unable, to go any further than to demand the elimination of the reprehensible aspects of the slave trade He would not, or could not, at that stage, prohibit the importation of slaves into the Ottoman Empire However, it was during his tenure of office that the first measures of restriction were applied to the African slave trade Between the years 1848 and 1850, the Porte prohibited the transportation of slaves in government vessels, and issued instructions to prevent all slave traffic to

[30] FO 84/774/170-5, Reade (vice-consul, Tripoli) to Palmerston, 24 8 49, and Gagliuffi (vice-consul, Marzūq) to Reade, 1 8 49

[31] Hamdı Atmar, "Zenci ticaretinin yasaklanması " *Belgelerle Turk Tarih Dergisi*, vol I, no 3 (December, 1967), pp 23-5 (Belge II, Mustafa Reşit Paşa to the *Vâli* of Tripoli, 21 Muharrem 1266/28 11 49)

the island of Crete and to the province of Janina. But the first restrictive measure was taken against the involvement of government officials in the slave trade. In December 1847 Palmerston received information that the governor of Tripoli was personally involved in the slave trade. He then instructed Cowley to ask the Ottoman government to prohibit its officials from engaging in the trade. Nothing was done. A while later, more information reached the Foreign Office concerning the *Vâli*'s shipments of slaves to Izmir, and Cowley embarked on serious negotiations with Âli Efendi on the matter. Finally, orders were issued to the governor of Tripoli to prevent government officials from pursuing the slave trade. The British consul-general in Tripoli reported, however, that the orders were interpreted as applying only to officials appointed directly from Istanbul, thereby excluding some of the most active culprits. A new and clear instruction was issued by Âli on 28 August 1848 and, reportedly, the local official most implicated in the slave trade was forced to give up the practice.[32] However, before a year had elapsed, this instruction too was alleged to have been violated.

The British vice-consul in Tripoli reported to the Foreign Office in August 1849 that the governor had sent sixteen slaves to Istanbul for sale.[33] Some of these slaves, the vice-consul wrote, had been given to the governor as a gift by

[32] FO 84/691/38-9, Palmerston to Cowley, 29.12.47; FO 84/737/2-3, Palmerston to Cowley, 10.2.48; *ibid.*/6-33 (excluding 12, 15-23), correspondence—Palmerston, Cowley, Alison, and Canning, until 10.18.48; FO 84/774/120-1, Crowe to Palmerston, 2.3.49. In the absence of the Turkish text of these instructions, we have to rely on the French translation, which was given to the British Embassy by the Porte. Such translations are often inaccurate and particularly misleading when one is looking for tone and subtlety of expression. Changes in translation were often made by the Porte deliberately in order to produce a favorable impression on the foreign reader. Thus, the French translation of the first order to the *Vâli* said that the slave trade was not "une chose louable", the translation of the second order included the following clause: "Or je n'ai pas besoin de vous répéter que ce commerce est par sa nature une mauvaise chose   ." (FO 84/737/29, 33). These expressions of disapprobation seem to be too strong for the time and might read quite differently in the Turkish original.

[33] FO 84/774/164, Reade to Palmerston, 3 8.49.

Hasan Paşa, the *Kaymakam* of Marzūq. Though open violations by such high-ranking officials became less frequent with
time, there is little doubt that secret evasion of government
orders by middle- and low-level officials was not infrequent.
A great deal depended on the actions of provincial governors
and the ability of the Central Government to impose its will
on them.

In July 1849 Sir Stratford Canning was apprised of the
transportation of slaves from Tripoli to Istanbul in vessels
belonging to the Ottoman government. He remonstrated,
but without any results. A year later he was informed that
400 slaves had been transported on the same route aboard a
government ship, and he decided to press the Porte on the
matter more vigorously than he had before. Canning's point
was that although no specific order against such practice existed, the prohibition concerning slave trading by government officials made it illegal to transport slaves on board
government vessels, where, presumably, all were government employees. This argument failed to impress Foreign
Minister Âli Paşa, but further negotiations with Grand Vezir
Mustafa Reşit Paşa produced better results. On 13 November 1850 Canning was given a copy of an instruction from
the Grand Vezir to the Kapudan Paşa prohibiting the use of
government vessels for the transportation of black slaves.
When in May 1853 government criers proclaimed in the
market of Tripoli that an Ottoman frigate would take slaves
to Istanbul for a fee, it was promptly reported to the *Vâli* by
the British consul. The governor acted immediately to carry
out the existing orders and prevented the embarkation of the
slaves.[34] Mustafa Reşit Paşa's instruction remained in effect
until the adoption of the general prohibition of the African
slave trade in 1857.

---

[34] *Ibid* /20-1 Canning to Palmerston, 19 7 49, FO 84/815/31-2, Canning
to Palmerston, 18 6 50, and *ibid* /35, Canning to Palmerston, 19 8 50, French
translation of the Grand Vezir's instruction to the Kapudan Paşa, in *ibid* /43,
FO 84/919/181, 197-200, correspondence—Herman (consul, Tripoli) and
Clarendon (Foreign Secretary), 22 5-26 7 53

THE PROHIBITION OF THE CIRCASSIAN AND
GEORGIAN SLAVE TRADE, 1854–1855

While concentrating its efforts on the Tripoli-Istanbul slave route, Britain attempted in 1851 to extend its efforts to the Circassian slave trade. Since this branch of the trade was considered to be within the Russian sphere of influence, and owing to its peculiar and sensitive nature, the Foreign Office had refrained from any interference with it before. However, with Canning as ambassador in Istanbul, action was taken upon the receipt of information that the Circassian slave trade was on the increase and that an Ottoman frigate was involved in transporting slaves to Istanbul. Sir Stratford urged the Foreign Office to pursue the matter with the Russians in St. Petersburg. The Russians, who had impeded the passage of slaves from the Caucasus until the mid-1840s, resorted thereafter to a policy of non-interference, if not as yet to that of overt encouragement, toward the slave trade. Contacts between the British ambassador in St. Petersburg and the Russian Foreign Minister Count Nesselrode produced no results. The Count, reportedly irritated by the question, said: "Que voulez-vous que nous fassions avec des gens qui s'enfuient? " Later, however, he promised to investigate the matter. In Istanbul, Sir Stratford held a meeting with the Russian ambassador in which both agreed that so long as slavery was legal in the Ottoman Empire, the slave trade from Russia could not be effectively suppressed, Canning, however, wondered why the Russians did absolutely nothing to impede it, not even using their consular officers for that purpose.[35]

It appears that the Russians had given up earlier hopes to

---

[35] FO 84/857/53-7, Brant (consul, Erzurum) to Palmerston, 5 5–7 6 51, ibid /35-45, correspondence—Palmerston, Canning, Brant and Stevens (vice-consul, Trabzon), 19–27 5 51, ibid /50-1, Canning to Palmerston, 26 8 51, Accounts and Papers, 1852-3, vol II, pp 648-9, in July of 1847, a British consul reported that many Circassians, believed to be slaves, arrived in Trabzon with Russian passports as immigrants to the Ottoman Empire (FO 84/691/253, Brant to Palmerston, 8 7 47), FO 84/857/35-45, correspondence—Palmerston, Canning, Brant, and Stevens, 19–27 5 51

win over the Circassian population of the Caucasus and decided to relax their blockade of the coast that was aimed at
preventing the slave trade. Openly, as a "civilized Christian
power," they still opposed the trade, but otherwise they turned
a blind eye to it. Not until after the Crimean War did the
Circassian immigration into the Ottoman Empire assume mass
proportions, but the flow was already steady in the early
1850s.[36] The slave trade contributed to the population movement by creating additional incentives for migration, as well
as an effective transportation network under the control of
the slave dealers. It should also be noted that the great majority of the slaves were women of child-bearing age, a fact
which had its own demographic implications. Thus, the slave
trade was welcomed by Russians and Ottomans alike, and
British attempts to check it were flatly rejected.

Fuat Efendi told Canning in 1851 that the prohibition concerning the transportation of slaves in government vessels
applied only to black slaves.[37] He was right, of course. The
Ottomans were always very careful not to implicate the slave
trade in whites whenever they issued orders restricting the
trade in blacks. The *ferman* of 1847 which prohibited the slave
trade in the Persian Gulf, as well as later orders pertaining to
the Mediterranean trade, specifically referred to black slaves.
British officials, eager to wrest concessions from the Ottoman government and often unaware of the intricacy of Ottoman domestic affairs, at times failed to understand what
these concessions really meant or, more importantly, what
they did not mean. They had to learn from experience, and
they did.

When in August 1851 Sir Stratford brought up the Circassian slave trade in a conversation with Âli, he was told that
there was no prospect of any Ottoman action to suppress
it.[38] The question was "one of great delicacy," Âli reportedly
said. Nothing was done about the Circassian slave trade in
the next three years.

[36] See Shaw, *History*, vol. II, pp. 115-6.
[37] FO 84/*loc.cit.*
[38] FO 84/857/50-1, Canning to Palmerston, 26.7.51.

The Crimean War brought the British and French fleets to the Black Sea to join forces with the weakened Ottoman fleet against the Russians. As the latter lost their supremacy at sea, the last obstacles in the way of the slave trade were removed. Circassian and Ottoman slave dealers took full advantage of the situation and a significant increase in the traffic was reported.

On 29 August 1854, after receiving information to this effect, Canning instructed his Dragoman to go to the Porte and read a strongly worded remonstrance. The ambassador protested against a practice repugnant to the Allied forces, whose very presence in the Black Sea in support of the Empire enabled the slave trade to flourish with impunity. Sir Stratford concluded:

"So long as the trade is permitted or connived at, so long as preventive measures, capable of enforcement, are loosely, or not at all employed, the Turkish authorities will justly be open to censure, and incur, to their peril, the charge of acting upon principles inconsistent in spirit and effect with the existing alliances. Let them beware of producing throughout Christian Europe, a total relaxation of that enthusiasm for the Sultan's cause which has hitherto saved his empire from the grasp of Russia."

In a shorter and less flamboyant communication dated 3 September 1854, the French, too, made known to the Porte their displeasure with the situation.[39]

The British and French remonstrances were brought before the Council of Ministers on 22 September 1854. A day later, the Grand Vezir Kıbrıslı Mehmet Emin Paşa reported to the Sultan on the Council's deliberations and decisions.[40] He wrote that, owing to the withdrawal of the Russians from their posts near the Georgian border and on the Circassian coast, and as a result of actions taken by the Allied fleets in

---

[39] For Canning's remonstrance, see Accounts and Papers, 1854–1855, vol. LVI, pp. 810–2; text of French protest in BA/İrade/Hâriciye/5553, enclosure, the Grand Vezir's report, 3.9.54.

[40] *Ibid.*, the Grand Vezir to the Sultan, 28 Zilhicce 1270/23.9.54.

the Black Sea, the slave trade was being carried out with "complete freedom" (*serbestiyet-i kâmile ile*). A difference existed between Circassians and Georgians in regard to the slave trade, the Grand Vezir explained. Circassians had a strange custom (*adet-i garibe*) of selling their children and relatives into slavery. Georgians, on the other hand, were being "stolen" by force and reduced to slavery against their will. Out of hatred for the Russians, Georgians willingly enlisted as soldiers in the Imperial Ottoman Army. But while the men were away on duty, their wives and children would be seized by the Lâz and other people to be sold as slaves. When the soldiers would return home and find out what happened, they would change their mind about the military service and refuse to go back to the army. This was a known problem, remarked the Grand Vezir. He then concluded his argument by saying: "Whereas the Circassians belong to the Muslim *ümmet* (and therefore cannot be legally enslaved), it is also forbidden to buy and sell for money, as if they were chattels or animals, the members of other religions." This enlightened statement is the earliest official condemnation of the slave trade that survived in writing.[41] It asserted that the practice was illegal on religious grounds in regard to the Muslim Circassians and on humanitarian grounds in regard to the Christian Georgians. This explanation was probably designed to appeal to the religious members of the Council; the other conservative members were offered the following arguments.

The abolition of slavery became the goal of all civilized nations, the Grand Vezir wrote. Britain and France expended large amounts of money in order to suppress the Atlantic slave trade and would not tolerate the practice in the Black Sea, where it was carried on under the eyes of their fleets sent to help the Ottoman Empire against Russia. Thus, if the European Powers were not given satisfaction on this matter, the war effort of the Empire would suffer greatly. In other words, Kıbrıslı Mehmet Emin Paşa was telling the Council

---

[41] Sultan Abdülmecit reportedly denounced the slave trade in an audience granted to the first Dragoman of the British Embassy in January 1851 (see below, p. 146).

of Ministers that European pressure could not be resisted at that time.

The Grand Vezir then outlined the various options open to discussion. Complete abolition of the slave trade was undesirable, as was also the complete freedom of action exercised by the slave dealers. Something had to be done and given publicity if the European pressure was to be eased. Although slave trading on a limited scale had been possible before the war, this was no longer the case. If nothing was done about it, there would soon be no alternative to a complete prohibition of the trade. Therefore, in order to satisfy the European powers and the Georgian people, and to prevent the future need to prohibit all slave trading, the Council decided to take the following steps:

(1) To issue two instructions to Mustafa Paşa, Commander of the Imperial Army of Batum. One would prohibit the slave trade from Georgia under severe penalty to both seller and buyer. The other would order the Commander to advise the Circassians that selling their children and relatives was contrary to humanity and should be given up. Mustafa Paşa would be instructed to take measures to ensure that exportation and transportation of slaves stopped; he should apprise the army officers at Batum, Çürüksu, and other places under his jurisdiction of the new regulations.

(2) Since slaves were being sold openly in many streets of Istanbul (the old city) and the quarters of Bey Oğlu and Galata, orders would be issued to the police, market, and customs authorities to prevent open trade in slaves. The discreet trade conducted inside houses should be pursued with caution.

(3) To instruct the Foreign Minister to inform the British and French Embassies in writing of the Council's decisions.

The Sultan endorsed the Council's recommendations two days later. In the letters sent to the two embassies it was stated also that captured Georgian slaves would be manumitted, and, if so desired, returned to their homes. No similar statement was made about the future of seized Circassian slaves. The Austrian Embassy was informed that the Austrian Lloyd's Company would be prohibited from transporting Circassian and Georgian slaves in its vessels.[42]

During the following months, arrangements were made for cooperation between the Allied and Ottoman naval forces in order to carry out the government's instructions Britain asked that her squadron in the Black Sea be allowed to assist in the suppression of the slave trade. The Ottoman government agreed and issued orders to that effect to both the commander of the Batum Army and *Vâlı* of Trabzon.[43] Although the French had not asked for a similar permission, the orders included them too, for the Grand Vezir felt that they would be interested in that matter as much as the British and, if excluded, they might be offended. It was not specified what kind of assistance was expected, or how it would be rendered. This was presumably left to the discretion of the military commanders in the area, and they indeed tried to devise the proper measures.

Mustafa Paşa, commander of the Batum Army, suggested that four steamers, two from each of the British and French squadrons, be put under Ottoman supervision for the suppression of the slave trade He thought such a move would benefit the Imperial Army in other ways, not necessarily connected to the slave trade in the Black Sea. However, the Allies, understandably, rejected the idea. Otherwise, they were quite willing to cooperate with the Ottomans, and did so[44]

---

[42] Sultan's assent in BA/*loc cit*, the *Baş Kâtıp* to the Grand Vezir, Selh-ı Zılhıcce 1270/25 8 54, for letters to embassies, see BA/Irade/Hâriciye/5601, an instruction to the *Baş Tercuman*, enclosure 2, the Grand Vezir to the Sultan, 7 Sefer 1271/30 10 54, *ibid*, enclosure 1

[43] BA/Irade/Hâriciye/5645, the Grand Vezir to the Sultan, 6 Rebiulevvel 1271/27 11 54, *ibid*, enclosure 1, the Grand Vezir to the commander of the Batum army and to the *Vâlı* of Trabzon n d, but probably shortly after the *Irade* was granted on 7 Rebiulevvel 1271/28 11 54

[44] BA/Irade/Hâriciye/5790, the Grand Vezir to the Sultan, 12 Cemaziyulâhır 1271/2 3 55, and Mustafa Paşa to the Grand Vezir, 11 Cemaziyulâhır 1271/30 1 55, Accounts and Papers, 1854-5, vol LVI, p 818, Stratford to Clarendon, 15 11 54, *ibid*, pp 819-21, correspondence—Clarendon, Stratford, Vice-Admiral Bundas, *et al*, 8-9 12 54

On 30 January 1855 Mustafa Paşa reported to the Grand Vezir that progress had been made in the efforts to put an end to the Circassian and Georgian slave trade.[45] Strict orders had been issued to the *Vâli* of Trabzon, the *Mutasarrıf* of Canik, and the *Kaymakam* of Sinop to prevent the trade in Georgians, the Commander wrote. In those places, he remarked, Georgians and slave dealers generally mingled in pursuit of the slave trade. The Sultan's orders were read in public, and some moral advice to refrain from selling children and relatives was given to the Circassians in the region. All smuggled slaves had been assembled and sent to him, reported Mustafa Paşa. Orders were given to the border patrol commanders to prevent the passage of slaves; investigations were conducted to discover hidden slaves. Officers of the Anatolian army were ordered to discontinue small-scale slave trading, which had been previously practiced by them. And, as for results, Mustafa Paşa reported that the Georgian trade was almost completely suppressed, but that, owing to the unstable situation in Circassia and the difficult weather conditions (it was the middle of winter then), success had been rather limited in regard to the Circassian slave trade.

With this report, Mustafa Paşa enclosed a draft, in French, of a letter he proposed to send the vice-admirals commanding the British and French squadrons in the Black Sea.[46] After vowing to carry out in full the Porte's orders concerning the suppression of the slave trade, the Commander of the Batum army wrote to the vice-admirals: "Je considère cette initiative de la Sublime Porte comme l'un des plus beaux faits de son alliance avec les gouvernements de S.M. l'Empereur des Français et celui de S.M. Britannique et je mets tout mon zèle à contribuer à la réalisation de ce progrès dans mon pays." But in January 1855 the commander of one of the British ships reported to his superior that the Ottomans did not seem

[45] BA/İrade/Hâriciye/5790, Mustafa Paşa to the Grand Vezir 11 Cemaziyülâhir 1271/30.1.55.

[46] *Ibid.*, enclosure 2, Mustafa Paşa to the vice-admiral commanding the French squadron in the Black Sea (text in French), 21.12.54.

to be too eager to cooperate in suppressing the slave trade.[47] They claimed, he wrote, that they could not distinguish between slaves and non-slaves. A not too sympathetic observer, Brigadier-General William F. Williams—later first Baronet "of Kars"—wrote a month later to Clarendon, then Foreign Secretary:

> "When I saw Mustafa Pasha quit the camp at Kars, and fawn upon the soldiers drawn out in a line to salute him who had robbed and starved them, he was closely followed, and that at noon-day, by two Georgian slaves under an escort of Regular Cavalry. They had been bought the day previous to his departure, and this traffic was notorious throughout the camp . . . all which had been said or may be written about abolitionary firmans simply adds mockery to crime and woe."[48]

On the other hand, the British consul in Erzurum reported at the same time that the governor of Kars was quite cooperative when approached by the consul on behalf of some kidnapped slaves.[49] Though he received no orders regarding the Circassian slave trade, the governor said he would assist the consul out of friendship toward England and France, the Ottoman Empire's allies.

What, then, was the significance of the prohibition of the Circassian and Georgian slave trade? What did it mean in the larger context of the suppression of the slave trade in the Ottoman Empire? The available sources, both Ottoman and British, provide us with a fairly clear answer. As for the Ottoman side, this policy was adopted only in order to relieve European pressure at a sensitive time when the Empire depended on the military and political support of Britain and France. The Ottomans also needed to ensure the supply of Georgian soldiers to the Imperial Army at a crucial stage in the war. The sacrifice seemed minimal at that point and was viewed as part of the war effort, perhaps to be rescinded

---

[47] Accounts and Papers, 1854–5, vol. LVI, p. 822, Captain Lord John Hay to Rear-Admiral Sir Edmund Lyons, 8.1.55.

[48] *Ibid.*, p. 832, Williams to Clarendon, 6.2.55.

[49] *Ibid.*, pp. 829–31, Brant to Clarendon (and enclosures), 10.2.55.

when peace returned. Ottoman interest in the continued supply of white slaves was in no way diminished; it in fact made the government realize that an overt public engagement in the trade could be harmful in the long run and would invite foreign pressure. To be sure, the Ottomans saw no connection between their actions against the Circassian and Georgian slave trade and the trade in blacks, to which a separate, and quite different, set of rules applied. The Porte was willing to give up the Georgian branch of the trade, which, at any rate, never equalled in volume the Circassian one. Thus, enforcement followed policy, and measures taken to check the Georgian traffic were more efficient than those aimed at the Circassian trade. The results matched the efforts.

On the British side, perceptions differed considerably. At the time, the Foreign Office still saw the struggle for the suppression of the slave trade in the Ottoman Empire as a one-dimensional issue. A simplistic view of slavery in the Empire prevailed: a slave was a slave, regardless of color, origin, or usage. Certainly, all white slaves were in one and the same category, Georgian or Circassian, and the complexity of the situation entirely escaped British policy-makers. Based on no knowledge of the language and but little understanding of the culture and social institutions of the Ottoman Empire, reports like Williams' continued, in most cases, to form the basis for the misconceived notions of the Foreign Office. Adolphus Slade was the exception rather than the rule. But much of this was to change later; the Gordons, the Elliots, and the Layards were still to come.[50]

For what it was worth, the prohibition of the Circassian and Georgian slave trade would be Britain's greatest success in that direction. From then on, her attempts to interfere in this type of traffic were rejected and she had to come to terms with the situation. However, the road was left open to further and more intensive action toward a total prohibition of the trade in Africans.

[50] More on British perceptions and attitudes, see Chapter VIII, below. On Slade, see Lewis, *Emergence*, p. 125.

CHAPTER IV

Prohibition and Resignation—
The African Versus the Caucasian Traffic
in the Late 1850s

As the British saw it, progress toward the suppression of the slave trade was like a ladder. What they had to do was to induce the Ottomans to climb it with them from restriction to prohibition to convention. Each rung was higher and more effective, but also harder to reach. The late 1850s would show that there were actually two separate "ladders": on the African, climbing would continue from restriction to prohibition and, with delays, even beyond; but on the Caucasian, the Ottomans would leave the British on the rung of prohibition, descend to restriction, and go it alone from there, in their own special way. In this chapter we shall follow developments on both "ladders."

Prohibition of the Traffic in Africans
to Crete and Janina

Until 1855, Britain sought mainly to limit the transit slave trade via North Africa into the Ottoman Empire rather than to have this traffic fully suppressed. But in a policy change early that year, the British began to focus their efforts on a number of provinces, demanding that slave trade to or through them be completely stopped. Following reports of active trading via Crete, the Foreign Secretary directed Lord Stratford "to urge the Porte . . . to put a stop to the Trade in African slaves between the coast of Barbary and Candia." Mustafa Reşit Paşa promptly responded and on 18 March 1855 issued a letter to the *Vâli* of Tripoli forbidding all slave trade to Crete [1] Similar success was achieved a few months later with regard to the slave trade from Tripoli to Albania.

Reports of an increase in the importation of slaves into Albania reached the Foreign Office in June 1855. However, the governor of Janina, Izzet Paşa, was praised by the British consul for his energetic efforts to prevent the trade and to pursue the dealers. Lord Stratford, supported by the Austrian ambassador, brought up the matter before the Porte, while, on his part, İzzet Paşa wrote to the Grand Vezir requesting approval of his actions and asking for further instructions. In response, Âli Paşa—now Grand Vezir—wrote to the *Vâli* and praised the steps he had taken against the slave trade in blacks. These steps, Âli stated, would prevent suffering and increase the prestige of the Ottoman Empire in the eyes of foreign powers. Later attempts to infer from Âli's letter a more general prohibition of the slave trade from Tripoli were rebuffed. Both the Grand Vezir and his Foreign Minister, Fuat Paşa, insisted that the instruction to the *Vâli* of Janina was intended for local application only [2]

Whereas the prohibition of the slave trade to Janina seemed to be holding, constant violations of the same instructions concerning Crete were reported in 1855-1856. On 9 July 1856 the British consul in Tripoli wrote to Clarendon "It is however but justice to the Pasha to state to Your Lordship that his efforts to arrest the evil are unceasing," though, owing to the lack of means at his disposal, smuggling was rife.[3]

[1] Accounts and Papers, 1854-5, vol LVI, pp 823-4, Clarendon to Stratford, 21 2 55, ibid , p 824, Stratford to Clarendon, 19 3 55

[2] For reports of increase in traffic, see FO 84/974/103-11, Saunders (consul, Parvesa) to Stratford, 9 6 55, ibid /118-20, Saunders to Stratford, 28 6 55, ibid /99-101, Saunders to Clarendon, 30 6 55, for Stratford's remonstrance and Izzet Paşa's letter, see ibid /62-72, 77, correspondence—Clarendon and Stratford, 31 5-4 10 55, ibid /126-7, Translation of the letter from Âli Paşa to Izzet Paşa, 19 Şevval 1271/15 7 55, for position of Âli and Fuat, see ibid /77, Stratford to Clarendon, 4 10 55

[3] Ibid /122-7, Saunders to Clarendon, 4 8 55, ibid /162-3, Ongley (consul, Canea) to Clarendon, 13 7 55, FO 84/1000/126-8, Ongley to Stratford, 10 4 56, ibid /9, Clarendon to Stratford, 26 4 56, ibid /259-62, Herman (consul, Tripoli) to Clarendon, 9 7 56, quote in text is from FO 84/1000/259-62, Herman to Clarendon, 9 7 59

As far as I could ascertain, no evidence is available at the moment in the Ottoman archives to substantiate charges of insincerity on the part of the Central Government regarding the prohibition of the slave trade to Crete and Janina. Despite the absence of explicit documentation, it is plausible to assume that the Ottomans tried to give an important ally, Britain in this case, some satisfaction in a matter believed to be of great concern to her. It is quite possible also that such concessions in regard to the African slave trade were used by the Ottomans as a sort of "safety valve" to temper down Britain's anger over her failure to stop the Circassian traffic.[4] Also, there is no reason to doubt the government's desire to reduce as much as possible the suffering of black slaves imported into the Empire. Expressions of such feelings abound in both Ottoman and British sources. Yet a gap began to develop, which grew wider with time, between the professed policy as enunciated in the various edicts and instructions of the Central Government and the application of this policy by Ottoman officials in the provinces. This gap raises questions of motivation, credibility, and effective control, which will be treated at a later stage.[5] Suffice it to say here that the Ottoman government, faced with increasing foreign pressure, embarked in the mid-1850s on a course of policy unmistakably leading to the suppression of the African slave trade.

Growing British Pressure for the Suppression of the African Slave Trade

British pressure intensified toward the end of 1855. In August, Lord Clarendon, usually reluctant to interfere too overtly in Ottoman domestic affairs,[6] wrote to Stratford de Redcliffe regarding the African slave trade:

[4] As we shall see below (pp. 138-9), during 1855-1856 the British were engaged in attempts to induce the Porte to put an end to the Circassian slave trade.

[5] See below, pp. 199-200, 204, 219-20, 228-9, 238, 243.

[6] See, for example, Harold Temperley, *England and the Near East: The Crimea* (London, 1964), pp. 487-8. On positions within the Foreign Service, see below, pp. 249-61.

"Her Majesty's Government observe with extreme regret the increase in this nefarious Traffic in Ottoman
Vessels, evidently protected by Ottoman Authorities. No
means for the prevention of these proceedings appear to
be taken by the Porte, and Her Majesty's Government,
however reluctant they may be to bring discredit upon
the Turkish Flag, will be compelled to send cruizers to
the Mediterranean for the purpose of checking the Trade,
and chastising the Traders."[7]

He asked Stratford to bring the content of this instruction
to the knowledge of Fuat Paşa, then Foreign Minister. Since
no progress was made, the Foreign Secretary, in Paris for
the Peace Conference following the Crimean War, wrote again
to Lord Stratford in March 1856. He instructed the Ambassador "to state to the Turkish Government that at this moment when Peace is about to be concluded, the Porte could
do nothing more acceptable to Her Majesty's Government
and the British nation than to adopt measures which should
be really effectual for putting an end to the Slave Trade."[8]
This time there was more success. A month later, the Grand
Vezir Âli Paşa ordered the *Vâli* of Tripoli to prevent all importation of slaves into the province. "This traffic in slaves
is not only contrary to the dictates of humanity, but is pro-
vocative likewise of representations from abroad," Âli wrote.
The exportation of slaves from the province was also prohibited. But conditions in Tripoli itself made it almost impossible to carry out the Grand Vezir's orders. Famine and
pestilence rendered virtually hopeless attempts to care for the
slave population, which had increased in the preceding months
owing to market conditions. Slaves were perishing in the
ports of the province for lack of provisions, and the governor had to ask the Porte to defer the application of the new
order by a year.[9]

[7] FO 94/974/31, Clarendon to Stratford, 9.8.55. For reports on the increase in the slave trade from Tripoli, see FO 84/1000/236-41, Herman to
Clarendon, 26.1.56.

[8] FO 84/1000/5, Clarendon to Stratford, 13.8.56. See also *ibid.*/7-9, Clarendon to Stratford, 29.3.56.

[9] *Ibid.*/53-4, Translation of an order from Âli Paşa to the governor of

In the course of the following months, numerous violations of Âli's order were reported by the British consuls in Tripoli, Rhodes, and the Dardanelles.[10] The governors of the Dardanelles and the islands of Rhodes, Mytilene, Scio, and Cyprus—all entrepôts for the slave trade from Tripoli—were not given any instructions by the Porte and, therefore, could not act to prevent passage of slaves through ports under their jurisdiction. It is open to speculation whether this was mere oversight on the Porte's part, or a calculated measure to render the order to the *Vâli* of Tripoli practically ineffective

It became almost a matter of routine for the British ambassador to make remonstrances to the Porte concerning violations of the prohibition, but with little or no result In September 1856 the governor of Tripoli introduced new regulations in an attempt to comply with the government's wishes Slaves were to be embarked only after manumission, which would be effected in the presence of a kadı They would be furnished with a copy of the certificate of manumission, another copy remaining in the hands of the captain of the transporting vessel to be delivered to the authorities upon arrival at the port of destination Evasions of these regulations were reported soon after their introduction [11] Indeed, opportunities for evasion offered themselves quite readily

The slaves—transplanted into a totally unfamiliar environment, whose language they did not speak, whose manners

Tripoli, 19 4 56, *ibid* /51-2, translation of a letter from the governor of Tripoli to the Grand Vezir, 22 2 56, *ibid* /242, Herman to Clarendon, 28 4 56

[10] *Ibid* /171-2, Campbell (consul, Rhodes) to Stratford, 4 6 56, *ibid* /01-9, Stratford to Clarendon and Fuat Paşa, 10 7-29 9 56, *ibid* /153-8, Calvert (consul, Dardanelles) to Clarendon, 9-11 56, *ibid* /244-6, Herman to Clarendon, 20 6 56, *ibid* /293, Herman to Clarendon, 26 12 56, *ibid* /33-4, Clarendon to Stratford, 26 12 56, FO/1028/2-3, Clarendon to Stratford, 2 1 57, *ibid* /65-70, Stratford to Clarendon, 12 1 57

[11] For governor's regulations, see FO 84/1000/268-70, Herman to Clarendon, 6 9 56, the British consul in Crete reported that in one case 26 black slaves were declared free in a single document signed by the kadı, but no individual certificates of manumission, or copies thereof, existed (FO 84/1000/143-5, Ongley to Clarendon, 23 12 56), *ibid* /289-91, Herman to Clarendon, 12 12 56

they did not know, and in which they were recognizable at sight by their color—continued to obey the slave dealers, who could easily dispose of their certificates of manumission at will. Once the cooperation of the captain was secured, slaves could be disembarked and sold at any of the entrepôts visited en route. With no measures taken in ports like Istanbul and Izmir to ensure that manumitted slaves indeed remain free, the orders of the Grand Vezir were in fact a dead letter. Besides, with worsening conditions in Tripoli and the real prospects of starvation and death, slaves were at least as much interested in getting out as were the slave dealers and the local authorities in transporting them. Aware of the situation, yet no less frustrated and angry, the British consul in Tripoli described to Clarendon in late 1856 "the imperturbable audacity with which the orders of the Central Government are evaded not to say mocked at in this remote province of the Empire. Thus, My Lord, either by open infraction, or by legal fiction, the action of the Imperial Firman[12] is absolutely nullified."[13] Although the Porte's instructions were not fully applied, the mere fact that they were issued and their partial enforcement constituted for Britain progress toward the suppression of the African traffic in the Mediterranean. As we now turn to the Hijaz, it becomes clear that these measures and the prohibition of the Circassian and Georgian slave trade did not pass unnoticed in the southern provinces of the Empire.

THE SLAVE TRADE AND THE REVOLT OF 'ABD AL-MUṬṬALIB IN THE HIJAZ, 1855-1856

During the years 1855-1856 the Ottomans were faced with an open, violent, and serious challenge to their rule over the Holy Cities. The conflict was rooted in the precarious balance between the provincial government and the *Şerifs* of

[12] In all probability, the consul refers here to the Grand Vezir's instruction, for the *ferman* prohibiting the slave trade was not promulgated until two months later (see below).

[13] FO 84/1000/281-5, Herman to Clarendon, 16.11.56.

Mecca. Though appointed and remunerated by the Sultan, the holders of this prestigious office often managed—by virtue of the complex tribal and urban structure of the population and the weakness of the Ottoman military and administrative presence—to accumulate considerable power. The Ottomans tried to maintain their own position in the province by playing tribal factions against each other. Control of the Hijaz was essential to the Empire if it was to remain the leading Sunnī power and the heir to the Caliphate.

As seen by the incumbent Şerif, 'Abd al-Muṭṭalib, the Crimean War had weakened the Ottomans and increased their dependence on the European powers, thereby offering an opportunity to expel them from the Hijaz. Exploiting popular resentment of European commercial and consular presence in the *Vilâyet*, mainly in Jidda, he carefully conspired during 1855 to overthrow the Ottoman government of the Hijaz.[14] 'Abd al-Muṭṭalib knew well that the slave trade, with its important commercial and religious implications, was an issue around which he could easily mobilize opposition to the Ottomans.

Information about the steps taken by the Ottoman government against the Circassian and Georgian slave trade[15] reached the Hijaz, and the restrictions which were placed on the North African traffic created the feeling that a prohibition of the trade in Africans was imminent. On 1 April 1855 some of the prominent merchants of Jidda addressed a letter to the leading *ulema* and *şerifs* of Mecca expressing their deep

[14] For details of 'Abd al-Muṭṭalib's stormy career, see Ismail Hakkı Uzunçarşılı, *Mekke-ı Mükerreme Emırlerı* (Istanbul, 1972), pp 128-137. The most detailed account of the events in the Hıjaz during the revolt of 'Abd al-Muṭṭalib is provided by Cevdet Paşa (*Tezakır*, no. 12, pp 101-52). It relies on Ottoman archival material and on the private papers of Ferık Raşıt Paşa, the general who was sent by the Porte to quell the revolt. Many of these documents are cited in full by Cevdet; they throw much light on Ottoman-Arab relations in the Hıjaz. This account was written from the viewpoint of a high-ranking Ottoman official. On these events and the question of the Hijaz traffic, see also Ochsenwald, especially pp. 118-19.

[15] See above, pp. 115-23

concern about these developments.[16] They wrote that the governor of Suez, acting on instructions from Istanbul, had issued an order to return to the Hijaz all slaves exported from there in the future. It was rumored, the merchants said, that a general prohibition of the slave trade would soon be effected throughout the Empire as part of the *Tanzimat* reforms. Given the fact that all slaves imported were being converted to Islam, they added, a prohibition of the trade would be anti-Islamic. Citing examples of other anti-Islamic, Western-inspired reforms which the Ottomans allegedly were contemplating, the Jidda merchants asked the Meccan notables to intervene against this policy.

The letter stirred up emotions in Mecca and set in motion a wide range of anti-Ottoman activities under the coordination of 'Abd al-Muṭṭalib. According to Cevdet, it was the *Şerif* himself who initiated the letter in order to provide a focus to the opposition movement.[17] He then invited the head of the *ulema* (*reisülulema*), Shaykh Jamāl, to Ṭā'if to discuss the revolt. During their conversation 'Abd al-Muṭṭalib reportedly told Jamāl that the outcome of the Crimean War would be disastrous to the Empire, whichever way it ended; the foreign debt would crush the Ottomans, he said. Besides, the Turks were in fact apostates (*mürted*), but had chosen to conceal their apostasy, which they would reveal at a later stage. Thus, the *Şerif* observed, the war offered an opportunity to rid the Hijaz of them, and the suppression of the slave trade was a good pretext (*bahane*). Though the prohibition had not as yet been extended to the Hijaz, he argued, it was in force everywhere else in the Empire and would soon be applied to the Hijaz as well. However, 'Abd al-Muṭṭalib suggested that open revolt be postponed until after the pilgrimage season, during which Ottoman military presence in the Hijaz was normally increased. In the meantime, he continued to organize his followers.

'Abd al-Muṭṭalib's anti-Ottoman activities became known

[16] Cevdet, *Tezakir*, no. 12, pp. 102-3 (letter dated 13 Recep 1271/1.4.55).
[17] *Ibid.*, p. 103.

to the Porte before the pilgrimage season was over. A high-ranking officer, Ferik (divisional general) Raşit Paşa, was sent to the Hijaz to investigate the situation and, if need be, to pacify the province.[18] In case it was proved that the *Şerif* had indeed conspired against the Ottoman government, Raşit Paşa was empowered to remove him and reinstate his predecessor and rival Muḥammad ibn ʿAwn, who was residing at the time in Istanbul. Raşit Paşa reached Jidda on 25 October 1855, the pilgrimage season having already passed, the province ready to rise in revolt, and ʿAbd al-Muṭṭalib waiting in Ṭāʾif for the right moment.

Two days after the arrival of Raşit Paşa in Jidda, and as a result of his consultations with the *Vâli* of the Hijaz, the Ottomans began to pursue a decisive policy in the province which led to the total defeat of ʿAbd al-Muṭṭalib by June of 1856.[19] Raşit Paşa wrote a conciliatory note to the *Şerif*, to which he received only a formal acknowledgment. Direct confrontation seemed unavoidable. The *Vâli* sent an order to the *Kaymakam* of Mecca, prohibiting the slave trade. The latter was instructed to read the order at the court in the presence of the *ulema* and *eşraf*. He did so on 30 October 1855, all the notables expressing their willingness to comply. At that point, ʿAbd al-Muṭṭalib—informed of the event while in Ṭāʾif—decided to act.

On his instructions, the head of the *ulema* Shaykh Jamāl issued a *fetva* condemning the prohibition of the slave trade as being contrary to the *Şeriat* and denouncing the Turks as polytheists (*muşrik*).[20] They were also accused of adopting other anti-Islamic innovations, their blood was allowed to be shed without revenge (*heder*), and the enslavement of their children made legal. Besieged by Meccan notables, the Kadi and *Kaymakam* were verbally abused and physically assaulted; the Kadi was then forced to sign an *ilâm* against the prohibition of the slave trade. All over the city the Ottoman garrisons were attacked by the crowd, as were also some

[18] *Ibid.*, pp. 106–10.
[19] *Ibid.*, pp. 110–1.
[20] *Ibid.*, p. 101.

protégés of foreign powers. In the streets of Mecca a Holy War was proclaimed against the Ottomans (*"Jihād 'alā 'l-Nasārā wa-l-mushrikīn yā mu'minūn"*—O believers, a Holy War [is being proclaimed] against the Christians and the polytheists).

The hostilities which followed in various parts of the Hijaz and the Ottoman suppression of the revolt[21] do not concern us here. What does concern us is the role which the slave trade played in these events and the extent to which it was used by both sides in their efforts to achieve their own goals. In this respect, 'Abd al-Muṭṭalib's manipulation of the issue is rather obvious and presents few problems. He knew well that would be easy to rally the people against a prohibition of the slave trade. The trade in the Hijaz was at once a lucrative business and a volatile religious issue, slavery being allowed in Islam and the Muslims commanded not to forbid what God had permitted. This and other reforms were attributed to European pressure, and the resentment of British and French presence in Jidda—blamed on the Ottomans— was effectively mobilized by the *Şerif.* On the Ottoman side, things were more complicated.

The British vice-consul in Jidda asserted, after the suppression of the revolt, that the slave-trade issue had been used by the Porte in order to create a disturbance in the Hijaz which would compromise 'Abd al-Muṭṭalib and enable his deposition.[22] Though this assertion is perhaps too sweeping, it cannot be completely ruled out. For the order from Istanbul against the slave trade, and especially its timing, raise a num-

---

[21] Detailed description can be found in Cevdet, *Tezakir*, no 12, pp 112-51 Cf the accounts of the British and French Consulates in Jidda MAE/Corr Pol and Cons /Turquie/Djeddah/vol I (1841-57), pp 190-1, Dequié (consul, Jidda) to the Foreign Minister, 4 11 55, pp 192-5, Dequié to the Foreign Minister, 9 11 55, pp 201-7, Beillaire (Gérant, Jidda) to the Foreign Minister, 7 12 55, pp 276-82, Lavalette de Montbrun (consul, Jidda) to the Foreign Minister, 15 5 56, pp 283-8, Lavalette to the Foreign Minister, 29 5 56, FO 195/375, Page (acting vice-consul, Jidda) to Cumberbatch (consul-general, Istanbul), 13 11 55, Page to Stratford, 4 8 56, FO 78/1170, Despatch no 14, Stratford to Clarendon, 4 1 56

[22] FO 195/375, Page to Stratford, 4 8 56

ber of questions; to these, I can at present offer only limited
answers. The original instruction could not be located in the
Ottoman archives, nor could copies of translations of it be
found in the British and French archives. If the order was
indeed a genuine Ottoman effort to curb the Hijaz slave trade,
it is reasonable to expect that—in hope of easing some of the
mounting British pressure to act against the African traffic—
the Porte would apprise Britain that such an order had been
issued. This was never done. Nevertheless, no documentation is available at the moment which enables us to preclude
the possibility that the Ottoman government ordered the
suppression of the Hijaz slave trade in late 1855 without ul-
terior motives and with the full intention of putting a stop
to the practice.

As we have seen, during the same period the Ottomans
were in a process of grudgingly giving in to British pressure
and restricting various aspects and routes of the African slave
trade in the Mediterranean; a year earlier they agreed to prohibit the traffic in the Circassians and Georgians. It should
be noted, however, that in her dealings with the Porte at the
time, Britain actually did not bring up the question of the
Hijaz slave trade. But even if we assume that the Ottomans
were motivated in this case by genuine abolitionist feelings,
their new initiative was shortlived. For, in an effort to win
over the rebels, following the Ottoman recapture of Mecca,
the *Şeyhülislam* addressed a conciliatory letter to the Meccan
notables.[23] The letter denounced as lies the allegation, among
others, that the Ottoman government had any intention of
prohibiting the slave trade. So as to avoid publicly contra-
dicting the earlier instruction on the matter, the letter was
confidentially communicated to the notables and given no
publicity.

Why, then, did the Ottomans choose to use the slave trade
as the bone of contention in their effort to subdue 'Abd al-
Muṭṭalib's revolt in the Hijaz? The choice was probably dic-
tated by the fact that it was the *Şerif* himself who decided to

[23] Cevdet, *Tezakir*, no. 12, pp. 133-5 (Arabic text), 136-8 (Turkish translation), letter dated 3 Cemaziyülevvel 1272/11.1.56; *ibid.*, p. 139.

make free slave trading a major cause of his anti-Ottoman campaign. As Raşit Paşa arrived in Jidda, he was still prepared—on the Porte's instructions—to negotiate with the *Şenf.* When his overture was ignored, it became clear to the Ottomans that a show of force would be inevitable. In the circumstances, they preferred to bring 'Abd al-Muṭṭalib to commit an open act of disobedience which would in turn justify his replacement. Any attempt to carry out anti-slave trade measures was sure to provoke the *Şenf* into action; therefore, it is likely that the instruction sent by the *Vâlı* to the *Kaymakam* of Mecca was intended for just that purpose. Indeed, it produced the expected result.

In any case, the events of 1855-1856 proved beyond a doubt how sensitive an issue the slave trade of the Hijaz actually was. When peace returned to the Holy Cities, the trade was allowed to resume without interference.[24] And, throughout the nineteenth century, the Red Sea and Hijaz traffic would prove most difficult to suppress—so much so that when the general prohibition of the trade in Africans was issued in 1857, the Hijaz was recognized as a special case to be exempted from the prohibition.

GENERAL PROHIBITION OF THE AFRICAN SLAVE TRADE— THE *Ferman* OF 1857

On 1 November 1856, Âlı was replaced as Grand Vezir by Mustafa Reşit Paşa To Stratford de Redcliffe, who hastened to approach him about the African slave trade, the Grand

---

[24] In a related development, a revolt broke out in Massawa—which administratively belonged to the *Vilâyet* of Hijaz It seems that there, too, earlier grievances existed, and the slave-trade prohibition served only as a catalyst The *Kaymakam* reportedly said that the prohibition depleted the treasury, whose chief source of revenue had been the duties levied on slaves Owing to that, he refused to honor government money orders (*havale*) A settlement was reached by March 1856, and with it the slave trade was resumed (MAE/*loc cit* , pp 201-7, Beıllarıe to the Foreign Minister, 7 12 55, *ibid* , pp 245-9, Beıllarıe to the Foreign Minister, 17 2 56, FO 195/375, Plowden (consul, Massawa—with responsibilities in Ethiopia) to Stratford, 17 2 56, *ibid* , R Barronı (Massawa) to Stratford, 12 5 56, *ibid* , Page to Stratford, 31 5 56)

Vezir promised "an early and liberal" consideration of the matter by the Council of Ministers. Before the year was out, Lord Stratford was confidentially informed that the Council had agreed on measures to suppress the slave trade in blacks. A month later, the Porte notified the British Embassy that the Sultan had issued a *ferman* to this effect, and added that this step was taken "indeed as a preliminary to the acceptance of the principle of the abolition of Negro Slavery." The first text of the *ferman*, that addressed to the *Vâli* of Tripoli, was dated 27 January 1957.[25]

Sultan Abdülmecit's *ferman* to the *Vâlis* of Egypt, Tripoli, and Baghdad is a major landmark in the history of the suppression of the slave trade in the Ottoman Empire It began by describing the suffering of the black slaves on the way from their homes in central Africa into the Ottoman provinces. Many of them perished in the desert, while others, unaccustomed to the colder climate of the Mediterranean, contracted pulmonary and other diseases Since this was contrary to humanitarian principles, especially with so many of the slaves being young children thus deprived of the joy of life, the Sultan stated, a total and permanent prohibition of the slave trade in blacks was necessary. From the receipt of the *ferman* onward, no slaves were to leave the abovementioned provinces, and all slave dealers were to be apprised of the prohibition. A grace period of eight weeks was allowed for dealers in remote places, after which they would not be permitted to sell their slaves in Ottoman territory. Slave dealers who would bring slaves with them thereafter

---

[25] FO 84/1000/73-5, Stratford to Clarendon, 8 12 56, *ibid* /86-7, Stratford to Clarendon, 29 12 56, FO 84/1028/79-84, note from the Porte to the British Embassy, 29 1 57, Ottoman text—BA/Yıldız/K33/73/1403/91, translation—FO 84/1028/106-13, the *ferman* to the *Vâli* of Tripoli is dated 1 Cemaziyulâhır 1273/27 1 57, all the others are dated 15 Cemaziyulâhır 1273/10 2 57 (see BA/Irade/Meclis-ı Vâlâ/16623, encl 70) A letter from the Grand Vezir to each of the governors accompanied the *ferman*, essentially, it urged compliance with the Sultan's instructions and repeated them almost verbatim Text of letters is in BA/Irade/*loc cit* , enclosure 14, the Grand Vezir to the *Vâli* of Tripoli, 27 Cemaziyulâhır 1273/22 2 57, translation in FO 84/1028-114-9

would be compelled to manumit them. One year's imprisonment was set for the first offense, and one additional year imposed for each recurrent violation.

Since it was deemed unsafe for the manumitted slaves to be returned to their countries of origin, the Sultan decreed they would be given proper housing and maintenance allowances in order to facilitate their permanent settlement in the Ottoman Empire. It was made clear that only slaves imported after the promulgation of the *ferman* would be eligible for manumission. All other black slaves could be liberated only at their masters' will As public sale was forbidden, owners were advised to dispose of their slaves "in a proper manner, that is, in a generous way."[26] Slaves caught while being transported by sea would be taken to Istanbul and restored to freedom there.

The *ferman* was also to be in force in the islands of the Mediterranean, for which a six-week grace period was granted in order to enable proper promulgation. For the same reason, a deferment of three months was set for the Persian Gulf area. The Hijaz slave trade was exempted from the prohibition, for it was considered too sensitive and risky to tamper with.

To Britain, the *ferman* gave the long-sought-after legal and moral basis on which to pursue its anti-slave trade policy in the Ottoman Empire. From then onward, the British would constantly refer to the *ferman* and demand its full application. On the Ottoman side, feelings must have been quite ambivalent. Of the many reforms proclaimed during the *Tanzimat* period—some as recent as the *Hatt-ı Humayun* (the *Islahat Fermanı*) of February 1856—the prohibition of the African

[26] This could be a subtle encouragement to owners to manumit slaves after long service, rather than resell them In an explanatory note which was sent to the British Embassy together with the *ferman*, the Porte asserted that it was customary in the Empire to manumit slaves after two to three years of service, or eight to ten years at the most Thus, the government argued, slavery would gradually disappear from the Ottoman Empire as a result of the prohibition of the slave trade (FO 84/1028/79-84, the Sublime Porte to Stratford, 29 1 57)

slave trade was perhaps one which the Ottomans understood and assimilated the least. Nevertheless, there is no reason to doubt the sincerity of the humanitarian sentiments expressed in the *ferman*; the Sultan and his ministers—and for that matter, Islamic law in general—always condemned cruelty toward slaves. Still, it is hard to avoid the impression that, in bowing to British pressure and promulgating the *ferman* of 1857, the Ottomans undertook to abolish a practice which, in principle, they did not oppose.

The *ferman* left the door open to further British interference in matters concerning the slave trade. As the following pages will attempt to show, this interference—which until the late 1850s applied to the traffic in both Africans and Circassians—would in the post-prohibition period be tolerated by the Ottomans only with regard to the African slave trade. The British, however, did not give up easily.

COMING TO TERMS WITH THE CIRCASSIAN SLAVE TRADE

Following the prohibition of the Circassian and Georgian slave trade, the British made an attempt to maintain some kind of momentum to ensure effective enforcement of the Porte's decision. Already in March 1855, Lord Stratford suggested to the Ottomans a convention with Britain for the suppression of the traffic in Circassians and Georgians. He was promptly rebuffed by the Grand Vezir Mustafa Reşit Paşa. It was therefore not surprising that in the following year the flow of Circassian slaves into Ottoman territory increased; in 1856-1857 it was reported that the Istanbul market was glutted and that prices fell to an unprecedented low level. Violations of the government orders were said to be common. Under a liberal policy of immigration, many slaves—not easily detected by the European observer or the unwilling Ottoman official—were allowed to enter the country. The Russian ambassador told his British colleague that, owing to her protracted war with the Circassians, Russia was now "indifferent" to the slave traffic. What he would not say, obviously, was that the Russians must have rejoiced at the depopulation of the Caucasus, which they would later encourage much more aggressively and by force of arms [27]

In London, the Anti-Slavery Society severely criticized Lord Palmerston, who in answering a question in the House of Commons, said that the government representations concerning the Black Sea slave trade had been completely successful. On 1 April 1856 the *Anti-Slavery Reporter* wrote·

> "Lord Palmerston's reply, we regret to say, was calculated to produce a very erroneous impression on the public mind. From it anyone would conclude that the slave trade, from the eastern coast of the Black Sea—that is the traffic in Georgians and Circassians—had been suppressed. This, however, is notoriously not the case, as we shall presently prove by extracts from the last papers on the slave-trade that were presented to Parliament. We are therefore left to surmise, either that his Lordship answered Mr. Bigg's question in ignorance of facts, or that he stated what he knew to be inaccurate."[28]

Throughout 1857 the British Embassy made numerous presentations to the Porte about the Circassian slave trade, but to no avail Mustafa Reşit Paşa and his Foreign Minister Âli Paşa consistently replied that the prohibition was limited to the war time. They stressed the special and mild nature of slavery in the Ottoman Empire and refused to allow any intervention in the matter.

In February 1857, Lord Stratford wrote to the Earl of Clarendon " . it is humiliating to confess how little can be done by any exertions of this Embassy to counteract the existing infractions of the law. The prohibition itself was indeed a result in great measure of our influence, but the en-

[27] FO 84/974/58, Stratford to Clarendon, 22 3 55, for situation in Istanbul market, see ASR, 3rd Series, vol IV (1856), p 202, reports on violations are in FO 84/974/82-3, Stratford to Clarendon, 13 10 55, and FO 84/1028/210-2, Stevens (acting consul, Trabzon) to Stratford, 8 10 57, for Russian position, see FO 84/1028/121-40, correspondence—Stratford, Stevens and Cumberbatch (consul, Istanbul), 19 8 57

[28] ASR, 3rd series, vol IV (1856), pp 81-2

forcement of it in spite of so many counteracting circumstances may well defy the powers of diplomacy . . . in the present instance I know not what to do beyond communicating (the infractions) to the Porte. . . ." It became clear that Britain had reached the limit of her influence and could not press for more concessions; the Ottomans stood firm. In October of the same year, Lord Stratford observed that only a strong combined remonstration with France might change the Porte's attitude, and added: "I would not answer for the efficiency even of that combination."[29]

Her efforts frustrated, Britain gradually realized that she was alone in her opposition to the Circassian slave trade. With the Georgian trade almost extinct, all parties involved in the Circassian traffic were keen on keeping it up. Seller, buyer, and slave were all united in supporting the continuation of the slave trade. The Russians were only too happy with the situation, and the French, as always, were very realistic about the chances of effective suppression. Aware of the state of affairs, Palmerston remarked in a note dated 6 November 1857 that "the only complaint we have ever heard from the Circassians has been against our attempts to stop the traffic." Shortly after, the Foreign Secretary Lord Clarendon finally formulated a policy which was to remain the principle of conduct in future dealings with the Porte regarding matters of the slave trade. He wrote to Lord Stratford de Redcliffe: "It is in vain however to continue to urge the Turkish Government to put a stop to this traffic, and it may be better policy for the future with a view to accomplishing some good, to continue our efforts for the suppression of the trade in African slaves in Turkey."[30]

Ottoman resistance to British pressure was adamant and

[29] For British presentations, see: FO 84/*loc.cit.*; FO 84/1028/96–101, Stratford to Clarendon, 26.2.57; *ibid.*/158–65, Stratford to Clarendon and Simmons, 21–22.6.57; *ibid.*/176–88, Stratford to Clarendon, 12.8.57; *ibid.*/204–8, Stratford to Clarendon, 21.10.57; *ibid.*/236, L. Moore (Dragoman) to Stratford, 29.10.57; *ibid.*/231–2, Stratford to Clarendon, 30.10.57. Quotations from: *ibid.*/96–101, Stratford to Clarendon, 26.2.57, and *ibid.*/231–2, Stratford to Clarendon, 30.10.57.

[30] Quotations from *ibid.*/221–3, Palmerston, 6.11.57, and *ibid.*/47–8, Clarendon to Stratford, 12.1.57.

ultimately successful. It demonstrated how important the Circassian slave trade was to Ottoman society. It also made Britain well aware that there was a limit to its ability to intervene in sensitive domestic affairs of the Empire. Given his well-known interventionist approach,[31] it is especially remarkable that Lord Stratford de Redcliffe would be the first to realize the situation and actually accept it. To be sure, Britain continued to put pressure on the Ottomans to suppress the slave trade, but after 1857 this pressure was primarily directed at the traffic in Africans and only rarely at the trade in Circassians. The latter was left exclusively to Ottoman initiative, and, as we shall see, the Porte did not fail to act when action was necessary. Also, we shall be talking more about the trade in the Circassians, rather than in the Circassians and Georgians, since the Georgian traffic was noticeably on the wane in the late 1850s.

THE DECLINE OF THE GEORGIAN SLAVE TRADE

In May 1857 the *Mutasarrıf* of Lâzistan (to the southeast shores of the Black Sea) sent to the Grand Vezir a report on the complaints of the Russian consul in Batum about the renewal of the Georgian slave trade.[32] The Russian consul had repeatedly asserted that some people from the *Kaza* of Çürüksu were crossing the border to Georgia, kidnapping children and selling them as slaves upon their return to Ottoman territory. The problem was referred to the *Mutasarrıf*, who, having examined it, referred his observations to the Grand Vezir and requested instructions.

It was true, the *Mutasarrıf* stated, that some rude (*edepsiz*) people from Çürüksu were buying and selling Georgian children—though very rarely—but no kidnapping was involved. Rather, the governor continued, many of the Georgians themselves served as middlemen and were selling slaves to

[31] Harold Temperley, *England and the Near East: the Crimea* (London, 1964), pp. 223 ff.; Stanley Lane-Poole, *The Life of Stratford Canning* (London, 1888), especially Vol. II.

[32] BA/İrade/Hâriciye/7672, enclosure 2, the *Mutasarrıf* of Lâzistan Mahmut Paşa to the Grand Vezir, 13 Ramazan 1273/7.5.57.

merchants of Çürüksu. Since the authorities were well informed of this traffic, fear of being caught induced the dealers to pass on the slaves as quickly as possible and for a low price. The slaves were then taken through the mountain routes to Erzurum, Harput, and the Arab provinces. When questioned, all involved in the trade denied having any connection to it. In view of the situation, the *Mutasarrıf* suggested that officers in the area and government officials in Erzurum, Harput, and Çıldır be ordered to observe and enforce the prohibition on slave trading in the Georgians. He also recommended that, following the Russian example, guard-houses be erected along the Ottoman side of the border in order to obtain accurate information about and to prevent the passage of slave dealers and slaves.

The Grand Vezir referred the *Mutasarrıf*'s report to the *Serasker*, the commander-in-chief of the Imperial Army, for his opinion. The Council for Military Affairs reviewed the governor's recommendations and decided to accept them. Upon completion of the demarcation of the eastern border of Anatolia, the *Serasker* wrote, guard-houses would be built and manned by the army. In the meantime, the local authorities should assign guards to prevent further infractions of the prohibition. On the recommendation of the Grand Vezir, the Sultan endorsed these measures on 7 August 1857.[33]

It thus appears that the Ottoman government continued its policy, first adopted in September 1854, which sought to suppress the Georgian slave trade. The Russians—in contrast to their strategy in Circassia—did not seek to depopulate and resettle Georgia; they therefore opposed the traffic in Georgians. This also gave them an opportunity to assert their authority in the newly, and by then still vaguely delineated, Ottoman-Georgian border. In spite of the reported transgressions against it,[34] it seems that, by and large, the

[33] *Ibid.*, enclosure 1, the *Serasker* to the Grand Vezir, 12 Zikâde 1273/3.8.57; *ibid.*, the Grand Vezir to the Sultan, 15 Zilhicce 1278/6.8.57, and the *Baş Kâtip* to the Grand Vezir, 16 Zilhicce 1278/7.8.57.

[34] The British consuls at Erzurum and Trabzon reported ın September 1869 that kidnapping and sale of Georgian children were taking place at the

prohibition of the traffic in Georgians was holding well. At the time, the Ottoman market was being generously compensated for the loss of Georgians by the steadily growing influx of Circassian slaves from the Caucasus.

★ ★ ★

At this point it may be opportune to discuss briefly the positions of some of the prominent Ottoman statesmen with regard to the suppression of the slave trade. Faced with an external political and diplomatic challenge—often presented in moral terms—the "Men of the *Tanzimat*" were clearly put on the defensive; thus, it is the *reaction* of some of them which we shall try to examine.

SULTAN ABDÜLMECIT, MUSTAFA REŞIT PAŞA, AND ÂLI PAŞA ON THE SUPPRESSION OF THE SLAVE TRADE IN THE OTTOMAN EMPIRE—SOME OBSERVATIONS

The nature of the Ottoman records for the period we are dealing with makes it difficult to attribute expressed views to the specific individuals who expressed, or merely held, them. In official reports, reference to an existing controversy is often subtle; one is left with the impression that more was said, especially in private, than written. Most readily available are the notes regularly exchanged between the Grand Vezir and the Sultan, which convey the views of these two personages. Individual reports, solicited and unsolicited, from ministers, governors, generals, and other high-ranking officials—when extant—offer some insight into the opinions and beliefs of their authors. But, generally, the Ottoman records have an inescapable air of anonymity about them. Unfortunately, foreign sources can do little to make up for this deficiency.

British ambassadors and other representatives who came

---

border areas and connived at by the Ottoman authorities. But even they put the trade at no more than 100-150 children annually, not including the traffic to Istanbul via the Black Sea, which presumably was somewhat larger (FO 84/1305/251-7, Taylor to Clarendon, 20.9.69; *ibid.*/456-9, Palgrave to Clarendon, 21.9.69).

into contact with Ottoman officials sometimes recorded in their reports the impressions they formed of the attitude of individual officials toward a particular issue. Interesting as these impressions may be, they ought to be considered with great caution. In many cases, differences of language and culture distorted the true picture. At other times, views were deliberately expressed to a foreign representative which differed from views expressed to colleagues and compatriots in the councils of state. In some instances, reporting was influenced by personal likes and dislikes toward Ottoman politicians. Thus, Stratford was a great supporter of Mustafa Reşit Paşa but was rumored to have been less enthusiastic about Âli. Bearing all this in mind, we may try now to examine the attitudes of Mustafa Reşit and Âli Paşas to the suppression of the slave trade in the Ottoman Empire as reflected in British reports on contacts with the Porte until 1857 regarding this question.

When Âli was first told by Lord Cowley, the British ambassador, in December 1847 that the governor of Tripoli was personally engaged in slave trading, he refused to instruct the *Vâli* to desist from doing so. He said that it was perfectly legal. In July 1849 Canning reported to Palmerston on his conversation with Âli regarding the transportation of slaves in government vessels. The Foreign Minister, he wrote, entered—as on previous occasions—into a defense of slavery in the Ottoman Empire and compared it favorably with slavery in other countries. In May 1850 Canning wrote to Palmerston that Âli had said that the consular reports on the "horrors" of the slave caravans en route to Tripoli were exaggerated. A few weeks later, Canning went to see Âli again about the use of government vessels in the slave trade and demanded that the practice be prohibited. He wrote: "From Aali Pasha I received no expression of sympathy or concern. That Minister, enlightened as he is in many respects, and open to views of humanity, appears to forget the horrors of the traffic in its earlier stages, and to think, that an ample atonement for them is to be found in the kind and generous treatment experienced for the most part by slaves in this country." In December 1856 Lord Stratford complained again about Âli Paşa's conduct. This time he wrote to Clarendon that Âli went out of office as Grand Vezir without doing anything about the slave trade, although he had promised to formulate a policy on the matter.[35]

The Ottoman archives, at this stage, neither confirm nor deny these reports, nor do they give us other information about Âli's attitude to the suppression of the slave trade in the Empire. How adamantly he held the views attributed to him by the British, if he held such views at all, is hard to assess, for in all the above-mentioned instances further negotiations with him and Mustafa Reşit Paşa ultimately produced compliance with the British demands. If he indeed opposed the policy of the Grand Vezir on the issue, he never openly refused to carry it out. In the case of the involvement of government officials in the slave trade, it was Âli himself who issued the instructions to the *Vâli* of Tripoli against the practice.

Mustafa Reşit Paşa, on the other hand, was more willing than Âli to accommodate the British on slave-trade matters. Whenever he was approached on the subject, as happened in all the aforementioned cases, orders were issued which placed restrictions of various degrees on the traffic in Africans. It was Mustafa Reşit Paşa who was credited with the promulgation of the 1857 *ferman* which prohibited all slave trading in blacks. "The credit of this signal compliance with the wishes of Her Majesty's Government is primarily due to Reshid Pasha," wrote Lord Stratford in January 1857. He later added: "I have no doubt that the Grand Vizir is serious now at length in carrying a complete measure of abolition into effect."[36] But, whatever his intentions were, before a year had elapsed the great reformer was dead; and for the next thirteen years

[35] FO 84/691/190-1, Cowley to Palmerston, 17.12.47; FO 84/774/20-1, Canning to Palmerston, 19.7.49; FO 84/815/24-5, Canning to Palmerston, 10.5.50; *ibid.*/31-2, Canning to Palmerston, 18.6.50 (for passage quoted above); FO 84/1000/73-5, Stratford to Clarendon, 8.12.56.

[36] FO 84/1028/57, Stratford to Clarendon, 51.1.57 (first quote); *ibid.*/62, Stratford to Clarendon, 12.1.57 (second quote).

it would be Âli's intentions and policies, along with Fuat's, that would be carried out.

In January 1851, after the instruction prohibiting the transportation of slaves in government vessels had been issued, Canning sent the First Dragoman of the Embassy to express to the Ottomans the appreciation and gratitude of the British government. The Dragoman was received by the Sultan himself, and in his report[37] we have a unique account of Abdülmecit's view on the slave trade as expressed in that audience. The Ottoman documents tell very little about Abdülmecit's position on the issue; in the slave trade matters referred to him, he always accepted the recommendations of the Grand Vezir of the time, and issued the *İrades* accordingly. In the audience granted to the First Dragoman of the British Embassy, the Sultan reportedly said that

> ". . . he exceedingly regretted not being able to go further at present, but he hoped ere long to abolish the nefarious trade within his dominions. It is a shameful and barbarous practice, continued His Majesty, for rational beings to buy and sell their fellow creatures. Though slaves in Turkey are treated better than elsewhere, yet are they sometimes very ill-used. Are not these poor creatures our equals before God? Why then should they be assimilated to animals?"

Again, we should not take these observations for more than what they are—impressions formed by foreign diplomats of views expressed to them by Ottoman statesmen. Direct quotations are somewhat more helpful, but they are rare. What we can learn from this information, however, is how these Ottoman statesmen wanted their position on the slave trade to be perceived by foreign representatives. Clearly, both Abdülmecit and Mustafa Reşit Paşa desired the British to be favorably impressed by their position; Âli, on the other hand, did not consider the effort worthwhile. He did not even attempt to convey an impression that he held "enlightened"

---

[37] FO 84/857/27-8, Canning to Palmerston, 24.1.51.

views on slavery or the slave trade. He made it clear to the British that he thought these were practices which they did not quite understand, and certainly had no cause to interfere with.

★ ★ ★

By 1857 the basic principles which were later to guide Ottoman policy regarding the slave trade were set. The traffic in Africans was prohibited by *ferman*, and the Porte was willing to review all British remonstrances concerning violations of this prohibition. The Circassian slave trade was legally pursued, and foreign interference in it on any grounds would not be allowed by the Porte. On her part, Britain was gradually coming to terms with reality; she would concentrate on guarding against evasion of the *ferman* and would not interfere in the Circassian traffic. The abolition of Ottoman slavery—a cause championed by abolitionists in the 1840s—became a long-term, ideal goal of British foreign policy, only rarely and feebly mentioned. The suppression of the African slave trade clearly replaced it as a revised and more realistic target.

We shall, therefore, continue our discussion of the suppression of the slave trade in the Ottoman Empire according to the distinction which emerged in the late 1850s between the Circassian and the African slave trade. Thus, in Chapter VI we move away from the sphere of Anglo-Ottoman dealings regarding the African traffic and into the realm of Ottoman domestic policies, where the government had to supply its own answers to the questions of Circassian slavery and slave trade.

CHAPTER V

Circassian Slavery and Slave Trade— an Ottoman Solution

CIRCASSIAN SLAVERY and slave trade in the Ottoman Empire in the second half of the nineteenth century took on a number of forms which, though interrelated, were nevertheless different. The main two types of slaves were agricultural[1] and domestic (or harem) slaves; both had the same legal status and belonged to the Circassian slave class. Normally, it was the members of this class—most often women intended for harem service—who changed hands and were exported from the Caucasus to the Ottoman Empire as part of the slave trade. The Russian-forced dislocation of the Circassian population of the Caucasus in the late 1850s and early 1860s turned the Ottoman traffic in Circassians from an import trade to an essentially domestic commerce. A large agricultural slave population was introduced into the Empire, and many domestic female slaves were thrown on the market. The problems caused by these developments and the ways in which the Ottoman government dealt with them will be examined in this chapter.

Unlike the prohibition of the African slave trade—which, as we have seen, owed a great deal to British pressure—reforms concerning Circassian slavery and slave trade were entirely the result of Ottoman initiative. Motivated by internal considerations, the Porte moved gradually and with caution during the last third of the nineteenth century to *de facto* abolish agricultural slavery among the Circassian immigrants. In-

[1] Throughout this work I shall use the term "agricultural slavery" in order to avoid confusion with other practices—notably serfdom—in other societies. Agricultural slaves had the same legal status as all other slaves. Customary law, especially that of the Circassians, reflected some of the social differences among slaves in various occupations, but this had no effect on Islamic law in the Ottoman Empire (see also pp. 182-3, below)

voluntary traffic in female slaves was also limited to a great extent. But, in order to understand these processes, we should first turn to review the events in the Caucasus during the period following the Crimean War

EARLY EFFECTS OF THE CIRCASSIAN IMMIGRATION ON SLAVERY AND THE SLAVE TRADE

After the Crimean War, the Russians intensified their efforts to subdue the Caucasus, committing greater resources and changing their strategy.[2] A systematic military advance aimed at clearing populated areas and resettling them with reliable elements replaced the pre-war approach of dealing only with pockets of resistance where they existed. The success of this strategy in the eastern Caucasus, which ended in the defeat of the Circassian leader Şamil in 1859, was soon followed by its application in the western Caucasus starting in 1860. Circassians in conquered territories were given a choice to emigrate either to the interior of Russia or to the Ottoman Empire.

In December 1863 the tribal federation of the Abaza surrendered, and 150,000 of them were ordered to leave the Caucasus by the following spring. Four months later, the last Circassian tribe—the Ubikh—was defeated and ordered to emigrate; the Russians reportedly offered the lands to the Azov Cossacks and to government employees who had served in the Caucasus ten years or more.[3] Military operations in the Caucasus ended in May 1864, but the flow of emigrants continued into 1866.

Transportation of the Circassians became a major problem, and the Russian government, obviously interested in speeding up the process, took an active part in it. The Rus-

[2] Marc Pinson, "Ottoman Colonization of the Circassians in Rumili after the Crimean War," *Études Balkaniques*, no 3 (Sofia, 1972), p 71 (hereafter, Pinson)

[3] FO 87/424, R C Clipperton (consul, Kerch) to Lord John Russell (Foreign Secretary), Confidential, 21 12 66, *ibid* , C H Dickson (consul, Sohum Kale) to Russell, Confidential, no 3, 13 4 64

sians were said to have contracted two merchants of Kerch to transport emigrants to Samsun at a rate of five roubles per person—three to be paid by the government, two by the Circassians themselves in money, cattle, or produce Although the Russians offered to pay five roubles per person for steamer transportation, ship owners in Odessa and Istanbul refused to get involved in what became a chaotic operation.[4]

The Ottoman government negotiated some arrangements with the Russians and sent vessels to carry the Circassians to various ports in the Black Sea. Emigrants intended for settlement in Rumelia were taken to Constanţa and Varna; those intended for Anatolia entered through Trabzon and Samsun Much to the Russians' delight, few emigrants were settled in border areas. The receiving ports were ill-equipped and could not cater to the basic needs of the emigrants Shortage of food supplies, absence of sanitary measures, inadequate medical facilities, and ineffective quarantine combined to exacerbate the already great suffering of the refugees. Smallpox, typhus, and dysentery took a heavy toll; mortality estimates varied from 200 to 300 people per day [5]

The available sources differ as to the number of Circassians who entered the Ottoman Empire between the years 1855-1866. Most of the Ottoman estimates are considerably higher than the Russian figures and run between 595,000 and 1,008,000, with one surprisingly low figure of 395,000 When the British ambassador in St. Petersburgh brought up the matter with Prince Gorchakov, the Russian Foreign Minister, in March 1864, the Prince observed that the estimate of 300,000 emigrants was greatly exaggerated Russia, said the

[4] *Ibid* , Clipperton to Russell, Confidential, 13 4 63, *ibid* , Clipperton to Russell, Confidential, 10 5 64 In November 1860, when emigration had not yet reached its mass proportions, the British consul at Sohum Kale reported that ships of the Russian Steam Navigation and Trading Company regularly transported Circassian emigrants to Trabzon (*ibid* , Dickson to Russell, Confidential, 17 11 60)

[5] *Ibid* , Sir Henry Bulwer (ambassador, Istanbul), to Russell, no 54, 12 4 64, Pinson, pp 73-4, 83-4, FO 97/424, Clipperton to Russell, Confidential, 10 5 64, FO 84/1204/224-5, Stevens (consul, Trabzon), to Russell, 4 8 63

Foreign Minister, regretted this emigration, but the Circassians had rejected the government's offer for their resettlement on Russian territory. The Ottoman Empire, he added, would nevertheless benefit from the Circassian immigration, which would increase her military manpower potential. It is open to challenge whether this was valid even as a long-term prediction, but the short-term problems created by the Circassian immigration certainly outweighted the benefits. The Prince was probably well aware of that. Despite repeated Ottoman pleas during 1864, the Russians refused to halt the emigration; though Prince Gorchakov claimed that an order to this effect had been issued, the Ottomans reported that the inflow of immigrants continued unhampered.[6]

The Circassian slave trade and the agricultural slavery peculiar to Circassian society were among the problems which accompanied this massive population movement. The Ottoman government estimated in 1867 that among the Circassian immigrants there were more than 150,000 persons of slave status.[7] Although this figure may be too high, it is clear that the number of slaves was very large indeed. The great majority of these slaves were peasants and their families; they were attached to their masters, commonly referred to in Ottoman and European sources as *emirs* (pl. *ümera*), or *beys*. In times of peace, the slaves cultivated the *bey*'s land; in war, they fought under his command. The slave holders were allowed to enter the Empire accompanied by their slaves without interference. Apart from this immigration of sizable slave population, the traffic in young Circassian, by then mostly female, slaves intended for the harems of Istanbul and other cities continued unabated.

[6] For a discussion of the migration estimates, see Pinson, p. 75 n.; Professor İnalcık quotes the figure 595,000, which is the same as that mentioned by Ubicini (Halil İnalcık, "Čerkes—iii. Ottoman period," *EI²*, vol. II [1960], p. 25); for British-Russian contacts on subject, see FO 97/424, Lord Napier (ambassador, St. Petersburg) to Russell, no 255, Confidential, 17.8.64; Pinson, p 77.

[7] BA/İrade/Meclis-i Mahsus/1407, the Grand Vezir to the Sultan, 24 Zilkâde 1283/30.3.67 On the class structure of Circassian society, see Marigny, pp. 47-50.

As the British were indeed told, the war-time prohibition, obtained under foreign pressure, was no longer considered to be in effect. In March 1858 the governor of Trabzon informed the British acting consul that he had been ordered not to impede in the future the passage of Circassian slaves through the area under his jurisdiction. It was after he had delayed the departure of some slaves to Istanbul in compliance with the acting consul's request. In December of the same year, the tax-farmer (*mültezim*) of the Trabzon customshouse complained to the governor that he had difficulties collecting dues from the slave dealers. He asserted that although the new tariff which was sent to him specifically mentioned the duty on slaves (*pencik resmi*), the dealers were told that it should be paid in Istanbul and not, as before, at the port of entry. In any event, it was "business as usual"; the trade was openly carried on and legally recognized by the authorities.[8]

THE IMMIGRATION COMMISSION AND THE SLAVES

Faced with the host of problems created by the Circassian, and earlier Tatar and Nogay, immigration, the Ottoman government decided on 5 January 1860 to establish the Immigration Commission (*Muhacirîn Komisyonu*, sometimes, *Muhacirîn İdaresi*).[9] Headed by the former governor of Trabzon and including mostly sub-cabinet-level officials from the various concerned ministries, the Commission was charged with coordinating all Ottoman efforts to cope with the immigration problems. Only few documents relating to the Commission's actions on Circassian slavery and slave trade

[8] For contact of acting consul with the governor of Trabzon, see FO 84/1060/126-7, Stevens to Lord Malmesbury (Foreign Secretary), 23.3.58; tax farmer's complaint in BA/İrade/Meclis-i Vâlâ/18167, the *multezim* of the Trabzon *Gümruk* to the governor of Trabzon, 12 Kânun-ı sânı 1274/ 24.1.58.

[9] For events leading to this decision, see Ahmet Cevat Eren, *Turkiye'de goç ve göçmen meseleleri* (Istanbul, 1966), pp 39-61.

have survived, or are presently accessible at the Ottoman archives. The most useful among these are the registers—a sort of *précis* books—in which was recorded the correspondence addressed to the Commission. However, it should be borne in mind that the information is as yet incomplete, and the conclusions, therefore, tentative.

In the early 1860s, the Immigration Commission dealt primarily with four types of problems concerning slavery and the slave trade:

(a) The most important task of the Commission was to supervise and facilitate the settlement of the immigrants and to provide them with the necessary means to cultivate the land and to establish their homes. Slave families followed their masters' households and often formed extended groups which had to be settled in one estate. The allocation of land for such purposes and the occasional need to relocate these extended units were among the problems which the Commission was called upon to resolve.[10]

(b) Then came the settlement of disputes which erupted among the immigrants between master and slave.[11] Many such disputes revolved around the slave's assertion that he was free and did not belong to the slave class. Cases of runaway slaves were also reported to the Commission by slave owners. In some instances, the Commission was asked to compel slaves by order to obey their masters (*itaat*). Crimes committed by slaves, especially murder and robbery, were laid before the Commission and its intervention was solicited. Conversely, slaves sought redress to their grievances by petitioning the Commission when ill used. The Commission

[10] For example, BA/BEO/Muhacirîn Komisyonu/vol. 758, entries no. (for the year 1278/1861-1862) 101; (for the year 1279/1862-1863) *fevkalâde* 2,259; (for the year 1281/1864-1865) petition 26, 31, 271; (for the year 1282/1865/1866) 29.

[11] For example, *ibid.*, entries no. (for the year 1278/1861-1862) 66, 126, 179, 403; (for the year 1279/1862-1863) *fevkalâde* 2, 209; (for the year 1280/1863-1864) 190; (for the year 1281/1864-1865) 167, 282; (for the year 1282/1865-1866) *fevkalâde* 1, petition 7.

did not, however, act as a court; it supplemented court action either by enforcing court orders, or by acting when and where the courts were ineffective

(c) The mass Circassian immigration created conditions which were conducive to excesses and abuses committed by powerful and privileged immigrants against their weaker and nonprivileged kin Sensing the inability of the Ottoman government to enforce the law strictly in that period of transition, such individuals would sell into slavery persons who belonged to the free classes but who could not—under the circumstances—effectively resist them Others also took advantage of the situation Captains of the transporting boats were said to exact passage fee by taking immigrants' children—one child per thirty passengers, according to one report—whom they would later sell as slaves It is difficult to estimate how common these practices actually were, but scattered evidence exists which indicates that both individuals and groups among the Circassian immigrants were subjected to them Complaints about such incidents were referred to the Immigration Commission, which tried to prevent their occurrence In 1862, for example, the Commission ordered the manumission of a free-born immigrant who had been brought from Amasya to Istanbul by a certain woman who sold him there into slavery Orders were then sent to Amasya to prevent the recurrence of such cases Another measure taken for this purpose was a restriction imposed on the sale of slaves among the immigrants A number of applications by slave owners to allow them to sell their slaves—usually out of economic need—were submitted to the Commission. One such application was made in 1861 by the governor of Izmir, who asked that slave sales by Circassian immigrants settled in the *Sancak* of Aydın be allowed to resume [12]

---

[12] For children as passage fee, see FO 84/1225/166-7, Bulwer to Russell, 31 8 64, ASR, 3rd series, vol XII (1964), p 198, quoting the *Levant Herald* of 17 8 64 Examples of selling free-born into slavery are in BA/*loc cit*, entries no (for the year 1278/1861-1862) 179, 371, (for the year 1281/1864-1865) 91, 167, 218, (for the year 1282/1865-1866) *fevkalâde* 1 See also BA/İrade/Meclis-ı Mahsus/1407, enclosure 2, *Emirname-ı Sâmı*, 19 Sefer

(d) In addition to these three kinds of activities—which concerned primarily, though not exclusively, slave families engaged in agriculture—the Commission also dealt with problems related to the slave trade in individual immigrants, which was being pursued by slave dealers.[13] Extensive correspondence concerning the status of immigrant women bought by some slave dealers was carried on with the office of the *Şeyhülislam,* which handled the *Serî* aspect of the problem. When, in Instanbul in September 1864, eighty-five slaves aboard a Russian ship were found to be ill, presumably with smallpox or typhus, the case was referred to the Immigration Commission. On 12 December 1865 the Commission was petitioned in regard to the admission of two male slaves to the preparatory vocational school in Tophane. The two became the property of the Treasury (*Beytülmal*) after the death of the woman slave dealer Nâzir Hatun, to whom they belonged.[14]

There are indications that the Immigration Commission, even before 1864, tried to restrict in some measure the immigrants' freedom of movement within the Empire in general, and into Istanbul in particular. How effective this policy was is hard to establish, but stricter measures were needed in 1864, with the overwhelming wave of immigrants who were entering the Empire from the newly conquered Caucasus. In July 1864 the Governor of Trabzon was ordered

---

1281/24.7.64. For manumission in Amasya, see BA/BEO/*loc.cit.*, entry no. 371 (for the year 1278/1861-1862) Applications to governor of Izmir to allow sale in *ibid.*, entry no. 133 (for the year 1278/1861-1862); and see also, entries no (for the same year) 256, 358.

[13] The overlap occurred mainly in category (c).

[14] Correspondence with office of Şeyhülislam in BA/*loc.cit.*, entry no. 24 (for the year 1281/1864-1865) mentions the existence of 67 enclosures; sick slaves aboard Russian ship in *ibid.*, entry no 111 (for the year 1281/1864-1865); admission to school of two male slaves in *ibid* , petition no. 14 (for the year 1282/1865-1866) The British ambassador reported in August 1865 that the commission was preparing a new program of relief, under which an asylum would be established for children whose parents were in great destitution, so as to prevent their being sold into slavery. In the asylum, boys would be taught a trade, and girls would be trained for attendance in harems (FO 84/1246/125-6, Bulwer to Russell, 10.8 65).

not to send any more refugees to the capital. Probably around the same time, for an exact date could not be established, the Commission moved also to prohibit the entry of slaves into Istanbul and tightened its control over their movement in general.[15]

Although no record of such instructions could be found, a report (*mazbata*) drawn up by the Commission on 17 April 1865 reiterated a "former prohibition" on slaves against entering Istanbul, thereby confirming that previous orders to that effect had indeed existed. Government officials and the head of the Slave Dealers' Guild (*Esirciler Kethüdâsı*) were to be informed that, unless for an essential personal purpose, no slave would be permitted to enter the city. Slaves going for such purposes should carry documents, endorsed by government officials, attesting to that fact. No permits of passage (*mürur tezkeresi*) would be issued to slaves wishing to leave Istanbul unless they carried identity papers (*ilmühaber*) provided by the Immigration Commission. The *mazbata* was marked "urgent" and was sent to the High Council for Judicial Ordinances; a day later it was enacted and entered in the registers of the Imperial Council (*Mühimme Defterleri*).[16] The need to reissue the prohibition may be taken as an indication that previous attempts to control the movement of slaves in and out of Istanbul were not entirely successful.

As suggested above, restrictive measures were introduced in mid-1864, probably as a result of the increased immigration following the collapse of Circassian resistance in the

---

[15] For restrictions of movement see BA/*loc cit.*, entries no. (for the year 1278/1861-1862) 60; (for the year 1279/1862-1863) 139 Entry no. 34 (for the year 1281/1864-1865) refers to the existence of earlier orders restricting the entry of slaves into Istanbul. Order to governor of Trabzon in Pinson, p. 73.

[16] BA/*loc.cit.*, entry no. 34 (for the year 1281/1864-1865). In another entry (no. 37 for the year 1282/1865-1866), the Slave Dealers' Guild is referred to as having been abolished. A circular to the governors of all provinces, signed by the Grand Vezir Âli Paşa on 19 July 1971, seven weeks before his death, also said that the guild has been abolished (Aristarchi, vol. V, p 36). In the latter case, it is implied that the abolition took place when the Istanbul slave market was abolished. In any case, it continued to function unofficially.

Caucasus in May of the same year. In the coming years, the Immigration Commission handled a growing number of applications from Circassians who wished to move their slaves from one place to another within the Ottoman territory. Again, it is difficult to assess how effective the control was, but in October 1865 the Commission deemed it necessary to issue yet another order prohibiting the introduction of slaves into Istanbul.[17] The increased immigration also caused the government to formulate a better-defined policy on the question of slavery among the Circassian immigrants and the slave trade practiced by them.

RESTRICTIONS ON SLAVE TRADING IN CIRCASSIANS

On 24 July 1864 the government issued an instruction to its officials which laid down the ground rules for dealing with the problems of slavery and the slave trade among the Circassian immigrants.[18] The free but poor immigrants, the government said, were compelled, out of sheer want, to sell their children into slavery. Some shameless and base people, in conjunction with slave dealers, were taking advantage of the situation, gathering and enslaving a large number of freeborn boys and girls. The established practice was, the instruction continued, that when children were discovered who had been taken from their parents by deception, they were returned to them by the authorities after proper investigation. However it was well known that fraud and trickery were often being used to evade such measures as taken to retrieve the children, and many complaints about that had reached the government. "Free immigrants were being traded

[17] For restrictive measures, see also FO 84/1225/166-7, Bulwer to Russell, 31.8.64. Examples of applications to move slaves. BA/*loc cit* , entries no. (for the year 1281/1864-1865) 124, petition 21, 255, 261, petition 36; (for the year 1282/1865-1866) 29, petition 6, 80. New prohibition against entering Istanbul is in *ibid.*, entry no. 84 (for the year 1282/1865-1866); the *maz-bata* was sent to the High Council for Judicial Ordinances on 12 Cemazi-yülevvel 1282/3 10.65.

[18] BA/Irade/Meclis-i Mahsus/1407, enclosure 2, *Emirname-i Sâmi*, 19 Sefer 1281/24 7.64.

regularly and without impediment like sacrificial lambs" (*ahrar-ı muhacirîn âdeta bimuhaba kurbanlık koyun gibi satılıp alınmakta*), the instruction stated. It then went on to denounce and prohibit the practice.

The selling of free men and women into slavery was prohibited by the *Şeriat*, the government asserted. Moreover, it was contrary to humanity to violate the rights of helpless immigrants who came to the Empire seeking refuge and relying on the Sultan's compassion. The miserable life they were forced to lead would make them regret ever having immigrated to this country; it gave Islam "a bad name." Therefore, no further sales of free persons would be allowed, and offenders would be severely punished, the government declared. However, if parents sold their children out of their own free will, the sale—though clearly against the *Şeriat*—would be valid and the right of ownership and usage would not be affected. But parents should be warned, the instruction concluded, that by doing so they would incur the wrath of God.

The prohibition sought to stem forced reduction to slavery and to discourage all slave trading. Further instructions set a procedure to verify the status of persons claiming to have been forcibly enslaved.[19] Upon appearance before a *Şerî* court, attempts would be made to establish whether the plaintiff was a free person or a slave. If he failed to produce satisfactory evidence, attesting to his freedom, but asserted that he had relatives at his original place of residence who could testify to that effect, he would then be sent to that place, whereat the investigation would be resumed. This complicated procedure was often abused, or simply ignored, by the courts. The following test-case was used in 1867 to amend it.

Early in 1866, a slave dealer was caught by the police in Istanbul as he was about to sail to Egypt with five Circassian boys, four of whom claimed to be free.[20] The boys, said to

---

[19] *Ibid.*, the Grand Vezir to the Sultan, 24 Zilkâde 1283/30.3.67.

[20] *Ibid.*, enclosure 4, *Zaptiye Müşiriyeti* (signed Mehmet) to Osman Paşa (member of the High Council for Judicial Ordinances), 19 Rebiülevvel 1283/31.7.66; *ibid.*, enclosures 6-9, statements by slave dealer and the slaves, 21-9 Sefer 1283/5-13.7.66.

be from seven to eleven years old, had been brought to the capital from towns in eastern Anatolia and sold into slavery by members of their own families. At the Şerî court, they failed to prove that they were free, but they nevertheless insisted that they could find witnesses in their home towns who would back their assertion. Contrary to the established procedure, instead of pursuing the investigation, the court issued a statement affirming that the boys were of slave status. Thus the court was used—probably not uniquely—by the dealer in order to frustrate the government's efforts to prevent the enslavement of free persons. Faced with that situation, the Council of Ministers decided to change the procedure.

In a report dated 30 March 1867,[21] the Council ruled that testimony concerning personal status could be given by relatives in their places of residence and communicated to the court through the local authorities. This was clearly aimed at helping the enslaved; some officials were prepared to go even further.

Basing his decision on the prohibition of July 1864, Osman Paşa, a member of the High Council for Judicial Ordinances, ruled in September 1866 that individuals held as slaves by immigrant slave holders or by slave dealers would be considered free if it could be established that their relatives were free.[22] An official of the Ministry of Police wrote in July 1866, in a letter to Osman Paşa, that even if an individual was a slave, it was illegal to separate him from his parents and relatives, and he should be returned to them. Osman Paşa concurred in this view and suggested that all slave dealings among the immigrants be deferred until the process of settlement was completed. It is doubtful whether such policy could be enforced, since this transition period was the one

---

[21] *Ibid.*, the Grand Vezır to the Sultan, 24 Zılkâde 1283/30 3.67; BA/Aynıyat/vol. 1136, Memo from the Porte to the President (of the High Council for Judicial Ordinances?), 29 Ramazan 1283/4 2.67.

[22] Correspondence on matter in BA/İrade/Meclis-i Mahsus/1407, enclosure 3, Osman Paşa to the High Council for Judicial Ordinances, 21 Rebiülâhır 1283/3 9.66; *ibid.*, enclosure 4, *Zaptıye Müşiriyeti* (signed Mehmet) to Osman Paşa, 18 Rebiülevvel 1283/31.7.66.

which created the greatest economic need for selling slaves. Constant mobility and the lack of proper registration and means to impose law and order offered many opportunities for effecting sales.

Separation of slave families usually occurred through the sale of one or more members of the family, or through the sale of the whole family, but to different buyers. The established customs among the Circassians strongly militated against such practices, in an attempt to maintain the unity of slave families.[23] But the fact that the Council of Ministers had to address itself to the matter indicates that the hardships of emigration eroded the old and established customs The immigrant slaves resisted, as much as they could, any attempts to effect involuntary separation, and the unrest among them was partially caused by this issue The government was not unsympathetic towards the slaves' position, but had to contend with strong opposition from the Circassian slave holders and other conservative elements, which often prevented effective action on its part. The following case may serve to illustrate this point.

Four people, two men and two women, held in common ownership eleven Circassian male and female slaves [24] The eleven formed an extended family. a middle-aged woman, her son, his wife, and their four children; and the woman's two married sons and two unmarried daughters The owners' ways parted and they decided to divide the slaves among them. Six of the slaves were to remain in Tekfurdağ, where they had resided, and five were to accompany their masters to Istanbul. Even the smaller nuclear family consisting of the married couple and their four children was to be split up, two of the children remaining with their grandmother and three of her children. The slaves protested against the deal and demanded to be reunited in Tekfurdağ. The owners ob-

---

[23] BA/Irade/Meclis-ı Vâlâ/25956, enclosure 1, *Mazbata* of the High Council for Judicial Ordinances, 22 Cemaziyulâhır 1284/21 10 67

[24] *Ibid* , the Grand Vezır to the Sultan, 1 Cemaziyulâhır 1284/30 9 67, BA/Aynıyat/vol 1136, no 675, the Porte to Osman Paşa (member of the High Council for Judicial Ordinances), 8 Cemaziyulâhır 1284/7 10 67

tained a *Şerî* court order enjoining the slaves to obey their masters. The total value of the slaves was assessed at 20,000 *kuruş*, but they did not have that much money, and therefore could not purchase their freedom. The matter was brought before the Immigration Commission.

On 26 August 1867 the Commission referred the case, along with its own recommendations, to the High Council for Judicial Ordinances.[25] The Commission stated that to comply with the owners' demand to separate the slaves, though backed by the court's ruling, would be "contrary to observed principles of conduct and the *Şerî* command to heed the slaves' cry for help" (*usul-ı meriye ve üseranın istimâ-ı feryadi hükm-i Şerîye mugayır*). Taking into consideration the perseverance demonstrated by the slaves, and the failure of the parties to conclude a *mükâtebe*—a mutually agreed upon contract between master and slave, according to the *Şeriat*, to grant manumission in exchange for monetary, or other, compensation—the Commission proposed that the Treasury pay the 20,000 *kuruş* and secure the manumission of the whole family.

The High Council for Judicial Ordinances accepted the Commission's views, stating that, under the circumstances, justice demanded neither to follow the court order nor to set the slaves free against their masters' will.[26] The Sultan, acting on the recommendation of his Grand Vezir, agreed to pay the necessary amount, and the slaves were given their freedom. The government's desire to support the slaves on the issue of "family splitting" was impeded in this case by the *Şerî* court order; as we shall see, this was not a unique incident. Generosity could perhaps solve some isolated cases; it could not, however, take the place of a coherent and decisive policy.

[25] *Ibid.*, enclosure 2, the Immigration Commission to the High Council for Judicial Ordinances, 25 Rebiülâhır 1284/26.8 67.

[26] *Ibid.*, enclosure 1, *Mazbata* of the High Council for Judicial Ordinances, 22 Cemazıyulâhır 1284/21 10.67; *ibid*, the Grand Vezir, to the Sultan, 1 Cemazıyülâhır 1284/30.9.67, and the *Baş Kâtıp* to the Grand Vezir, 2 Cemazıyülâhır 1284/1 10.67

It should be noted here that the separation of families in general—that is, not only of slave families—became a serious problem during the Circassian immigration into the Ottoman Empire. In 1865, the Immigration Commission issued instructions to the governors of the various provinces which received and absorbed the immigrants.[27] Article 14 of these instructions provided for the reunion of families which had been separated, owing to the circumstances of emigration, and settled in different places. For this purpose, the Commission recognized only the nuclear family as eligible, including the family's slaves.

Orders concerning slavery and the slave trade among the Circassian immigrants were occasionally reiterated, and the government tried to bring the situation under control; slave dealers were caught and imprisoned for violations of these orders.[28] However, this was not enough to eliminate the practice, and, with the injured party receiving only partial satisfaction, discontent and anger among its members increased. On the other hand, the government went far enough in its measures to antagonize the slave holders, who opposed any interference with their right of ownership over their slaves. Thus, rather than satisfying all, the government's half-measures satisfied none. Exacerbated by this policy, the already existing tension soon led to open hostilities.

VIOLENCE AND A CHANGE IN GOVERNMENT POLICY— THE *Mukâtebe*

On 9 September 1866 the governor of the *Vilâyet* of Edirne reported to the Grand Vezir that violent clashes had erupted in the village of Mandıra between Circassian slave holders

---

[27] BA/Irade/Meclis-i Vâlâ/24269, enclosure 2, the High Council for Judicial Ordinances to the *Vâlis*, *Mutasarrıfs*, and *Kaymakams* of the provinces which absorbed immigrants, 12 Cemaziyulevvel 1282/13 10 65

[28] For examples of repeated orders, see BA/BEO/Muhacirîn Komisyonu/vol 758, entries no 34 (for the year 1281/1864/1865), 84 (for the year 1282/1865-1866) Arrest of slave dealers in BA/Irade/Meclis-i Vâlâ/24924 and 26185

and their slaves. The issue was the slaves' status. A few policemen were sent to stop the fighting, but they were barred from entering the village. When the authorities learned about this, they immediately dispatched more policemen under the command of a *binbaşı* (equivalent rank of a major). This time, the police managed to control the situation and put an end to the skirmish, but the dispute which had caused it still remained unresolved. The slaves demanded to be freed, and the slave holders refused to manumit them. The governor reported that he had sent to the village one of his staff officers to mediate between the factions. He was concerned, however, that with 400 households of immigrants—all armed—fighting could be resumed at any time. Therefore, the *Vâli* suggested that the villagers be disarmed, and he asked the Grand Vezir to authorize this move.[29]

This incident was not an isolated case, and the situation greatly alarmed the Ottoman government. The immediate effect was to stop the practice which had probably upset the Circassian slave holders most—that is, the issue of manumission papers by some *Şerî* courts to children of parents belonging to the slave class. This practice was apparently encouraged by the government even against the will of the masters, but in the face of violent opposition the Porte was obliged to retract its orders on the matter.[30] Two reasons were given for the change of policy.

[29] BA/İrade/Meclis-i Mahsus/1407, enclosure 5, telegram from Mehmet Hurşid Paşa, *Vâli* of Edirne, to the Grand Vezir, 21 Eylûl 1285 (5:10 p.m.)/1.10.69. It is not known what was done in this case, but a later document may shed some light on the fate of the villagers In a government report of 4 June 1879, the Circassians of the village of Mandıra are mentioned as having been moved to Anatolia and given land for settlement there; they were forbidden to return to Rumelia (BA/İrade/Meclis-i Mahsus/2926, *Mazbata* of the Council of Ministers, 13 Cemaziyülâhır 1296/4.6.79). It is possible that the relocation took place after further clashes, but it could be unrelated to these events altogether.

[30] BA/Ayniyat/vol. 1136, the Porte to the President (of the High Council for Judicial Ordinances?), 29 Ramazan 1283/4.2.67. For other violent incidents, see: BA/İrade/Meclis-i Mahsus/1407, enclosure 1, *Mazbata* of the High Council for Judicial Ordinances, 5 Zilkâde 1283/11.3 67; Blunt, pt. 1, p. 150.

One was that the slave owners considered the offspring of their slaves also as their own property, and the government was reluctant to tamper with old and established Circassian practices; this particular view, we may note, was not in conflict with the Şeriat. The large number of immigrants and the "savage and vile" nature of the majority of them were blamed for the difficulties. The other reason was legal—it was contrary to the Şeriat to effect manumission without the master's consent, unless ill-treatment could be proved. This, of course, raises the question of why such a policy was adopted in the first place, but no explanation is provided. Instead, the government decided that, when slaves complained, attempts would be made to reconcile the parties and induce them to conclude a *mükâtebe*.[31] But the Porte also realized that a more thorough review of the whole issue was necessary.

On 30 March 1867 the Council of Ministers discussed the recommendations of the Immigration Commission and the High Council for Judicial Ordinances on slavery and the slave trade among the Circassian immigrants.[32] The Circassian *emirs* traditionally held as slaves some of their people, the Council observed, and they continued to do so after their immigration to the Empire. As Muslims, and like all Ottoman subjects, the Circassian immigrants were entitled to the full benefits of Ottoman citizenship, among which freedom was one. Nevertheless, the Council ruled, the mere act of migration could not abrogate Circassian slavery, an old, well-established institution. Since the number of slaves in the immigrant population was estimated to exceed 150,000, measures had to be taken that would ensure that disputes over personal status were resolved in a peaceful manner.

Since earlier attempts to restore slaves to freedom without

---

[31] The *mükâtebe* (Arabic *mukātaba*) is an Islamic legal procedure, whereby the master and the slave voluntarily conclude an agreement to enable the slave to gain freedom in exchange for a set payment, the form and amount of which are decided by the parties. The slave is manumitted when the payment is completed.

[32] RA/İrade/Meclis-i Mahsus/1407, the Grand Vezir to the Sultan, 24 Zil-kâde 1283/30.3.67.

their owners' consent had met strong and often violent opposition, the ministers advocated the conclusion of a *mükâtebe* as the best possible solution. Being a voluntary contract,
the *mükâtebe* had the advantage of securing the manumission
of the slave while providing a fair compensation to the owner.
However, in order to induce a slave holder to enter such a
contract, the compensation (*bedel-i ıtk*, "manumission fee")
had to be worth his while. The slaves themselves could hardly
be expected to provide the necessary fee, so that leaving the
matter at that would have been tantamount to perpetuating
the stalemate. Aware of that, the ministers decided that the
government would have to bear the burden.

With the Treasury in chronic deficit and heavily in debt to
foreign creditors, all the government could offer was land.
During the period of settlement, land was allocated to the
immigrants for cultivation, and, with government approval,
adjacent lots were given to slave families for the same purpose. The authorities, the Council of Ministers noted, had
been treating the slaves as free immigrants, and gradually
some of them were manumitted. The ministers proposed now
to continue this policy, and to allow the slaves to use these
government lands as their manumission fee. To facilitate that,
a method of assessing the value of the land and that of the
slaves would be devised. The land would then be transferred
to the slave owner as a full or partial compensation, according to the *mükâtebe*, upon which manumission would be
granted. Slaves who would thus gain their freedom could,
with the consent of their former masters, remain on the land
and continue to work it.[33] However, if the freed slaves wished
to leave the estate, they could do so. In this way, the ministers observed, the land would be cultivated and inhabited,
many slaves would be manumitted, and the slave holders too
would be satisfied. It was nevertheless made clear that such
an arrangement would not be imposed by the government

[33] Although this provision was not mentioned in the Council's report, it
becomes apparent from a later *mazbata* on the issue (see, BA/Meclis-i Vükelâ Mazbata ve İrade Dosyaları/vol. 225, Draft of minutes of the Council
of Ministers, 19 Rebiülevvel 1299/8.2.82).

on the immigrants; officials were to be sent to explain the proposed policy to the leaders of the Circassians, obtain their reaction, and relay it to the Porte.

This decision of the Council of Ministers was a setback for the slaves. A *mükâtebe* could not be imposed on a slave owner who had not flagrantly mistreated his slave; it also gave greater leverage to the *Şerî* courts, before which such procedures were normally being conducted. Apparently, the government was unable to overcome the strong opposition of the Circassian slave holders, or simply preferred to avoid a direct, and undoubtedly bitter, confrontation with them. The readiness with which the *Şerî* courts were issuing orders supporting the position of slave owners against the claims of their slaves put the government in a different situation. In both cases cited above—that of the five boys who demanded their freedom, and that of the family which resisted separation—as well as in others,[34] the courts impeded the authorities' actions which were meant to benefit the slaves. This may be indicative of a general mood in religious circles, one which upheld the legality of slavery because it was sanctioned by Islam. The government, it should be stressed, was consistently careful in emphasizing that slavery, as distinct from the slave trade, was not to be interfered with. The Persian Gulf *ferman* of 1847, the prohibition of the Circassian and Georgian slave trade in 1854, and the *ferman* of 1857 against the traffic in blacks come to mind in this context. It was only the institution of agricultural slavery among the Circassians that the Porte was trying to dismantle, and that too—in the face of strong opposition—it did gradually, with great caution, somewhat diffidently.

It is interesting to note that in documents of the Council of Ministers concerning the above-mentioned *fermans* of 1847 and 1854, the term used to denote slavery in the context of abolition was neither *esaret* nor *kölelik*, but rather the less common *rıkkiyet*, the term usually employed in *Şerî* legal

[34] See, for example, BA/Ayniyat/vol. 1136, no. 210, the Porte to the Immigration Commission, 21 Sefer 1286/2.6.69.

language. This was, perhaps, an indication of how much slavery was still being considered within an Islamic context at the time. Religious and conservative opposition, which had played an important role in shaping government policy with regard to the African slave trade,[35] was probably also behind the decision of the Council of Ministers to prefer the procedure of the *mukâtebe* to more drastic measures and to make the application of the procedure contingent upon its acceptance by the immigrants' leaders, most of whom were slave holders

In the absence of the determination, or perhaps the ability, to formulate and implement a clear policy in regard to Circassian slavery and slave trade, there was no peace among the immigrants. Consequently, the authorities were often obliged to extinguish fires the outbreak of which they had failed to prevent.

Several times during 1872 the Ottoman government received information that groups of Circassian slave dealers in various parts of Anatolia were conspiring to continue the traffic despite government orders which restricted the trade and even suspended it altogether for a while Authorities in the *Vilâyet*s of Sivas, Konya, and Adana were instructed to check such activities. Similar allegations were being investigated in the province of Sinop in the same year. And in the *Vilâyet* of Hüdavendigâr and the *Sancak*s of Canık and Lâzistan, reports regarding the establishment of secret societies (sing., *cemiyet-i hafiye*) to promote the slave trade were investigated and found to be without foundation.[36]

However, the trade was still being carried on, mainly toward the capital. It consisted mostly of young women in-

---

[35] See above, p 99, n 12

[36] Orders to check activities in BA/Ayniyat/vol 1136, nos 211, 215, the Porte to the Immigration Commission, 28 Şevval 1288/10 1 72, ibid , nos 237, 239, the Porte to the Immigration Commission, 3 Zilkâde 1288/14 1 72 Sinop investigation is in ibid , no 127, the Porte to the Immigration Commission, 24 Rebiulâhir 1289/1 7 72 Secret societies mentioned in ibid , nos 237, 239, the Porte to the Immigration Commission, 3 Zilkâde 1288/14 1 72, ibid , nos 255, 256, the Porte to the Immigration Commission 12 Zilkâde 1288/23 1 72

tended for the harems of Istanbul and the other large cities of the Empire. After their settlement, Circassian parents continued to sell their daughters through slave dealers or, less frequently, directly to buyers. Whereas these dealings were largely conducted within the slave class, that is, slave holders selling their slaves' children owing to the hardships and opportunities created by the immigration, a growing number of free-born children were also being traded and reduced to slavery. British sources and an Istanbul newspaper in the English language reported in 1872-1873 that most steamers, many belonging to European companies, such as the Austrian Lloyd's Company, were regularly transporting Circassian slaves from Trabzon, Samsun, and other Black Sea entrepôts to Istanbul. It is unclear what, if anything, the Ottoman government did to stop the trade. When no coercion was involved, it seems that the traffic was allowed to go on undisturbed. The Penal Code of 1858 contained a number of clauses concerning kidnapping and enslavement, but the penalties were not too heavy. On 16 September 1867 these were amended to include further offenses and the penalties somewhat increased, perhaps as a result of the growing number of cases of abduction and enslavement.[37]

THE FAILURE OF BRITISH ATTEMPTS TO INTERFERE

Circassian slaves continued to contest their master's right of ownership over their person and to demand freedom.[38] In 1872-1874 the British government became aware of the situation, which again deteriorated to an open, and sometimes violent, conflict. Breaking with the policy of non-interference in Circassian slavery and slave trade, as formulated by

[37] Reports on transportation in European steamers in FO 84/1427/218-9. Francis (consul-general, Istanbul) to Elliot (ambassador, Istanbul), 29.11.72; *ibid.*/309-10, the U.S. consul in Malta to Lord Granville (Foreign Secretary), 1.1.73, quoting the *Levant Herald.* For 1858 Penal Code, see Articles 203-6, *Düstur,* vol. I (Istanbul, 1289), p. 582; and its amendment in Aristarchı, vol. II (Istanbul, 1873), p. 272.

[38] BA/Ayniyat/vol. 1136, no. 398, the Porte to the Immigration Commission, 21 Cemaziyülevvel 1286/29.8.69; *ibid.*, no. 265, the Porte to the Immigration Commission, 13 Zilkâde 1288/24.1.72.

Clarendon in November 1857, Britain tried to intercede on behalf of the slaves and help them secure their freedom.

Clarendon's policy was generally adhered to by the Foreign Office throughout the period under discussion, but there were some exceptions. In December 1860 the British ambassador in Istanbul, Sir Henry Bulwer, tried to discuss with Âli Paşa, then Foreign Minister, the war-time prohibition on the Circassian slave trade. He was told, as had been his predecessor, that the prohibition was intended only for the duration of the war; he was also informed that it was specific, not general, and covered the Batum area alone. When five years later, upon Lord John Russell's request, he tried to bring up the matter at the Porte, Sir Henry found the Ottomans more receptive than before. They informed him, Bulwer reported, that, contrary to earlier statements, the prohibition was actually in effect, but that there were some difficulties in enforcing it. He was also told that the Immigration Commission was in the process of framing new ideas to solve the problem. This contradiction can be explained by the change, mentioned above, in Ottoman policy regarding this issue.[39]

Reluctant to suppress the Circassian slave trade in the post-war years, the government then maintained that the prohibition had no force after the cessation of hostilities. However, when conditions resulting from the mass immigration moved the Porte to prohibit the slave trade once again, there was no longer a need to bluntly turn away British inquiries. The British, very much out of touch with the developments bearing on the situation, were unaware of the significantly different circumstances which lay behind the two prohibitions and which accounted for the difference between them in scope and detail. The Ottomans did not find it necessary, or desirable, to share with a foreign power information about such a highly complex and sensitive domestic matter. Considering the intimate British involvement in the suppression of the African slave trade to the Ottoman Empire, it is even more striking that, at the same time, they had so little to do

[39] FO 84/1120/5–6, Bulwer to Russell, 12.12.60; FO 84/1246/125–6, Bulwer to Russell, 10.8.65.

with the suppression of the Circassian traffic or, for that matter, with the phasing out of Circassian agricultural slavery

In August 1870 Sir Henry Elliot, the British ambassador in Istanbul, wrote to Foreign Secretary Lord Granville that he did not regard it possible to approach the Porte on Circassian slavery He added

> "With the knowledge not only that the wife of the Grand Vizier had been a Circassian slave, but that ladies in a still more exalted position had belonged to the same class, Your Lordship will understand that I should have been guilty of gross impropriety if I had gone to Aali Pasha and insisted upon the debasing consequences of an institution, which nobody can think more hateful than I do "[40]

This reference to Circassian harem slavery was made in the context of the traffic in young women, which was the aspect of Circassian slavery most familiar to foreigners But in 1873 Elliot became aware of the widespread sale of whole slave families and, worse, of the separation of such families which occurred as a result of sale This he found to be totally unacceptable, and he made a strong representation to the Foreign Minister Halil Paşa, writing "Je croirais très volontiers que l'on m'ait exagéré l'abus Mais je puis malheureusement vous garantir qu'il existe dans les proportions qui non seulement justifient, mais qui demandent impérieusement que le sujet reçoive l'attention sérieuse du gouvernement "[41]

In March 1873 the ambassador addressed Lord Granville again, describing the practice and asking for instructions The matter was discussed at the Foreign Office in late March-early April [42] W H Wylde, Head of the Slave Trade Department, wrote

[40] FO 84/1324/108-10, Elliot to Granville, 10 8 70

[41] FO 84/1370/42-3, Elliot to Halil Paşa, 21 1 73

[42] *Ibid* /28-31 Elliot to Granville, 3 3 73 Elliot mentioned the Circassian issue again in a remonstrance regarding the slave trade in blacks from Benghazi (*ibid* /47-9, Elliot to Safvet Paşa, 14 4 73) Quotation is from *ibid* /33-4, Minute by W H Wylde, 27 3 73

"The state of things described by Sir H. Elliot in this Dispatch is one which ought not to be passed over in silence. However much we might have been inclined to shut our eyes to the so called Circassian and Georgian slave trade when girls were sold by their parents and thought it a great privilege to become inmates of Turkish Harems with the chance eventually of becoming the Wives of Turkish Officials, yet a totally new state of things is depicted by Sir H Elliot which Lord Granville will perhaps think ought to be taken serious notice of. The Turkish Government and Authorities are not insensitive to Public Opinion in Europe, which might be brought to bear upon them by giving publicity to the iniquities of the Circassian Chiefs and Turkish Authorities as reported by Sir H Elliot. . . "

Elliot was instructed by Lord Granville to remonstrate strongly against the practice and "to use every effort to procure its suppression " But Wylde's suggestion to bring the matter to the attention of the public was rejected. Later, Elliot described his attempts to induce the Ottoman government to act on this matter as unsuccessful.[43] What it meant was that the Ottomans still refused to allow any British interference, or even the appearance thereof, in Circassian slavery and slave trade. They certainly did act on the issue, but kept the British in the dark as to developments and progress.

This policy was quite effective. Absorbed in their relentless efforts to induce the Ottomans to conclude a treaty for the suppression of the slave trade in Africans—for which purpose a great deal of pressure was being put on the Porte—the British were now resigned to the fact that they would not be able to affect the Circassian traffic. What in fact was a return to Clarendon's policy, occasionally ignored in the 1870s, was taking place at the Foreign Office In March 1880 Wylde wrote: "No machinery we could put in motion will

[43] *Ibid* /7, Granville to Elliot, 14 4 73, Wylde's suggestion appeared in his minute, but was struck out, probably by Granville FO 84/1397/173, Elliot to Lord Derbey (Foreign Secretary), 16 8 74

prevent the Traffic going on, and any attempt on our part to do so would only cause great irritation and give rise to hostile feelings against us, without in any way lessening the evil."[44]

MORE VIOLENCE, THE SLAVES, AND THE DRAFT

In August 1874 it was reported that in the area of Çorlu, a town in the *Vilâyet* of Tekfurdağ not far from Instanbul, a large number of Circassian slaves organized and demanded their freedom. The slave holders, also Circassian immigrants, refused to grant manumission unless it was purchased by the slaves; they tried to impose their will on the recalcitrants by force of arms. On the Porte's orders, the governor of Edirne moved immediately to subdue the slave holders. He brought troops and four field-guns to Çorlu and read to the *emirs* an instruction from the Porte enjoining them to lay down their weapons and to accept the government's terms. These terms conformed to the general policy as formulated in the above-mentioned decision of the Council of Ministers. Accordingly, the slaves were to be manumitted and the masters compensated by gaining ownership over the lands previously occupied and cultivated by the slaves. The exact value of the slaves and their plots, as well as the ways of making up the differences between land value and slave value where such existed, was to be determined by an *ad hoc* commission. If the government's demands were not met, the *Vâli* warned, the army would attack. The slave holders surrendered their arms and accepted the Porte's mediation.[45]

[44] FO 84/1570/140, Minute by W H Wylde, 1 3 80.
[45] FO 84/1397/180-1, Depuis (vice-consul, Edirne) to Elliot, 12 8 74. This arrangement was reported by the British vice-consul in Edirne in a somewhat confusing manner While the first dispatch asserted that no compensations would be paid by the slaves themselves, the second dispatch (*ibid* /184-5, Depuis to Elliot, 28.8.74) mentioned that a special commission would determine the amounts to be paid by the slaves This was probably a result of the vice-consul's ignorance of the Council of Ministers' decision of 30.3.67, as his reports do not indicate any awareness of the fact that this was not a

In the settlement that followed, the slaves were liberated and removed—some 250 "*araba* (carriage) loads" of them—from Çorlu to other parts of the *Vilâyet*. They were to be distributed among the villages in the interior, one family per village, and allotted land for cultivation. Some 90 of the most belligerent slave holders were arrested. Another fire was put out, but the unrest caused by master-slave relations continued to demand the government's attention in other parts of the Empire.

In 1878–1879 more groups of Circassian slaves claimed their freedom, and some even asked for permission to return to the Caucasus.[46] The legal ambiguity which enveloped the status of the immigrant slaves must have served the interests of the Ottoman government, for no serious attempt was made to clarify matters, say by issuing an imperial *ferman* which would set the basic guidelines. Decisions were being made to resolve specific cases, but when some government officials or local authorities tried—somewhat timidly, it appears—to interpret such decisions as having general applicability, the Porte moved to block their efforts. The confusion that necessarily resulted does not seem to have affected the situation too adversely, and might have actually served the Porte's ends best. To illustrate this point we may now turn to examine a few cases.

In September 1878 *Vilâyet* of Kastamonu addressed the Council of State (*Şura-yı Devlet*) in regard to a problem of ownership which arose among the immigrants.[47] A number of Abaza immigrants who had come to Kastamonu fifteen and twenty years earlier claimed ownership over a group of other Abaza immigrants who had recently moved into the

unique settlement, but rather a part of a broader policy based on precedents and formulated to deal with a large number of cases.

[46] See, for example, BA/BEO/Muharicîn Komisyonu/vol. 758, entries no. 89 (29 Şabân 1295/18.8.78), 168 (12 Şevval 1296/29.8.79); request to return is in *ibid.*, entry no. 196 (22 Zilkâde 1295/17.11.78).

[47] BA/Meclis-i Vükelâ Mazbata ve İrade Dosyaları/vol. 225, Draft of minutes of the Council of Ministers, 19 Rebiülevvel 1299/8.2.82 (reference to the letter from the *Vilâyet* of Kastamonu, 22 Ramazan 1295/20.9.78).

Empire from Sohum. The recent arrivals asserted that the Russian government, presumably acting in lieu of the absent owners, had concluded *mukâtebe* agreements with them and handed them certificates of manumission. Thus, the slaves claimed to be free and to owe nothing to their former masters. Although legally open to challenge—a non-Muslim government assuming the role of master over Muslim slaves, contracting with them as such, and manumitting them—the procedure was accepted by the Council of State, which rejected the claims of the former masters in a ruling of 24 October 1878.

The Council stated that "persons who immigrated to the Ottoman Empire should be considered free (*hür*)," which clearly implied general applicability. It was indeed taken to mean exactly that by no less an authority than the Porte itself. Early in 1879 the local authorities in the *Vilâyets* of Trabzon and Sivas were being confronted with strong demands from Abaza slaves to be freed from bondage, and the Central Government was called upon to help settle the dispute.[48] Basing its decision on the Council of State's ruling, the Porte apprised the governors of these provinces that all immigrants were in fact free and that it was therefore illegal to claim them as slaves. The governors were ordered to ensure that no improprieties were resorted to by the former slave holders and that the freedom of the slaves was guaranteed. However, it seems that this policy ran into difficulties which, in February 1882, caused the government to review its position.

The Ottomans expected that the Circassian immigration would contribute to the manpower potential of the Imperial Army. They were granted a 25-year exemption from military service but encouraged to enlist as volunteers.[49] Several cavalry units were formed for them, and many indeed agreed to serve in the Sultan's forces. The military offered food,

[48] BA/Ayniyat/vol. 1011, no. 148, the Porte to the Ministry of Justice, 12 Nisan 1295/25.4.79.

[49] Pinson, pp. 80-2. Pinson mentions a twenty-year exemption, but, according to Ottoman sources, the exemption was of twenty-five years (see BA/Meclis-i Vükelâ Mazbata ve İrade Dosyaları/*loc.cit.*).

shelter, clothes, and a way of life which many Circassians preferred to farming. But, after some time, these units had to be disbanded because of the unruliness of the immigrants, who resisted discipline and, reportedly, even killed some of their Ottoman officers. The army drafted only free men, and slaves who entered military service gained their legal freedom automatically. In the case of the Circassian immigration, the government soon found out that this arrangement left out a large number of potential soldiers.

Early in 1882, military authorities in the *Vilâyet* of Sivas attempted to register the immigrant slaves in the draft lists which were being drawn up in the province at the time.[50] The slave holders, of course, opposed the move, since it would have deprived them of their right of ownership over their slaves from the time of the men's entry into the army. The Council of State, to which the matter had been referred, acknowledged that a blanket conscription, regardless of personal status, was bound to create problems between master and slave and needed careful consideration. The Sivas authorities were therefore instructed to postpone action until a decision was reached by the Council of Ministers.

The Council of Ministers discussed the issue in detail on 8 February 1882. Already at the outset, the Council affirmed its support for the procedure of *mükâtebe* as the only way to redress the grievances of slaves and to grant them their freedom. The ministers ruled that the decision of the Council of State regarding the Abaza slaves from Kastamonu[51] applied only to that case. The declaration that all immigrants were actually free was based on error. The interior Ministry was instructed to clarify that point to the Immigration Commission and to ensure that the erroneous statement was corrected. Having laid down this basic principle, the Council proceeded to decide the question of the draft.

Here, the ministers confirmed the policy which granted the immigrants a twenty-five-year exemption from military service, and stated that a thorough investigation should be

[50] BA/*loc.cit.*
[51] See above, pp. 173-4.

conducted in each case to establish the length of time which elapsed from the date of the immigrant's entry into the Empire. Immigrants' children born in the Ottoman Empire were drafted upon reaching the age of twenty. In addition, the Council went on to establish an important principle.

Since in most places slaves had been given separate land near that allotted to their masters, it was "only natural," the ministers argued, that, after twenty-five years, they too would join the army. According to previously formulated guidelines,[52] a *mükâtebe* would then be concluded and the land cultivated by the slave would revert to his master to cover, wholly or in part, the manumission fee. The Council noted that even if the slave remained indebted to his master—the value of the land that he and his family cultivated falling short of his own market value—he first had to serve his term in the army, since "defending one's country is the highest of all duties." The debt could be paid to the master after the manumitted slave had completed his service. The specific case of drafting the Circassian slaves in Sivas was referred to the Council of State for further deliberation.

It appears that in its decision on the draft the Council wished to achieve two goals at once. On one hand, the ruling made a large number of slaves eligible for military service; on the other hand, it devised a mechanism for speeding up the manumission of the whole Circassian slave population. Stopping short of explicitly imposing a *mükâtebe* on the master, the Council implied a regularity of procedure which had to have general applicability. Nevertheless, nothing was said about the status of the families of slaves who would be drafted. Unfortunately, the paucity of available information on the matter makes it impossible at this stage to examine how the Council's decision was actually implemented, or what effects it had on the gradual process of manumitting the Circassian slaves. As regards the rest of the slave population—i.e., those not intended for military service, such as women, men over forty years old, disabled men, etc.—the cornerstone of government policy was still manumission through *mükâtebe*. On

[52] See above, pp. 164–6.

this, the ministers were clear and adamant—no device other than the conclusion of a *mükâtebe* was acceptable for resolving disputes between master and slave.

Thus the Council of Ministers was acting—by reaffirming the preeminence of the *mükâtebe*—to stifle the tendency, expressed by the declaration of the Council of State and its adoption by some local authorities and government officials, to grant automatic manumission to all the immigrant slaves. One can, of course, ascribe this inconsistency of policy within the various branches of the administration and the seeming confusion merely to bureaucratic incompetence on the part of the Ottoman government. This, however, would be simplistic and unsatisfactory. For after Abdülhamit II firmly established control over the government, no later than 1878, the Ottoman bureaucracy was fairly effective in carrying out the policies of the highly centralized administration. This is borne out by the available archival material, which can hardly support charges of laxity or ineptitude on the part of the Central Government even for much of the *Tanzimat* period; the situation in the provinces, of course, was quite different. We need, then, to look for explanations elsewhere.

ASSESSMENT OF OTTOMAN POLICY ON CIRCASSIAN SLAVERY AND SLAVE TRADE

As already mentioned above, it is feasible to assume that the ambiguity in the government's policy on Circassian slavery and slave trade actually served the interests of the Porte. It can be argued that the government deliberately refrained from clarifying matters in this area so as to enable itself to maneuver with greater ease between the rival factions in order to defuse the tension. On one side were the slaves, a sizable group, who demanded to be freed; on the other stood the slave holders, influential men whom the government needed in order to communicate effectively with and to control the whole of the Circassian population. Both parties had access to arms and were certainly capable of violence. Religious and conservative elements who opposed what could have amounted to the abolition of slavery in the Empire, or at least what they thought might be a significant step toward it, lent their support to the slave holders. The irony of this is, of course, that when in the Caucasus the Circassians were only nominally Muslim. They maintained their own customary law and traditions, which often contradicted Islamic law. After the migration, however, it was the *Şeriat* which offered the slave holders the best protection against government interference with their rights over their slaves. At the time, the Porte had neither the desire, nor perhaps the power, to side openly with one party, thereby bringing about a serious clash, probably an armed and violent one, with the other. So it chose the middle way.

All that notwithstanding, it is possible to say that the general mood of the Ottoman government was sympathetic to the slaves' demands. This becomes clear from the minutes of the Council of Ministers. Both in 1867 and 1882, when Circassian slavery was discussed, the Council stated that all Ottoman subjects were free persons.[53] In 1867 the ministers even rejected the use of the term "slavery" in reference to any Ottoman subject. In 1882 the existence of a prohibition on the slave trade in blacks was mentioned, and the continuation of Circassian slavery was decried as being contrary to the proper and just order. In both cases, the old and deeply rooted Circassian traditions, and the government's lack of desire to meddle in them, were cited as the reason for allowing the immigrants to maintain slavery. Here, derogatory remarks on the "wild, savage, vile, and uncivilized nature" of the Circassians abound.[54] But some of the government's actions spoke louder than words.

[53] BA/İrade/Meclis-ı Mahsus/1407, the Grand Vezır to the Sultan, 24 Zılkâde 1283/30.3.67; BA/Meclis-ı Vukelâ Mazabata ve Irade Dosyaları/*loc.cit.*

[54] See, for example, BA/Aynıyat/vol. 1136, the Porte to the president of the Immigration Commission, 29 Ramazan 1283/4.2.67; BA/İrade Meclis-ı Mahsus/1407, enclosure 3, Osman Paşa to the High Council for Judicial Ordinances, 21 Rebıülâhır 1283/3.9.66; BA/Aynıyat/vol 1011, the Porte to the Ministry of Justice, 12 Nısan 1295/25.4.79 Cevdet, who described the Circassians very favorably, nevertheless stated that no manners, as known to the civilized world, existed among them (*"beynlerinde âdab ve rusum-ı medeniye yoktur"*; Cevdet *Tarıh*, vol I, p. 295).

In a number of cases—e.g., the sale of the four free-born boys and the separation of the slave family, both mentioned above—the Porte challenged existing *Şerî* court orders regarding the status of the plaintiffs. An unorthodox *mükâtebe* between the Russian government and some Abaza slaves was recognized, and the claims of the former owners were rejected. In a similar case, the freedom of the slaves was upheld, though it was alleged that only a partial manumission fee (*bedel-i cüzi*) had been paid to the Russians. In other instances, manumission was granted to groups of slaves who could not reach a settlement with their masters. Even when accepting the principle of *mükâtebe* as the only legitimate way for slaves to realize their freedom, the government in fact offered to pay—with its own lands—the manumission fees.[55]

In the two recorded incidents of slave-master riots, the Porte's mediation was aimed at and resulted in the liberation of the slaves and their resettlement. Central and local authorities were instructed to prevent the kidnapping of free-born children and their sale into slavery. In one case the Ottoman consuls in Potide and Tiflis successfully negotiated with the Russians the release of more than forty people who had been enslaved by Circassians living in Russian territory.[56] These actions, probably just a sample of a more ramified whole, the records of which are either lost or at present unavailable, reflect the government's sympathetic attitude toward the slaves' complaints. Given this attitude, we may now ask what motivated the Porte to adopt it and, furthermore, what prevented a rigorous and uncompromising pursuit of a policy commensurate with this attitude.

It has been suggested that the Ottoman government wanted

---

[55] For the *Şerî* court cases mentioned before, see above, pp. 158–61; the Russian *mükâtebe* is in BA/Yıldız/K35/2027/44/109, the *Vâli* of Konya to the *Baş Kâtip*, decoded telegram 22 Mayıs 1307/3.6.91.

[56] BA/İrade/Hâriciye/12344, the Grand Vezir to the Sultan, 28 Zilhicce 1281/24.5.65 (and enclosures). Some of these people were sold, presumably against their will, and the others were captured and enslaved after their boat had been wrecked near the Russian coast. Russian cooperation in obtaining the release of the slaves is cited. The Ottoman vice-consuls at Potide was recommended for a medal on his part in the negotiations.

to put an end to the slave trade in adult men among the Circassian immigrants in order to channel as many of them as was possible into the army.[57] This, however, ignores the important class distinctions within Circassian society between freemen and slaves. Four points should be made clear in this respect. First, persons belonging to the slave class—and that included all the Circassian agricultural slaves—were ineligible for military service. Second, the Circassian slave trade was, for the most part, carried on in members of the slave class (*köle* or *cariye cinsi*, as the case might be).[58] Third, even when free-born persons were sold into slavery—which occurred more frequently during and after the Circassian immigration—they were mostly young girls, who would never be drafted into the army, or boys who would not have been eligible for service before another ten or fifteen years had passed. Fourth, the only group regarding which military considerations could have played a part were free-born adult males, or teenage boys, who were sold into slavery and thus became ineligible for military service. This group was very small and it would therefore be incorrect to suggest that the Porte's attempt to suppress the Circassian slave trade emanated from military calculations. Rather, it is more likely that in this area of child trafficking the main concern of the Ottoman government was to prevent the sale of free-born Muslims into slavery. As noted above, such sales were strictly forbidden by Islam. In sales of this kind, the government intervened, especially when deception was involved or the consent of the child's family had not been obtained.

What did have bearing on recruitment to the army was the existence of a large class of agricultural slaves among the Circassians. Since only freemen could be drafted, the manpower potential was, of course, reduced. Thus, the government's efforts to help these slaves to secure their freedom might have been motivated by the desire to make them eligible for the draft. There is no mention in Ottoman sources

[57] Pinson, pp. 81-2.
[58] For details, see above, p. 155, and pp. 184 ff., below.

of any such considerations before 1882. While this is no proof that they did not play a role in shaping the Porte's policy, there seems to be no reason why mention of them should have been avoided in memoranda or minutes of the various councils—the argument being of itself legitimate and even honorable. No attempt was made to conceal the military consideration when the imposition of the draft on immigrant slaves was discussed by the Council of Ministers in February 1882. In any event, the military factor cannot alone and by itself account for the government policy regarding the Circassian slavery and slave trade.

The possibility that the Porte acted favorably toward the Circassian slaves in order to impress upon the European powers its enlightened and progressive disposition should be discarded. Nor can we say that any of the Porte's actions were taken under European pressure. The Ottoman government never reported to the foreign powers, not even to Britain—naturally interested in the matter—any of its actions concerning Circassian slavery and slave trade. In 1865 the Porte told the British ambassador, in response to his inquiry, about some of the plans which were being prepared by the Immigration Commission to cope with the problem. The British remonstrances regarding the clashes between Circassian slave holders and their slaves were left unanswered. This was a domestic matter and the Ottoman government wanted to make sure that, unlike the traffic in Africans, it remained so.

We may, then, consider two other possible explanations, one pragmatic, the other cultural. Being practical-minded as they were, consecutive Ottoman governments realized full well that one of their most important tasks was to maintain public order (*hıfz-ı asayiş*). They had to contain sources of discontent which might disrupt law and order; failing to do so, they had to pacify the disturbance and restore order. The tension arising from the disaffection of the Circassian slaves by their masters, and from outrage over deceitful slave dealing, clearly endangered the public order in the Empire. Frequent kidnapping and small-scale violence, occasional outbreaks of serious hostilities, and actions of brigandage by bands of manumitted slaves who—through *mükâtebe* agreements—lost the land plots they had been cultivating[59] were some of the most conspicuous manifestations of the problem. The desire to defuse this growing tension has to be seen as the main driving force behind the government's actions regarding Circassian slavery and slave trade.

In forming the unfavorable attitude toward Circassian slavery, which the Ottoman government came to hold during and after the immigration, cultural differences certainly played an important role. Though ostensibly Muslim, the Circassians in fact retained many of their customs and practices, especially in the area of personal law, which also governed their concept of slavery. They were welcomed as immigrants to the Empire for reasons at once pragmatic and humanitarian, yet they were regarded by the Ottomans—and ample evidence of that is available—[60] as uncivilized and barbarian. The spirit of pluralism, though on the wane as a result of growing nationalism in the Balkans and of the increasing alignment between the minorities and the foreign powers, still held together this multi-national Empire. In this spirit, the Circassians were allowed to maintain their customs and social institutions, including their agricultural slavery.

Although slavery was practiced in the Ottoman Empire and the slave trade still pursued, agricultural slavery was rare, if at all extant, except among the Circassian immigrants. It had existed on a small scale in the fifteenth and sixteenth centuries, but gradually disappeared later.[61] Albeit subject to some restrictions of their freedom, mainly that of movement, peasants in the Ottoman Empire were free men, not slaves. Holding farm hands and their families in slavery was

---

[59] On this interesting phenomenon, see BA/Meclis-i Vükelâ Mazbata ve İrade Dosyaları/*loc.cit.*

[60] For some examples, see note 54, above.

[61] Ömer Lûtfi Barkan, "Le sérvage éxistait-il en Turquie?" *Annales ESC*, vol. XI (1956), pp. 54-60. The two notable exceptions to this were in Egypt (see Baer, p. 165) and Çukurova (see Lewis, *Emergence*, p. 451).

looked upon by the Ottomans with contempt and considered socially backward. Ottoman slavery was mostly domestic and, in its nature, milder than the agricultural slavery prevalent among the immigrants. The sale of children by their parents was also regarded as a "strange custom" (*adet-i garibe*), which—being un-Islamic—was sure to bring upon the sellers damnation both in this world and the next.[62] These views must have had their impact on Ottoman policy and most likely led to the government's favorable disposition toward the Circassian slaves and their demands.

Why then, we must ask, did the Porte fail to enact a strong and clear policy on the issue, which would then be rigorously enforced? The answer lies in the nature and events of the time. The problems caused by the mass immigration of the Circassian tribes to the Empire in the years 1864-1866 were indeed enormous. The government's lack of preparedness, and later its inability to cope with these problems, resulted in a chaotic process of settlement, which disrupted the life of the peasantry and exacerbated discontent and lawlessness in the countryside. This period of transition had also affected class relations among the Circassians themselves. The slaves felt less bound by the old social structure and, aware of changing realities and the breakdown of authority, challenged their masters' right of ownership.[63] Given the bellicose nature of the parties and the availability of arms, the situation was potentially explosive; and, whereas a one-sided policy might have produced a more rapid and drastic solution, it was also sure to result in a violent confrontation.

During the period under discussion the Ottoman government could not afford even to risk such a confrontation, which would have added to its already numerous and pressing problems. We should remember that these were indeed trou-

[62] To cite only one of many examples—BA/İrade/Meclis-i Mahsus/1407, enclosure 3, Osman Paşa to the High Council for Judicial Ordinances, 21 Rebiülâhir 1283/3.9.66.

[63] For assessment of the Ottoman efforts to absorb and settle the Circassian immigrants, see Pinson, pp. 80-1, 83-5; on challenge to masters' authority, see also Blunt, pp. 146-7.

bled years in Ottoman history, a time of almost incessant external and internal difficulties, which nearly brought the empire to its demise. Rebellions and attempts, ultimately successful, to achieve independence in virtually all of its European provinces, war with Russia on both the western and eastern fronts, trouble in Lebanon, and the loss of Tunis and Egypt to France and Britain, respectively, kept the government fully occupied. Internal dissent, the Palace-Porte power struggle, financial bankruptcy, the turmoil preceding and following the promulgation of the 1876 Constitution, and the constant meddling by the European powers in the Empire's domestic affairs left little desire in the councils of state for avoidable confrontations.

Thus, the government chose the middle road. It neither abolished Circassian slavery altogether, nor did it fully support the slave holders' rejection of any changes in the status quo. Rather, it advocated manumission through *mükâtebe*, and facilitated the conclusion of such contracts by offering state land as manumission fee. Involuntary slave dealings were prohibited, but the voluntary trade, though occasionally suspended according to circumstances, often had a blind eye turned on it. For the Ottomans made a fundamental distinction between Circassian agricultural slavery and forced slave trade, which they disapproved, and the traffic in Circassian girls intended for harem service, which they tacitly encouraged.

THE PROCUREMENT OF SLAVES FOR HAREM SERVICE— THE DECLINE OF THE PRACTICE

It was precisely this distinction which accounted for the continued supply of Circassian women to the Istanbul harems, especially those of the wealthy and powerful among the élite. The demand kept alive the traffic throughout the nineteenth century, the largest purchaser being the Imperial Harem, which set an example for the high functionaries of the state.[64] Smaller

---

[64] On the harem, see Uluçay, Durukan, and Penzer.

households in the provinces tried, in turn, to imitate the establishments of the capital. Though discreetly conducted, this type of slave trade was not illegal, nor was it considered dishonorable to engage in it. As late as 1893, publicly endorsed receipts were being exchanged between buyer and seller specifying the details of the deal. Among the papers of the Deputy Minister of the Interior, Ahmet Refik Paşa, there are a number of such documents attesting the purchase of some Circassian female slaves.

One complete set of three documents refers to the purchase of a nineteen-year-old female slave by the Deputy Minister.[65] In it the seller confirmed that the woman belonged to the slave class and had been in his possession for many years. The transaction was witnessed by six persons, among whom were the Deputy Governor of the *nahiye*, the village *imam*, and the village *muhtar*. We should note, perhaps, that it was the Ministry of the Interior which handled many of the problems relating to the slave trade. Along with the Ministry of Police it was responsible for the suppression of the traffic in Africans, and matters concerning the trade in Circassians, as well as slavery among them, were occasionally coordinated by its officials. Yet the second-ranking official of this Ministry did not even attempt to conceal the deal. This clearly demonstrates how various forms of what legally was one and the same institution, namely slavery, were in fact conceived to be different social phenomena and treated accordingly. Black and Circassian slavery were considered as being totally different, and so were Circassian agricultural slavery and Circassian harem slavery. Although they may all appear to the outside observer as having a great deal in common, especially from a legal point of view, they were certainly quite distinct in Ottoman eyes. The reasons for this, which deserve a separate and careful analysis, do not concern us in the present study. Suffice it here to say, that long-

---

[65] BA/Yıldız/K18/480/141/123/53, Dâhiliye Müsteşarı Ahmet Refik Paşa Evrakı, 3 documents, 27 Şâban 1310/16.3.93; see also *ibid.*/K18/480/ 136/123/53, 1 document, 19 Teşrin-i evvel 1308/31.10.92.

established practices and norms—and the stigma they produced over time—assigned different places in Ottoman society to Circassian and black slaves, to harem and agricultural slaves. The legal notions of the *Şeriat*, which does not recognize racial or occupational differences within the slave class, failed to eliminate discrimination among slaves. Social realities prevailed.

Let us turn now to the Imperial Harem in Istanbul in order to examine some of the ways in which it procured female slaves during the early part of the last decade of the nineteenth century. If what characterized the purchases made by the Deputy Minister of the Interior was the lack of secrecy in which they were effected, the same can hardly be said about the search conducted for the Palace by the Chief Secretary of Sultan Abdülhamit II, Süreyya Paşa. The Yıldız Palace archives contain a unique correspondence on the subject consisting of twenty-one letters and telegrams from the years 1891-1892.[66] The correspondents were the Chief Secretary Süreyya Paşa and the *Vâli* of Konya, Hasan Hilmi Paşa. Most of the telegrams were coded, and great care was taken to maintain secrecy. Though neither earlier nor later documents of this nature are available at this point, it is possible that similar exchanges took place between the Palace and other provincial governors at other times as well.

The *Vâli* of Konya was asked to procure the female slaves from among the Circassian immigrants who had been settled in the *Vilâyet*. The Palace was looking for beautiful and healthy girls over fourteen years old, who did not speak Turkish or acquire Turkish manners. Presumably, the reason for that was that the Palace wanted to give them the best possible upper-class Ottoman education in the tradition of the old *acemi* system, and to avoid lower-class "corruption" of their style. Such girls could be found, the Palace expected, among the newly arrived immigrants from the Caucasus; but earlier arrivals were also acceptable, provided they possessed all the

[66] BA/Yıldız/K35/2027/44/109; twenty-one documents. One of the letters in the file is from another province, the *Vilâyet* of Sivas (İbrahim Zühdi to the *Baş Kâtip* (?), 7 Muharrem 1310/1.8.92.

above-mentioned qualifications. The preferred features appear to have been blond hair and blue eyes.[67]

So as not to violate the prohibition on trading in free-born Circassians, the Palace expressed interest only in girls of slave status. In a few cases, however, free-born and freed women were also offered by the governor of Konya, who argued that since a suitable amount of money had been paid for these girls, they could be considered as belonging to the slave class.[68] But even so, the *Vâli* found it quite difficult to satisfy the needs of the Palace.

There were three reasons for the *Vâli*'s problems in this respect. The first was the paucity of women who possessed the necessary qualifications. Especially hard to accommodate was the requirement that candidates be ignorant of Turkish language and culture. By the 1890s, the number of new immigrants had decreased substantially, while most of the earlier arrivals, having lived in the Ottoman Empire for twenty-five to thirty-five years, had already been Turkified, or Ottomanized, to a large degree. Difficulties in absorption, such as occurred for example in the *Vilâyet* of Adana, offered an opportunity for recruitment, which indeed was seized upon by the *Vâli* when 250 families of immigrants were being transferred to his *Vilâyet* of Konya for re-settlement.[69] But disappointment awaited him there too.

He soon discovered that beauty was not easy to find among recent arrivals. During the process of migration and settlement, the immigrants endured great hardships, and they reached Konya in a most wretched condition. Under such circumstances, even beautiful girls retained only little of their original attractiveness. To remedy that, the *Vâli* suggested

[67] For palace requirements, see: *ibid.*, the *Baş Kâtip* to the *Vâli* of Konya, decoded telegram, 23 Mayıs 1307/4.6.91; *ibid.*, the *Vâli* of Konya to the *Baş Kâtip*, 11 Zilkâde 1308/18.5.91; *ibid.*, the *Baş Kâtip* to the *Vâli* of Konya, 22 Teşrin-i evvel 1307/3.11.91. On the *acemi* system see İnalcık, *The Ottoman Empire*, pp. 85-7. On preferred features: BA/*loc.cit.*, the *Vâli* of Konya to the *Baş Kâtip*, 20 Kânun-ı evvel 1307/1.1.92.

[68] BA/*loc.cit.*, the *Vâli* of Konya to the *Baş Kâtip*, 29 Ağustos 1307/10.9.91, and 11 Teşrin-i sâni 1307/23.11.91 (letter and decoded telegram).

[69] *Ibid.*, the *Vâli* of Konya to the *Baş Kâtip*, 20 Kânun-ı evvel 1307/1.1.92.

that those girls he had selected as potentially appealing would still be taken into the Harem And, he observed, if they were well fed and properly cared for—and sent to the bath (*hamam*) twice a week—they would regain their beauty in no time In the course of the correspondence, the governor became increasingly apprehensive about his judgment as he had been rebuffed once by the Sultan's chief secretary In an exchange of telegrams, the latter advised him not to send two more slaves who had been bought, if they were of the same quality as the last two he forwarded to the Palace [70]

The third obstacle in the governor's way was the apparent refusal of some of the parents to sell their daughters In one case, the parents were persuaded to sell only after the intervention of the head of the immigrant community in the area, though a large amount of money was being offered In yet another case, money was not enough, the *Vâli* reported Taking care not to implicate the Imperial Harem in any way, he was obliged to hint that the girls were intended for one of the large establishments in the capital, the parents then relented In this context, it may be interesting to refer once again to the aforementioned receipts, which were given to the Deputy Minister of the Interior by the seller of one of the female slaves he had bought The latter specifically noted in the document that arrangements should be made for the girl's parents to visit her once or twice a year [71]

There is not sufficient evidence to allow for any meaningful generalization regarding a possible change in the previously reported willingness of Circassian parents—mostly, though not exclusively, those belonging to the slave class— to sell their children to the highest bidder in the hope of

[70] *Ibid* , and the *Vâli* of Konya to the *Baş Kâtip*, 19 Eylûl 1307/1 10 91 For exchange of telegrams, see *ibid* , the *Vâli* of Konya to the *Baş Kâtip*, decoded telegram, 23 Şubat 1307/7 3 91, and the *Baş Kâtip* to the *Vâli* of Konya, telegram 25 Şubat 1307/9 3 91

[71] For resistance of parents, see *ibid* , the *Vâli* of Konya to the *Baş Kâtip*, 7 Şubat 1307/19 2 91, *ibid* , the *Vâli* of Konya to the *Baş Kâtip*, decoded telegram, 19 Temmuz 1307/31 7 91 Deputy Minister's receipts in note 65, above

bettering their and their children's lot. If such a change indeed occurred, which is supported by the little evidence that is available, it probably came as a result of the changes in the life-style of the immigrants brought about by their settlement in the Ottoman Empire. Most of the immigrants became cultivators, and the attachment to the land introduced a certain stability into their lives, which they had lacked before in the Caucasus, especially during the long and arduous years of incessant war against the Russians. It is possible that slave families—the main source for the slave trade—who had secured manumission through *mükâtebe* became reluctant to sell their children again into slavery. When still in bondage, many parents—with the consent of their masters—sought to better their children's lot, as well as their own, by selling them to harems in the big cities. Having gained their freedom, they might have become less eager to do so. In addition, we should note that under normal circumstances of settlement, free-born Circassians did not sell their children into slavery.[72] As pointed out, the *Vâli* of Konya also tried to purchase girls who belonged to the free-born and freed classes; the immigrants' reaction to that could, perhaps, be expected.

Displaying a great deal of energy and zeal, the governor conducted inquiries even beyond the limits of his jurisdiction. His searches spread into the *Vilâyets* of Sivas, Ankara, and Bursa. However, as he met with only partial success, the *Vâli* decided to explore other ways in order to achieve his goal. One such way was suggested by the head of a large group of Circassian immigrants, a thousand households, settled in the *Vilâyet* of Konya. The man, who according to the *Vâli* had great influence over his people as well as good contacts in the Caucasus, offered to set out on a searching mission in the Samsun area and in Russian-held territories. He would take with him, the man said, two pictures of girls whose beauty was according to the *Vâli's* requirements, and

---

[72] Cevdet, *Tarih*, vol. I, p. 292; FO 84/1596/93-9, Lieutenant Herbert Chermside to Colonel Wilson (consul-general, Anatolia), 15.3.81 (this is a very interesting and perceptive report, which displays a great deal of knowledge about Ottoman slavery and the slave trade).

bring back with him girls of comparable, or even greater, beauty. Although the governor wrote to the Palace in favor of the plan, there is no information as to what, if anything, ever came out of it.[73] In any event, an alternative course was soon adopted.

Owing to the existence of cultural, often including linguistic, barriers between Ottomans and Circassians, the governor wanted to engage the services of a trustworthy Circassian who could conduct the search on his behalf. He found such a man in the Miralay (equivalent rank of a colonel), Mehmet Bey. After serving in the 1877-1878 war against Russia, Mehmet Bey worked in settling immigrants in the *Vilâyet* of Konya, thus acquiring the necessary experience of dealing with them. The *Vâli* promised him a promotion to the rank of Mirliva (equivalent of major-general) if he could find suitable girls for purchase. Indeed, his knowledge would be especially useful, the *Vâli* wrote, in determining whether or not the girls were of slave status. In Russia, a number of Circassian slaves were manumitted by the Russian government for a partial manumission fee (*bedel-i cüzi*), the governor added. After their immigration, they were considered by the Ottoman government as freedmen. Other slaves whom the Russians had not manumitted tried to exploit the situation and present themselves also as free persons. Some of the ownership disputes which resulted were resolved by Mehmet Bey. Within a year after sending to Istanbul a number of girls who had been selected and purchased through the endeavors of Mehmet Bey, the *Vâli*, as promised, recommended to the Palace Mehmet's promotion to the rank of Mirliva.[74]

[73] *Vâli*'s searches outside Konya in BA/*loc.cit.*, the *Vâli* of Konya to the *Baş Kâtip*, 29 Ağustos 1307/10.9.91. For the headman's suggestion, see *ibid.*, the *Vâli* of Konya to the *Baş Kâtip*, 7 Şubat 1307/19.2.91.

[74] *Ibid.*, the *Vâli* of Konya to the *Baş Kâtip*, decoded telegram 22 Mayıs 1307/3.6.91, and letter, of 29 Ağustos 1397/10.9.91;*ibid.*, the *Vâli* of Konya to the *Baş Kâtip*, 22 Mayıs 1307/3.6.91. Promotion requested in *ibid.*, the *Vâli* of Konya to the *Baş Kâtip* 1 Kânun-ı sâni 1308/13.1.93; the *Vâli* used this opportunity to ask also for a personal favor: he solicited the Baş Kâtip's intercession in behalf of his brother, who wished to be transferred from the

The high prices paid by the Palace for these slaves and the small number that was ultimately procured indicate that by the early 1890s this kind of slave trade, i.e., in Circassian women intended for harem service, was being pursued only on a very limited scale. It is unlikely that more than fifteen or twenty girls were purchased in 1891 for the Imperial Harem, surely the largest customer in the Empire. Although slaves reached the Palace in other ways too—notably as gifts from upper-class ladies who had reared and trained them since early childhood—and taking account of the existence in Istanbul and other cities of sizable harems in addition to the Imperial one, still the total number of acquired slaves was considerably lower than in the previous decades.

As suggested above, the completion of the process of settlement and the gradual manumission of immigrant slaves through government-encouraged *mükâtebe* were the main factors in reducing the volume of the Circassian slave trade and in driving prices up. The generally worsening economic conditions in the Empire during the last decades of the nineteenth century, which also affected the wealthy and powerful classes, made the Circassian female slave, even more than before, a "luxury item" which only few could afford to buy. One must not be tempted to attribute the decline of Circassian harem slavery to the impact of Western ideas and lifestyle, though these had probably influenced the attitude of some Ottomans toward the practice. As long as the Imperial household continued to serve as a model to be imitated by the upper class, and as long as that household continued to maintain Circassian harem slavery, it was up to the market forces and economic realities to determine the extent to which the institution would persist.

---

position of battalion commander (in the Gendarmerie) at Kayseri to the equivalent position at Teke. The Governor's earliest request forwarded in conjunction with the *Vâli* of Ankara, was addressed to the *Serasker* but produced no results. This time, he suggested that the *Baş Kâtip* would talk about the matter with the Head of the Gendarmerie Commission (*Jandarma Komisyonu*).

CHAPTER VI

Between Prohibition and Convention—
The African Slave Trade to
the Ottoman Empire, 1857-1877

THE *ferman* of 1857 which prohibited the slave trade in Africans marked the beginning rather than the end of an era. The story of the suppression of the Ottoman traffic in the years that followed consists mostly of the incessant attempts to put this *ferman* into effect. The British saw in its promulgation a major success for their efforts and thereafter constantly pressed the Ottomans to live up to this commitment. The Ottomans, somewhat reluctantly drawn into an abolitionist policy, found the prohibition difficult—and in a number of provinces virtually impossible—to enforce. At times, a considerable gap existed between the Porte's official policy of suppression and the reality of unimpeded trading in the slaving provinces.

The Hijaz, Egypt, and Tripoli—by far the most important entrepôts of the African slave trade to the Empire—would alternate as the chief supply channel according to the changing circumstances. British pressure, sometimes backed by the use of naval power, was foremost among these circumstances. Thus, the history of the suppression of the African slave trade to the Ottoman lands is largely—though by no means exclusively—the political-diplomatic history of foreign pressure and the reaction thereto. Consequently, the present chapter is devoted to the dealings between the concerned governments regarding the suppression of the African slave trade to the Ottoman Empire and the results which they produced.

A lengthy chronological narration of the numerous incidents, British remonstrances, and Ottoman instructions issued to redress them in the twenty years under review here would obviously be tedious I shall, therefore, discuss only the main relevant developments, trends, and agreements of the time. On the "ladder" representing the suppression of the African traffic to the Empire, this was the arduous climb from the rung of prohibition to that of convention.

OTTOMAN EFFORTS TO ENFORCE THE PROHIBITION OF 1857

There are good reasons to believe that the Ottoman government indeed tried to enforce the prohibition against the slave trade in Africans Reports from the various provinces confirm that steps were taken during 1857-1859 to reduce, if not eliminate, the traffic. The British consul in Baghdad wrote to Stratford de Redcliffe that the authorities in Iraq were acting to prevent importation of slaves and to liberate slaves who had been smuggled into the province. The governor of Crete ordered the manumission of slaves who passed through the island on their way to Istanbul. Reports on similar actions came from Izmir, Diyarbakır, and Jerusalem [1]

In Istanbul, instructions were given to the customs-house to stop levying the duty on slaves (*pencik resmi*), and a special official was appointed to detect and to detain smuggled slaves.[2] One of the dragomans of the British Embassy, sent to investigate the situation at the port, was satisfied that the smuggling of large parties of slaves, i e , more than eight slaves, was virtually impossible. Similar steps were taken at the important port of Izmir, where the government, in a

[1] FO 84/1060/32-4, Kemball (consul, Baghdad) to Stratford, 17 12 57, *ibid* ,/184-6, Kemball to Clarendon, 16 3 58, *ibid* /188-9, J G Taylor (vice-consul, Basra) to Kemball, 17 12 57 On Crete action, see *ibid* /172-6, Ongley to Clarendon, 16 1 58, the *Vâli* was informed of their presence on board an Ottoman war ship by its captain, an officer who had been educated in England For other places, see FO 84/1028/141-2, Stratford to Clarendon, 25 4 57, FO 84/1029/58, W A Maltass (consul, Diyarbakır) to Clarendon, 25 6 57, FO 84/1060/192-3, James Finn (consul, Jerusalem) to Malmesbury, 26 5 58

[2] FO 84/1060/44-6, Phillip Sarell (an Embassy dragoman) to Alison (Chargé d'Affaires, Istanbul), 25 1 58

symbolic action, captured and manumitted forty-five slaves
For this interesting incident we have both the Ottoman and
British accounts, which give us an insight into some of the
complications involved in this seemingly simple act

Early in February 1857 the British consul in Tripoli reported to the Foreign Office that an Ottoman ship had left
the province for Izmir and Istanbul with sixty to seventy
slaves on board.[3] An attempt was made in conjunction with
local officials to detain the ship for examination, but it was
unsuccessful. This information was communicated to the
Istanbul and Izmir authorities, placing them on alert so that
they might act to free the slaves and arrest the dealers When
the ship arrived at the port of Çeşme, near Izmir, it was met
by the local police The slaves and dealers were taken into
custody, and the authorities began a lengthy debate concerning their future The case was not fully settled until October
1857, that is, almost eight months after the boat's departure
from Tripoli

The local councils of the *Kaza* of Çeşme and the *Sancak* of
Izmir, and the High Council for Judicial Ordinances reviewed the details of the case On 8 October the Sultan finally granted imperial assent to the proceedings and the decisions reached through them But the fate of the slaves was
decided much earlier, in fact upon their arrival in Izmir in
mid-April Out of the 45 male and female slaves discovered
on board the captured ship, 29 had been intended for sale in
Izmir and 16 in Istanbul [4] Of the 29 intended for Izmir, 12

---

[3] The British sources for this case are FO 84/1029/85-92, Herman (consul, Tripoli) to Clarendon, 8 2 57, *ibid* /75, J Chumarian (an Embassy dragoman) to Stratford, 18 4 57, *ibid* /77, G D Vedova (acting consul, Izmir)
to Stratford, 23 4 57 The Ottoman sources are BA/Irade/Meclis-ı Vâlâ/16623,
enclosure 13, *Mazbata* of the Council of the *Kaza* of Çeşme, 5 Şevval
1273/29 5 57, *ibid* , enclosures 15 and 29, *Mazbata* of the Council of the
Sancak of Izmir, 27 Şâban 1273/22 4 57, *ibid* , enclosure 71, *Mazbata* of the
High Council for Judicial Ordinances, 7 Sefer 1274/27 5 57, *ibid* , the Grand
Vezir to the Sultan, 17 Sefer 1274/7 10 57

[4] Detailed list of slaves, owners, dealers, etc , is in BA/*loc cit* , enclosures
28 and 68, additional information comes from the reports mentioned in
Note 3

belonged to the 5 slave dealers caught on the vessel; these slaves were manumitted in court by the dealers, presumably under government pressure. In the Izmir batch there were also 12 slaves who belonged to owners in Tripoli, and the owners of the remaining 5 could not be identified. Of the latter group, 1 died, 2 were hospitalized with unspecified illness, and 2 were classified as "mute" (*dilsiz*). These 16 slaves together with the 16 intended for sale in Istanbul were given certificates of manumission by the authorities, allowed to settle in Izmir, and placed as servants with local families, to be paid specified and individually fixed wages.

Following this arrangement, the 5 slave dealers petitioned the government and demanded compensation.[5] They asserted that when they left Tripoli, on 12 February 1857, they were unaware of the existence of a *ferman* prohibiting the slave trade. We should note that the *ferman* had been sent from Istanbul to Tripoli only sixteen days before the ship's departure, and it is possible that promulgation did not take place by that time. The dealers went on to say that they suffered a great financial loss by the action of the government since they could not recover the money they had invested in the slaves and their transportation. In addition, they were liable, they said, for the slaves whom they did not own themselves, but who had been entrusted to them by the owners in Tripoli for sale in Izmir and Istanbul. The High Council for Judicial Ordinances decided to give the dealers the benefit of the doubt, agreeing that it was possible that knowledge of the *ferman* was not widespread in Tripoli so soon after its promulgation. Therefore, the Council recommended that the dealers be recompensed by the Treasury of Izmir, but only for the slaves they personally owned, and at a rate clearly below market prices.

This was not a unique incident. A case similar in nature involved a group of 47 slaves detained in Crete by the *Vâli*

[5] The dealers presented three petitions: *ibid.*, enclosure 12, 8 Şevval 1273/1.6.57; *ibid.*, enclosure 14, 13 Şevval 1273/6.6.57; *ibid.*, enclosure 69, 4 Zilhicce 1273/26.7.57.

on their way from Tripoli to Istanbul.[6] The governor admitted that the slaves had left Tripoli before the promulgation of the *ferman* there, but reached Crete after it had been
read on the island. Nevertheless, he refused to return the
slaves to the dealer, citing the protest it would raise from
foreign consuls and the appalling conditions in which the
slaves reached his province. Some slaves, originally number-
ing more than 60, died of starvation, "and the rats on board
hastened to eat their bodies," the new *Vâli* wrote to the Grand
Vezir in support of his predecessor's action. Most of the slaves
were found lying sick, and the government had to spend a
large amount of money (24,000 *kuruş*) in order to feed, clothe,
and hospitalize them. They were then manumitted and, having acquired—through government-sponsored training—
various skills, joined the local free labor force. They could
not, would not, be returned to the dealer, the *Vâli* concluded.

In fact, a special investigator sent to Crete by the government recommended that the slave dealer's demand for the
return of his slaves be rejected. His petition to the Council
of the *Tanzimat* was also unsuccessful. However, the High
Council for Judicial Ordinances ruled that the dealer had a
case, mainly because he had paid customs duties for his slaves
before leaving Tripoli. The Council decided, therefore, to
compensate him for the loss of the slaves and to give him
back the amount he had paid to the Tripoli customs-house.
But, here again, the sum assessed by the Council per slave
was rather low by market standards. The Grand Vezir and
the Sultan accepted these recommendations, and the case was
closed in October 1858, more than twenty months after the
seizure of the slaves in Crete. However, the government was
not always so generous with the dealers. In December 1857

---

[6] BA/Irade/Meclis-i Vâlâ/17636, *Mazbata* of the High Council for Judicial
Ordinances, 6 Rebiulevvel 1275/14 10 58, ibid , the Grand Vezir to the Sultan, 16 Rebiulevvel 1275/24 10 58, and the *Irade*, 17 Rebiulevvel 1275/25 10 58,
ibid , the *Vâli* of Crete to the Grand Vezir, n d , but responding to inquiry
from the Grand Vezir dated 28 Muharrem 1275/7 9 58, ibid , petition of the
slave dealer Omer, 21 Muharrem 1275/31 8 58

another slave dealer—an Albanian operating between Tripoli, the Balkans, and Istanbul—was sentenced to six months imprisonment for violating the imperial *ferman*.[7] His partner, a well-known slave dealer from Istanbul, was banished from the capital for a period of three months.

There is also clear indication that the government ordered the removal of customs duties levied on slaves prior to the prohibition. The evidence here comes from the *Kaza* of Fezzan in the *Vilâyet* of Tripoli, for long one of the major slaving regions for the North African-Ottoman traffic The tax-farmer for that area petitioned the government in 1857 to release him from his commitment to the Treasury, which he could not meet owing to the abolition of the duties and to market taxes related to the slave trade [8] In October the Sultan granted him his wish and cancelled the lease. As we shall see, some sort of payment would still be exacted from slave dealers importing slaves into the Ottoman Empire, though, of course, unofficially and without proper registration in the customs-house books In many cases, this payment would take the form of a bribe paid to officials to cover for infractions of the prohibition Nevertheless, on its part, the Central Government officially adopted the concomitant measures necessitated by the 1857 *ferman*

In October 1857 the *Vâli* of Tripoli reported to the High Council for Judicial Ordinances that he had taken rigorous actions to enforce the prohibition More than 300 cavalrymen were deployed along the coast east and west of the port of Tripoli, covering the distance of a six-hour ride. An "intelligence network" was established in order to obtain infor-

[7] BA/Irade/Meclis-ı Vâlâ/16856, *Mazbata* of the High Council for Judicial Ordinances, 5 Cemaziyulevvel 1274/22 12 57, ıbıd , the Grand Vezır to the Sultan, 9 Cemaziyulevvel 1274/26 12 57, and the *Irade*, 10 Cemaziyulevvel 1274/27 12 57 We shall return later to the interesting letters exchanged between the two and seized by the authorities in Tripoli while searching for slaves smuggled into the province after the promulgation of the *ferman* (see below, pp 198-9)

[8] BA/Irade/Meclis-ı Vâlâ/16624, *Mazbata* of the High Council for Judicial Ordinances, 3 Sefer 1274/23 9 57, ıbıd , the Grand Vezır to the Sultan, 18 Sefer 1274/8 10 57, and the *Irade*, 19 Sefer 1274/9 10 57

mation about intended shipments, and slave dealers were being apprehended in their homes to check for illegally imported slaves In January 1858 British sources reported that the prohibition had an effect in Tripoli, and that slave dealers were abandoning slaves already imported because of difficulties in exporting them from the province The *Vâli* of Crete reported in September 1858 that the *ferman* was being strictly enforced on the island, and vowed to continue to implement measures which would ensure the suppression of the trade [9] There is evidence to substantiate his claims

Indeed, the effect of the measures taken by the Ottomans is reflected in the correspondence—alluded to above—between two slave dealers, Ismail Ağa of Istanbul and Bayram, an Albanian living in Tripoli The letters were captured by the police at Bayram's home in Tripoli during a search for smuggled slaves.[10] From this correspondence it becomes clear that measures were taken to enforce the prohibition in Tripoli, as well as in Crete and Izmir Ismail advised Bayram in July 1857 to avoid being detected by the authorities by embarking his slaves outside the port and from different points along the coast He also cautioned against touching at Crete and Izmir, and urged Bayram to proceed directly to Istanbul, where he would receive him and try to smooth out things Officially, he wrote, no permits were being given in Istanbul to dealers who wished to import slaves and the future seemed uncertain. However, beyond that, no one was prevented from dealing in slaves as he pleased Bayram reported that the prohibition was being enforced in Tripoli and slaves were hard to come by, though it was still possible to trade secretly As a result of the strict measures employed by the government,

[9] The Tripoli reports are in *ibid* /16856, enclosure 4, the *Vâli* of Tripoli Osman Muzhir Paşa to the High Council for Judicial Ordinances, 1 Rebiülevvel 1274/20 10 57, and FO 84/1060/36–40, Alison to Clarendon, 28 1 58, *ibid* /48–9, Slade to Alison, 25 1 58 For report of the governor of Crete, see BA/*loc cit* /17636, the *Vâli* of Crete to the Grand Vezir, n d , but responding to inquiry from the Grand Vezir dated 28 Muharrem 1274/7 9 58

[10] *Ibid* /16856, Bayram to Ismail, 15 Zilkâde 1273/7 7 57 and 5 Zilhicce 1273/27 7 57, Ismail to Bayram, 7 Zilhicce 1273/29 7 57 and 5 Muharrem 1274/26 8 57, *Mazbata* of the High Council for Judicial Ordinances, 5 Cemaziyülevvel 1274/22 12 57

he added, prices of slaves went up. He approached the governor on the matter, in the hope of obtaining permission to export some slaves, but was turned down. İsmail and Bayram seem to have been very well connected and to have maintained good relations with high-ranking officials in the province. İsmail asked Bayram to convey his regards to the private secretary of the governor (*Divan Efendisi*), the Kadi, and two colonels (*miralays*). They apparently tried to use these connections in order to evade the prohibition, for which and for violating the *ferman* they were later punished.

The Ottoman attempts to uphold the provisions of the *ferman* of prohibition were welcomed by the British.[11] Lord Stratford de Redcliffe wrote to the Earl of Clarendon in April 1857 about the sincerity with which the *ferman* was being implemented in Izmir. This followed the capture and liberation of the slaves who were landed at Çeşme. In the House of Commons, Mr. Baxton—a major advocate of the abolitionist cause in Britain—proposed a resolution in July of the same year, indirectly censuring Spain for its lack of cooperation on the suppression of the African slave trade. In his presentation he referred to the slave trade in the Ottoman Empire as having already been suppressed. The *Anti Slavery Reporter* also praised the Ottomans for their efforts to put down the trade in Tripoli. Before long, however, reports would reach London reflecting a somewhat different situation, which in turn would give rise to a new series of British remonstrances against and public criticism of Ottoman actions in this regard.

During 1858–1859 British consuls reported from the Balkans, Baghdad, and Tripoli on increasing violations of the slave trade prohibition.[12] The authorities in the Balkan prov-

[11] FO 84/1028/141-2, Stratford to Clarendon, 25.4.57; *Hansard's Parliamentary Debates*, 3rd series, vol. CXLXVI, p. 1501; the resolution was passed on 14 July 1857; ASR, 3rd series, vol. VIII (1860), pp. 155-6.

[12] FO 84/1060/151-4, Blunt (consul, Monastir) to Alison, 2.6.58; FO 84/1090/73-8, Brunt (consul, Skopje) to Longworth (consul, Monastir), 15.3.59; FO 84/1060/184-6, Kemball to Clarendon, 16.3.58; FO 84/1090/80-1, Herman to Blunt, 12.6.58.

mces did not receive the *ferman*—addressed only to the *Vâlis* of Egypt, Tripoli, and Iraq—so they did not feel obliged to prevent importation of slaves into their ports In other provinces, accusations were made of official connivance at the trade, and in June 1858, the British consul in Tripoli wrote "Since the prohibition of the exportation of slaves from this Regency   every ingenious device and surreptitious maneuver has been resorted to from the highest to the lowest authority in the country to neutralize its operation "[13] Whether this was so from the promulgation of the *ferman* is at least debatable, but what this dispatch can tell us is that at the time it was written, a year and a half after the prohibition had been issued, the consul had reason to believe that the slave trade was still being carried on, and that he could do little to stop it

British protests caused the Porte to issue fresh instructions to the *Vâli* of Tripoli and the *Kaymakam* of Benghazi to enforce the prohibition in the *Vilâyet*, this occurred in two separate instances during 1858 The *Kaymakam* of Benghazi was summoned to Istanbul and put on trial for misconduct and infraction of the slave trade *ferman* With the change of governors in Tripoli early in 1859, new attempts were made to stop the traffic Both Izzet Paşa and Mahmut Nedim Paşa, who served as *Vâlis* between 1859-1867, tried to put an end to the raids which were being organized from time to time in the province for the procurement of slaves from Waday, near present-day Chad They were said to have returned to their homes women and children seized in these raids [14]

In May 1860 Izzet Paşa—acting on information supplied by the British consul—dispatched an expeditionary force to

---

[13] FO 84/1090/80-1, Herman to Blunt, 12 6 58
[14] Instructions to governors of Tripoli and Benghazi are in FO 84/1060/82-5, translation of a letter from the Grand Vezir to the governors of Tripoli and Benghazi, 18 Şevval 1274/1 6 58, *ibid* /98-101, translation of an order from the Grand Vezir Mehmet Emin Âli to the governor of Tripoli 9 11 58 Trial of the *Kaymakam* of Benghazi is in *ibid* /80, Alison to Lord Malmesbury (Foreign Secretary), 4 6 58 For actions of Izzet Paşa and Mahmut Nedim Paşa, see BA/Yıldız/K39/2128/129/118, a report (*lâyiha*) by Muhammad Bashālā of Tripoli, 6 Şevval 1311/12 4 94

intercept a raiding party on its way to Egypt with a large number of Tiboo and Touareg captives intended for sale. How large were the forces involved may be gathered from the size of the contingent committed by the *Vâli* on this occasion: 1 batallion of riflemen, 2 squadrons of cavalry, 1 light field battery, and 600 mounted irregulars—all under the command of a colonel. After a 600-mile march in extremely difficult desert conditions, the Ottoman force surprised the marauders' caravan, captured the leaders, and took possession of the slaves and stolen property. Expressing his appreciation for this action, the British consul wrote in his report to the Foreign Secretary: ". . . while it reflects the highest credit on the skillful execution of the officer in command, [the expedition] exhibits at the same time the extraordinary power of endurance of the Turkish soldier."[15] In this and another expedition, close to 500 captives were freed, who otherwise would have been sold into slavery in Tripoli, Benghazi, and Egypt; many of them would have ultimately reached the various cities of the Levant and Balkans.

One of the consequences of these Ottoman efforts to enforce the prohibition of the African slave trade—indeed, an indication of the efficacy of these measures in the *Vilâyet* of Tripoli—was the attempt to divert the trade routes. In May 1858 it was reported that 17 merchants from Ghudāmis and the Fezzan had sent a petition to the *Vâli* of Tripoli.[16] They complained that in Ghāt, a major market town and inlet on the southwestern border of the province, the only acceptable barter was in slaves. As a result of the Ottoman prohibition, the petitioners asserted, they could not trade in Ghāt nor exchange the merchandize they had brought down from the northern parts of the province. Slaves were still being transported to Ghāt, but were now bought by Algerian merchants. The outcome was the decline of the Tripolitan trade and the prosperity of the Algerian one. Notably, the peti-

[15] FO 84/1120/156-65, Herman to Lord John Russell (Foreign Secretary), 2.7.14-9.60.

[16] *Accounts and Papers*, 1859 (session 2), vol. XXXIV, p. 516, Herman to Malmesbury, 22.5.58 (including the translated text of the petition).

tioners did not demand the relaxation or abrogation of the prohibition, but rather that it be applied universally, that is, to all merchants trading with sub-Saharan regions, so that legitimate commerce could replace the now illegal slave trade.

The Ottoman government could do little to control such remote areas where it had neither jurisdiction nor the necessary military forces. It could do even less to affect the Algerian trade, which was directed and partly financed by the French. Indeed, allegations were made by British observers—which nevertheless are not substantiated by other sources—that Frenchmen, if not the French government, were involved in the Ghāt slave trade. Several reports in 1858-1859 mentioned the presence of French agents who accompanied the large caravans coming from Algeria to Ghāt to buy slaves.[17] The dealers were looking for male and female slaves between the ages of fifteen and twenty, and had in their possession large amounts of money. A group of 500 slaves from Ghāt was turned back by the Ottoman authorities of Tripoli in January 1858; it was reportedly sold to the Algerians later in Ghāt. The French were said to have instructed their agents and the Algerian merchants to procure as many slaves as possible, with the intention of enrolling them in the army. Such slaves were to be manumitted upon purchase.

Thus it seems that, despite connivance on various administrative levels, and though violations of the prohibition continued to occur, the Ottoman effort to enforce the 1857 *ferman* in Tripoli was sincere and successful. This is not to say, however, that the supply of African slaves to Istanbul and to other Ottoman cities was cut off; other sources were found and other routes were used. Nor does it mean that the days of the slave trade in Tripoli were over; in later years, and according to developments and circumstances in Tripoli and other slaving provinces, the trade would be revived from time to time. It would not, however, assume the same proportions as before the promulgation of the *ferman*.

---

[17] *Ibid.; ibid.*, pp. 516-7, F. H. Crowe (vice-consul, Benghazi) to Herman, 3.5.58; *ibid.*, p. 517, Reade (acting consul-general, Tripoli) to Malmesbury, 20.7.58; FO 84/1090/151, Reade to Malmesbury, 15.1.59.

As noted above, the Hijaz was excluded from the prohibition, owing to past experience which demonstrated the sensitivity of the issue in that province. However, in June 1859, the Grand Vezir Âli Paşa ordered the governor of Jidda to suppress the slave trade in and out of Massawa—the main outlet for the Ethiopian traffic to Arabia, often used also for the exportation of black Sudanese.[18] This order was issued in response to presentations by the British ambassador in Istanbul, Sir Henry Bulwer. A few months later, early in 1860, reports reached Sir Henry that the Hijaz was on the brink of yet another uprising in connection with the question of the slave trade.

On orders from Istanbul, the governor of the Hijaz issued an instruction to prevent the slave trade in the Red Sea.[19] Future importation was forbidden, but slaves already in the province could be sold locally and exported. In a conversation with the British consul in Jidda, the governor voiced his concern that strict enforcement would cause major agitation, which could threaten the safety of Christians and Europeans in the Hijaz. The initial reaction to his order was calm, for the merchants thought it would not be carried out. Fuat Paşa, at the time Foreign Minister, did not share the *Vâli*'s concerns, but agreed that caution should be exercised in applying the Porte's orders in regard to the suppression of the slave trade. Recalling the revolt of 'Abd al-Muṭṭalib in 1855–1856 and the attacks on Europeans in 1858, neither the Porte nor the provincial authorities were too eager to provoke the local population by harsh enforcement of the prohibition in the Red Sea.

So for the years 1860–1864 we have a somewhat inconsistent picture of the Red Sea traffic.[20] British representatives

---

[18] For earlier events in the Hijaz, see above, pp. 129–35. Âli's order is quoted in FO 84/1090/21, the Grand Vezir Mehmet Emin Âli Paşa to the governor of Jidda (translation), 21.6.59.

[19] FO 84/1120/9–14, correspondence—Stanley (consul, Jidda), Bulwer, Russell, 18.3–4.4.60.

[20] For this period see: *ibid.*/1, Russell to Bulwer, 22.6.60; *ibid.*/101–3, Barroni (vice-consul, Massawa) to Stanley, 17.10.60; FO 84/1144/193, the Grand

wrote of Ottoman connivance but also mentioned some positive steps and serious efforts to suppress the slave trade. The
volume of the traffic did increase, nonetheless, a phenomenon attributed by British observers to the death of Sultan
Abdülmecit on 25 June 1861 and the accession to the throne
of Abdülaziz. The new Sultan was perceived in the region—
probably owing to his conservative and religious reputa-
tion—as being favorable to the slave trade. Even so,
throughout 1864, the British would still do no more than
remonstrate to the Porte against each reported violation and
demand full application of the prohibition *ferman*.

However, Britain was gradually realizing that Ottoman
power in the Hijaz was insufficient to risk the confrontation
with the local population, a confrontation which was generally expected to result from a serious attempt to put down
the slave trade. Having to preserve a delicate balance of power
in the Hijaz, the provincial authorities could be expected to
affect the trade only marginally and temporarily. Aware of
this, the Porte did not press for harsh measures, but rather
counselled caution. Nevertheless, an important principle was
established by the late 1850s: the Hijaz no longer enjoyed
official immunity from the efforts to suppress the slave trade.
In recognition of the Porte's difficulties, the British looked
for a regional power which would be both willing and able
to put a stop to the trade. Having failed to affect importation
into Arabia, they now aimed at the exportation from the
African coast. For a price, they would find an eager ally in

Vezir Kıbrıslı Mehmet Emin Paşa to the governors of Jidda and Massawa
(translation), 26 Cemaziyülâhir 1277/9.1.61; *ibid.*/209-12, Stanley to
Colquhoun (consul-general, Egypt), 21.1.61; *ibid.*/ 215-6, Colquhoun to
Russell, 5.3.61; *ibid.*/219-23, correspondence—Colquhoun and Barroni to
Russell, 7.9-1.11.61; *increase is reported also in*—FO 84/1181/87-9, Stanley
to Colquhoun, 21.1.62; *ibid.*/15-7, E. M. Erskin (for Bulwer) to Âli Paşa,
14.3.62; *ibid.*/30-1, the Grand Vezir to the governors of Jidda and Massawa
(translation), 7 Zilhicce 1278/23.6.62; FO 84/1225/157-8, Russell to Bulwer,
28.11.64; *ibid.*/159-60, Russell to William Stuart (Chargé d'Affaires, Istanbul), 29.12.64; FO 84/1246/50-60; correspondence—Stuart, Russell, Âli Paşa,
1-4.65; *ibid.*/154-60; correspondence—Colquhoun, Russell, Calvert (acting
consul, Jidda), 30.1.64-22.2.65.

the semi-independent governor of the Ottoman province of Egypt.

THE PLACE OF EGYPT IN THE OTTOMAN SLAVE-TRADING NETWORK

From the early 1860s to the British occupation of Egypt in 1882, and to an extent even in the following decade, the importance of Egypt in the Ottoman slave trade and in the efforts to suppress it greatly increased. Here we shall concentrate only on the role Egypt played within the network of routes supplying slaves to the Ottoman markets. But Egypt was also a major market in itself, with a complex web of supply routes drawing mostly on the Sudan as a source for slaves. Nevertheless, the Egyptian "sub-system" deserves special attention and will not concern us in this study. Instead, we shall focus on how slaves were chanelled through Egypt by both land and sea and on the impact that this question had on the demarcation of borders in the Red Sea.

The Demarcation of Borders in the Red Sea Area and the Slave Trade

The ports of Massawa and Sawākin—for a long time the most active outlets of the Red Sea slave trade—belonged to the *Vilâyet* of Hijaz and remitted their revenues to the treasury of Jidda. By *ferman* of 11 September 1846, issued on the request of Mehmet Ali Paşa, they were attached to the *Vilâyet* of Egypt in exchange for a fixed amount of money to be paid to the Jidda treasury.[21] During the reign of Abbas Paşa, Egypt relinquished these ports and they reverted to the administration of Jidda. Thus, it was considered the responsibility of the Ottoman government and its representatives in the Hijaz—rather than the responsibility of the Egyptian administration—to suppress the slave trade in the Red Sea.

---

[21] BA/İrade/Mesail-i mühimme-i Mısır/787, the *Vâli* of Egypt İsmail Paşa to the Grand Vezir, 27 Recep 1281/26.12.64.

Since the Ottomans were in possession of both the exporting
and the importing Red Sea ports, Britain continued to exert
pressure on them during the early 1860s to act decisively
against the traffic.

To counter accusations that the *Kaymakam* of Massawa was
conniving at the trade, the governor of Jidda asserted that
Pertev Efendi had actually been appointed to the Massawa
position, with specific orders from Istanbul to suppress the
slave trade. If indeed this was so is hard to determine, but it
is certain that Pertev studied the problem well and wrote
long reports to the *Vâli* of the Hijaz and to the *Şerif* of Mecca,
suggesting ways to solve it.[22] In his reports he described the
raids carried out by nomad tribesmen of the Eritrean and
Somali coast against the sedentary population of the Ethiopian interior. In strong language he condemned the cruelty
of the marauders and lamented the suffering of the enslaved.
He then went on to propose that force be used in order to
suppress the trade completely, which he saw as an Ottoman
obligation.

With the 200 local militiamen he had at his disposal, the
Kaymakam argued, he could only increase foot patrols and
try to intimidate the tribal chiefs, but more was needed. The
Egyptian soldiers deployed in the Sudan, Pertev asserted, were
also considered as Ottoman soldiers and should be employed
against the dealers and raiders. If put under an Ottoman officer with appropriate instructions, these troops could enter
the province of Ḥubāba and "within a few hours" punish the
offenders and suppress the slave trade. Pertev was also critical of the British and French vice-consuls in Massawa and
the consuls in Jidda, whose interference in slave-trade matters often complicated the situation rather than improved it.

The Porte's reaction to the suggestion of the *Kaymakam*
was not too enthusiastic. The Grand Vezir wrote to the Sul-

[22] The governor's defense of Pertev is in FO 84/1144/209-12, Stanley to
Colquhoun, 21.1.61, and Pertev's reports are in BA/İrade/Meclis-i Vâlâ/
19711, Pertev Efendi to the *Vâli* of the Hijaz and the *Şerif* of Mecca, 23
Rebiülevvel 1277/9.10.60.

tan, praising Pertev's ideas and the steps he had already taken, but warned that he should proceed with caution so as to give no party any excuse to complain about Ottoman policy.[23] There was no mention of the use of Egyptian troops, nor was an alternative course proposed by the High Council for Judicial Ordinances, which reviewed the reports and submitted them to the Grand Vezir. That probably signaled to the *Kaymakam* that some action to avoid overt infractions of the prohibition was necessary to placate the British, but that too rigorous action to effect complete suppression might alienate the local population, and was therefore undesirable.

The result, however, was to bring upon Pertev British accusations of connivance at and promotion of the slave trade. But he was successful in his efforts to maintain law and order in his jurisdiction, and early in 1865 was even commended by a British official in the area on his cooperation with Britain in her efforts to check the traffic. At the same time, the governor of the Hijaz reportedly issued an instruction to the governors of Massawa and Sawākin not to impede the passage of slaves of Jidda, in what is perhaps the best indication of the efficacy of Pertev's actions. The British took the matter to the Ottoman Foreign Minister Âli Paşa, who, annoyed and surprised, ordered an investigation and an immediate reversal of the governor's instruction.[24] This incident and the apparent inconsistency of Ottoman performance, as in Pertev's case, convinced Britain that a different arrangement had to be found in order to improve the situation in the region.

At that time, the British were approached by the governor of Egypt İsmail Paşa, later the Khedive İsmail, who asked them to support in Istanbul his efforts to re-attach Massawa

---

[23] BA/*loc.cit.*, the Grand Vezir to the Sultan, 2 Şaban 1277/13.2.61, and the *İrade*, 3 Şâban 1277/14.2.61; *Mazbata* of the High Council for Judicial Ordinances, 27 Recep 1277/8.1.61.

[24] Documents concerning Pertev's case are in FO 84/1246/165-9, H. Rassam (First Assistant to the Political Resident at Aden, on special mission to Ethiopia) to Calvert, 11.3.65; *ibid.*/171-3, the French vice-consul in Massawa (name omitted) to H. Rassam, 9.3.65; *ibid.*/100-1, Stuart to Russell, 22.4.65.

and Sawākın to Egypt.[25] İsmail asserted that the Porte could
not check the slave trade because of distance and lack of sufficient means, such as cruisers and troops, in the area. If put
in possession of the ports, he said, he would abolish the trade.
In fact, at that point İsmail had already written to the Grand
Vezir, requesting that the ports be leased to him. In his letter
he listed two reasons for his desire to acquire Massawa and
Sawākın: the need to subdue the nomad tribes of the Eritrean
coast and the need to suppress the slave trade. The nomads
were lawless and unruly, he said, and harbored their fugitive
brethren who escaped from Egypt to avoid paying taxes.
The tribesmen fleeing Egypt did not, of course, pay taxes to
the Ottoman administration of Massawa and Sawākın. Rather,
they engaged in various kinds of "harmful and corrupt" activities. They must be brought under control and made part
of the Ottoman Empire, Ismail concluded. He then addressed himself to the slave trade

Pledging his intention to suppress the traffic, İsmail promised to bring civilization and progress to the area that he
would control Officials would be stationed in the ports of
Massawa and Sawākın, who would take the necessary measures to ensure that the slave trade cease completely İsmail
then stated his loyalty to the Ottoman government and his
willingness to pay the Jidda treasury any amount deemed
suitable by the Porte. He might have added that the two
ports had great strategic importance for communication with
and supply of expeditionary forces in Ethiopia and the eastern Sudan. They would later serve the Egyptians exactly for
these purposes in their campaigns in the region.

The Council of Ministers debated İsmail's request in January 1865.[26] Though agreeing in principle to grant him his

[25] *Ibid* /81, Stevens (staff member of the Consulate in Egypt) to Bulwer,
7 1 65 For Ismail's application to the Porte, see BA/Irade/Mesail-ı muhimme-ı Mısır/787, Ismail Paşa to the Grand Vezir, 27 Recep 1281/26 12 64
[26] Documents relating to Ismail's request are in BA/*loc cit* , the Grand
Vezir to the Sultan, 13 Şâban 1281/11 1 65, *ibid* /791, enclosure 13, the *Vâli*
of the Hıjaz Mehmet Vechı Paşa to the Grand Vezir, 18 Şevval 1281/16 3 65,
ibid , the Grand Vezir to the Sultan 1 Zilhıcce 1281/27 4 65 *ibid* /974, Ismail

wish, the Council decided—owing to administrative changes which resulted from the Law of the *Vilâyet*s promulgated in 1864—to solicit reaction to İsmail's request from the *Vâli* of the Hijaz. The latter supported leasing the ports to Egypt and said that it was impossible for him to suppress the trade with the limited forces at his disposal; İsmail would be in a better position to enforce the prohibition, he concluded. Âli Paşa, however, told the British Chargé d'Affaires in Istanbul that he doubted the efficacy of the measures proposed by İsmail to check the traffic. The British supported the Egyptian request, in the hope that İsmail would be able to live up to his promises. Ultimately, the Grand Vezir recommended to the Sultan that the two ports be leased to İsmail Paşa for life at an annual rate consisting of their revenue at the time plus 50 percent. The terms were to be re-negotiated after three years. We shall soon discuss the effect on the slave trade in the Red Sea of this change of jurisdiction

Considerations related to the slave trade continued to play a role in the demarcation of boundaries on the Somali coast during the following years This is not to say that the slave trade was the sole, or even the most important, factor in the calculations of the three governments involved—the Ottoman, the Khedival, and the British. But the issue was used by the Khedive in order to mobilize British support for requests that he put to the Porte to extend his jurisdiction along the western coast of the Red Sea. The British were guided by a number of considerations, foremost among which was their concern for the safety of the sea route to India, especially after the opening, in 1869, of the Suez Canal—to a great extent a French enterprise Britain was also genuinely interested in the suppression of the slave trade in that region The Ottomans—realizing their inability to exercise effective control over the Eritrean and Somali coasts—resigned them-

Paşa to the Grand Vezir, 20 Zilhicce 1281/16 5 65, FO 84/1246/102-4, Count Pisani (Embassy dragoman) to Stuart, 3 8 65, *ibid* /105-8, Stuart to Russell, 8 5 65, FO 84/1246/64-6, Stuart to Russell, 16 3 65 (the British, on their part, considered Ismail more capable than the Porte of suppressing the slave trade in the Red Sea *ibid* /91-2, Bulwer to Russell, 10 4 65)

selves from the mid-1870s onward to the lesser evil of Egyptian rule over that territory, where they did not wish to see direct European domination.

The next development regarding the African coastline came in 1875, with the transfer of the port of Zayla' to the Khedive in return for an annual payment to be paid directly to the Imperial Treasury.[27] The Secretary of State for India, Lord Salisbury, supported this change, for it would prevent, he observed, any other foreign power from gaining hold over that territory. He added, however, that Egypt's poor record with regard to the slave trade might adversely affect British efforts to suppress the Red Sea traffic. During 1875-1876 Britain formulated her policy on the whole question of boundaries in the region and entered into negotiations with İsmail in order to conclude an agreement on the matter.

The British goals in this respect were defined as being the following three:[28]

(1) To obtain a firm commitment that the territory which Britain would recognize as Egyptian would not be ceded to any foreign power.

(2) To have the ports of the African coast—primarily Zayla', Tajūra, Berbera, and Bulhar—declared free to commerce. No monopolies would be allowed, and there would be unrestricted importation of livestock and provisions to Aden.

(3) To make progress toward the suppression of the slave trade from the Somali coast between Zayla' and Tajūra, and to obtain an agreement which would afford facilities for suppression in Egyptian waters and neighboring seas.

In exchange for the fulfillment of these demands, Britain offered to recognized Egyptian sovereignty over the coast as far as Cape Guardafui. During the negotiations which were conducted from August to October 1876, the Khedive did not agree to turn Zayla' and Tajūra into free ports and asked

---

[27] BA/*loc.cit.*/918, the Grand Vezır to the Sultan, 27 Cemazıyulâhır 1292/31.7.75. For Salısbury's view, see FO 78/3183/86-8, Louıs Mallet (India Office) to the Under-Secretary of State for Foreıgn Affaırs, 23.3.75.

[28] FO 78/3189/282-93, Memo by George E. March (superıntendent of the Treaty Department, Foreıgn Office), 1 5.77

for an extension of his jurisdiction to Rās Ḥāfūn. The British
agreed to that, but other issues surfaced. The bargaining continued until February 1877, when Britain served the Khedive
an ultimatum which finally produced a treaty in April.

Further negotiations were needed to clarify matters concerning the slave trade.[29] The British demanded the right to
search and seize in Egyptian waters vessels suspected of slave
trading. The article on the slave trade, Article IV, in the final
form of the treaty signed on September 1877 read as follows:

> "With respect to the Slave Trade and the Police of the-
> Seas, the Government of His Highness the Khedive en-
> gages to prohibit all export of slaves, to suppress this
> traffic (as within the rest of Egyptian Territory) and to
> maintain order as far south as Berbera. Between Berbera
> and Ras Hafun, His Highness's Government can only
> pledge itself for the present, and until such time as its
> authority can be regularly established along this line of
> coast, to use every endeavour within the means at its
> disposal to suppress the Slave Trade, and to maintain
> order.
>
> "The Government of His Highness consents that British
> cruisers employed in the suppression of the Slave Trade
> may detain and send for trial any vessel which they may
> find engaged in this traffic or which they may have good
> reasons to believe to be destined for this traffic in the
> territorial waters of Egypt on the Somali coast."

The Ottomans were left out of the negotiations and presented with a *fait accompli*, though the necessary language
was employed to maintain their suzerainty over the said territory. Their main concern, which surfaced again in 1884-
1885, was to prevent any foreign power from gaining pos-

[29] *Ibid.*/325-8, Lord Derby (Foreign Secretary) to H. Vivian (consul-general, Egypt), 4.7.77. For text of the Treaty, see *ibid.*/351-3, draft of the
confidential treaty between Egypt and Great Britain (signed by Şerif Paşa
and Vivian), 7.9.77.

session over what they considered to be Ottoman territory.[30] But little was done in this respect beyond the exchange of a few notes through diplomatic channels

The Diversion of the Tripoli Traffic— The Overland Routes to Egypt

As we have already seen, the efforts to enforce the prohibition in the *Vilâyet* of Tripoli caused a diversion of some of the traffic to Algeria, but a more significant diversion for the Ottoman slave trade was the increasing use of the desert road to Egypt.[31] The coast and inland roads connecting the two provinces were considered unsafe and were in fact closed for a long time—twenty years, according to an Ottoman report—but were reopened by strong military action of the governor of Egypt. The renewal of commercial activity along these routes probably meant that some slaves were also carried by the trading caravans, though we have no specific reports to establish that. The first evidence of an actual slave caravan heading from the province of Tripoli, via the Fezzan, toward Egypt is from August 1859, that is, after the 1857 *ferman* had already been implemented in Tripoli.

Further reports implying that the overland trade in slaves from Tripoli to Egypt was carried out on a rather regular basis were received at the Foreign Office in April and November 1863.[32] Slaves not sold in Egypt were exported to

[30] For the Ottoman reaction, see BA/*loc cit* /966, enclosure 3, *Mazbata* of the Council of Ministers, 5 Şâban 1296/25 7 79, *ibid* , enclosure 6, the Khedive to the Grand Vezir (telegram), 1 Eylûl 1295/13 9 79, BA/Meclis-ı Vukelâ Mazbata ve Irade Dosyaları/vol 225, draft translation of a telegram to be sent by the Foreign Minister to the Ottoman Embassy in London (signed by all the ministers), ca 1302/1884-5, *ibid* , a similar telegram, 4 Rebiulâhır 1302/21 1 85, FO 84/1482/73-5, W H Wylde to Derby, 22 10 77

[31] For the diversion to Algeria, see above, p 202 For the situation on the road to Egypt, see BA/Irade/Mesail-ı muhimme-ı Mısır/586, enclosure 3, the *Vâli* of Tripoli Mustafa Paşa to the Grand Vezir, 15 Şevval 1270/11 7 54, FO 84/1120/156-60, Herman to Russell, 2 7-14 9 60

[32] FO 84/1204/258-60, Herman to Russell, 30 4 63, *ibid* /286-8, Herman to Russell, 12 11 63

Istanbul, Izmir, and ports in the Balkans and the Levant. Four caravans carrying 300 slaves each were said to have left Marzūq for Egypt during that year with the connivance of local authorities. Again, the change of route was attributed to the effects of the prohibition in Tripoli.

The British vice-consul in Benghazi reported in June 1874 that the caravan route to Egypt was being regularly used to transport as many as 2,000 slaves annually.[33] The consul-general in Egypt thought the number exaggerated since the difficult conditions on the road allowed for only small-scale trading by the Bedouins. He added that some of the Darfur trade to Upper Egypt might have been diverted through the Fezzan, owing to the Egyptian military operations in the Sudan. However, after an investigation conducted by the Consulate Dragoman, he revised his earlier assessment. Three caravans a year, he wrote, reached Alexandria and other towns in Lower Egypt from Benghazi carrying up to 200 slaves each. Bedouins and others bought the slaves in Benghazi and transported them along the coast route to Egypt. Other caravans, of which he had no precise information, reached Cairo and its vicinity directly from the Fezzan. The Khedive promised the consul-general to watch the land routes and to confiscate all camels and property of caravans carrying slaves. On instructions from the Foreign Secretary, the subject was brought up with the Ottoman Foreign Minister, who agreed to send orders to the governor of Tripoli to prevent such traffic in the future.

At this point it may be interesting to note that five years later, in November 1880, the consul-general in Egypt speculated in a dispatch to the Foreign Office on the reasons for Khedive İsmail's policy in regard to the slave trade.[34] Puzzled

[33] Documents regarding the report and its ramifications are in: FO 84/1428/76-9, Henderson to W. H. Wylde, 22.6.74; FO 84/1397/269-71, Stanton to Derby, 14.8.74; *ibid.*/280-2, Stanton to Derby, 3.9.74; *ibid.*/165, Derby to Elliot, 25.9.74; *ibid.*/192, Elliot to Derby, 17.10.74.

[34] FO 84/1572/347-53, Malet to Granville, 10.11.80. On the attempts to suppress the slave trade in Egypt, including İsmail's position on the matter, see Holt, *Modern History*, pp. 65 ff., and Baer, pp. 176 ff.

over the fact that İsmail gave Colonel Gordon full powers in
the Sudan, knowing that he would attempt to suppress the
trade, the consul-general offered the following explanation:
İsmail must have feared the growing power of the chief slave
dealers in the Sudan, who threatened his policy of expansion
in that region. Therefore, he allowed Gordon to deal a blow
to their source of power, i.e., the slave trade, but at the same
time opened the western overland routes in order to keep
Cairo well supplied in slaves from other sources. I found no
evidence to support this speculation; it may or may not be
true.

The late 1870s and early 1880s witnessed greater control
over the land routes.[35] In 1876 the British consul-general in
Egypt estimated that, owing to the Egyptian occupation of
Darfur a year earlier, the number of slaves introduced into
the country by the overland routes from the west had decreased substantially. No large slave-carrying caravans coming through the Libyan Desert could escape Egyptian detection, he wrote, and smuggling—a relatively easy enterprise
on the Siwa-Nile route—was on a small scale only. In May
1880 the Khedive appointed an Italian officer, Count della
Sala, as the commander of a special force assigned to suppress the overland slave trade to Egypt. The Count was in
contact with the British and kept them apprised of his actions.

Count della Sala's authority was limited to checking the
overland routes feeding slaves into Egypt between Alexandria in the north and Aswān in the south, and did not include
the Red Sea or the Sudan trade. His headquarters was set at
Asyūṭ. He deployed his force in 5 locations in Upper Egypt—
2 companies with 72 camels, and ½ squadron of cavalry—
and in 4 locations in Lower Egypt—1 company with 30 cam-

---

[35] For some of the documents relating to this period, see FO 84/1450/317-
8, Stanton to Derby, 17.2.76; Della Sala's appointment is in FO 84/1572/122-
8, Malet (consul-general, Egypt) to Lord Granville (Foreign Secretary), 11-
12.5.80; BFASS/Mss. Brit. Emp./S18/C162/26, T. V. Lister (for Granville)
to the Secretary of the Anti-Slavery Society, 8.1.81; FO 84/1572/325-9, Count
della Sala to Malet, 8.11.80.

els, and ½ squadron of cavalry. Della Sala reported that he
received from the Egyptian government all the necessary help
to carry out his assignment. In the following years the overland routes were no longer mentioned in reports on the slave
trade filed by the various sources. As we shall see, other
routes took their place in supplying the Egyptian and Ottoman markets.

The North-Bound Slave Trade from Egypt—
The Mediterranean Routes

During the late 1860s and early 1870s Egypt became the most
important entrepôt on the supply routes to the Ottoman
markets. This was the result of a number of factors, foremost among which were the decline of the Tripoli trade as
a result of the *ferman* of 1857, the diversion of the overland
routes from the west, the opening of the Suez Canal, and,
last but not least, a government willing to turn a blind eye
on the traffic, if not tacitly supporting it. Slaves were exported from Alexandria and other Delta ports to Istanbul,
Izmir, and ports in the Levant and Balkans. The extensive
trade from the Red Sea which developed in the 1870s will be
discussed separately.

Most of our evidence regarding the Egyptian–Ottoman slave
trade in the Mediterranean is from 1869 onward. This is partly
because of increased attention to this subject, which resulted
in a larger-than-usual number of reports from one of the two
major ports of entry—Izmir. The appointment of Robert W.
Cumberbatch—an energetic and often over-zealous abolitionist—as the British consul-general in that city brought
frequent reporting about even the most minute occurrences
relating to the slave trade. We should not, however, let
"over-reporting" and the sheer amount of evidence mislead
us to perceive an increase in the traffic from Egypt to Izmir
and the Aegean islands. A gradual increase probably occurred during the early years of İsmail's reign (1863–1879)
and persisted throughout most of his rule. Still, it is to the

period between 1869 and 1874 that most of our evidence belongs.

Slaves were brought to Izmir mainly from Alexandria and by steamers of the Aziziye Company, which was controlled by the Khedive. They usually carried certificates of manumission issued by the Egyptian authorities. But these were often taken from them after debarkation and police inspection, and they were then sold in the various towns The British consul-general in Istanbul submitted in December 1869 a report on the Egyptian slave trade, in which he argued that this fiction of manumission was useless in coping with the trade and only increased corruption [36]

Slaves were also carried by the Austrian Lloyd's Company and often sold on the way, mainly in the Aegean islands of Scio, Mytilene, and Rhodes In addition to the steamers' trade, slaves were carried by sailboats. They were reportedly taken to the islands of Cos and Laros, where they stayed a while to recover from the rough journey, and then proceeded to the markets. Those "markets" were in the private houses of dealers, generally known to the public, to which interested buyers would come to make their purchase. Some of the slaves were discovered and freed through consular contacts with local authorities, but detection was difficult and cooperation not always readily offered [37]

In June 1869 the Egyptian traffic was brought up by the British ambassador in Istanbul in a conversation with the Grand Vezir.[38] The Grand Vezir promised Elliot to order the immediate liberation of all slaves discovered by the port authorities and to communicate with the Khedive on the mat-

[36] FO 84/1305/335-7, Cumberbatch to Clarendon, 8 6 69, ibid /125-33, Sir Phillip Francis to Clarendon, 1 12 69

[37] Ibid /385-7, Cumberbatch to Clarendon, 21 8 69, ibid /391-3, Cumberbatch to Clarendon, 26 8 69, ibid /395-7, Cumberbatch to Clarendon, 28 8 69, ibid /411-3, Cumberbatch to Clarendon, 10 9 69, ibid /417-8, Cumberbatch to Clarendon, 24 9 69, FO 84/1324/293-5, Cumberbatch to Elliot, 4 8 70, FO 84/1341/180-1, Charles Roboly (acting vice-consul, Mytilene) to Cumberbatch, 3 11 71

[38] FO 84/1305/61-2, Elliot to Clarendon, 22 6 69, ibid /96, Elliot to Clarendon, 19 9 69, ibid /98-9, Elliot to Clarendon, 3 10 69

ter. Three months later, Sir Henry wrote that he was satisfied that slaves arriving from Egypt aboard the Aziziye
steamers were now being promptly manumitted by the Ottoman authorities. The men were taken into the service of
the police or the arsenal, and the women were given manumission papers and placed as servants in the harems of Istanbul and other cities. But less than a month later, Elliot acknowledged that the trade on board the Egyptian steamers
was still carried on, though on a smaller scale than before.
In his view, the Ottomans were doing their best, but the task
was difficult.

Gradually it became clear that the slave trade could not be
effectively checked by applying measures only at the Ottoman ports of destination. Action was needed at the Egyptian
ports of embarkation as well. The Egyptians suggested that
all slaves detected upon arrival be returned to the ports of
origin.[39] The Grand Vezir Âli Paşa rejected this proposal and
accused the Khedive of insincerity about the slave trade, for
it was principally on board his Aziziye steamers that slaves
were being exported to Istanbul. He insisted that it was more
humane to liberate all slaves who were discovered rather than
to send them back to Egypt. Âli also charged that Aziziye
steamers were landing slaves on the coast prior to their arrival in Istanbul in order to avoid detection by the police.
The British realized that pressure had to be exerted on the
Khedive.

In February 1870 Foreign Secretary Lord Clarendon instructed the British consul-general in Egypt to demand that
the Khedive issue an official order prohibiting the transport
on board Aziziye steamers of slaves intended for sale.[40]
However, effective measures were not taken until late in 1872.
The Egyptian government asserted that it had recently discovered that the slave trade from Egypt to Istanbul and Izmir
was carried on largely by Iranian dealers. Strong representations were reportedly made by the Egyptians to the Iranian

[39] FO 84/1324/68-70, Barron (Embassy staff member) to Clarendon, 1.2.70.
[40] *Ibid.*/130-2, Clarendon to Stanton, 21.2.70; FO 84/1354/300-1, Stanton
to Granville, 19.8.72.

consul-general, who assured the government that the chief offender had been ordered out of the country. The government also decided to register all manumitted slaves, as well as domestic slaves accompanying their masters, who were leaving Alexandria by boat. Servants were to be registered too. Thus, it was hoped, it would be easier to verify charges of slave trading by comparing lists with information received from Istanbul and other ports.

In September 1872 the British consul in Alexandria reported that strict measures were indeed in effect, and that even slaves accompanying their masters were manumitted and told that they were free to take employment wherever they wanted.[41] He wrote that the authorities issued passports to all manumitted slaves, and that the few irregularities which had been discovered at the passport office were corrected and the culprits punished. These steps reduced the number of slaves still being registered. In June 1874 the consul-general in Egypt reassured the Foreign Office that these measures to prevent the export were still in effect in Alexandria.

However, by then the focus of attention had already shifted to the Red Sea slave trade. It seems that by the mid-1870s the Mediterranean traffic was brought under control and that infractions of the prohibition were on a relatively small scale. Little could be done, either by foreign pressure or by well-meaning instructions from the Porte, to eliminate those violations. This will become clear when we shall deal with the slave trade from Tripoli during the 1860s and 1870s. Egypt—in possession of Massawa and Sawākin since 1865, of Zayla' since 1875, and the custodian of the Suez Canal, which was opened in 1869—became the main target for British pressure. She controlled the most active slave routes from the Hijaz, and was considered to be in a position to suppress the traffic. It was during the early and mid-1870s that Britian negotiated an anti-slave trade convention with the Khedive, which was finally signed in September 1877. However, before we ex-

[41] *Ibid.*/326-9, Stanley to Granville, 10.9.72; FO 84/1397/258-61, Stanton to Derby, 15.6.74.

amine these negotiations and their outcome, we should look into the developments in the Red Sea since the time its major exporting ports came under Egyptian rule.

THE RED SEA SLAVE TRADE BETWEEN 1865 AND 1877

The transfer to Egypt of Massawa and Sawākin, and later of Zaylaʿ and the Somali coast town of Rās Ḥāfūn, divided the responsibility for the Red Sea slave trade between the Sultan, who controlled the Arabian coast, and the Khedive. Britain had hoped to suppress the trade through the Khedive, but was obliged instead to exert pressure on both. This situation led to a number of complications, mostly unforeseen by the British, and enabled the dealers to pursue the trade into the 1880s. Negotiations between Britain and the two governments, the Egyptian and the Ottoman, produced an Anglo-Egyptian treaty for the suppression of the slave trade in 1877 and an Anglo–Ottoman one in 1880. Both of these treaties were concerned, to a great extent, with the Red Sea slave trade, and will be discussed in Chapter VII. They provide convenient breaking points for the examination of the Red Sea traffic. Let us now look into this traffic during the period between the transfer of the ports to Egypt and the conclusion of the Anglo-Egyptian Convention.

Soon after the transfer of Massawa and Sawākin to Egypt, the British found that their expectations for effective suppression of the exportation of slaves from these ports were too high.[42] In an internal consultation at the Foreign Office in August 1867, the Head of the Slave Trade Department commented: "We have supported at Constantinople the Pacha's application to have the Ports of Soukim and Massowah in the Red Sea made over to him, solely on the ground that he undertook if he were put in possession of them to put a stop to the export of Slaves from the Soudan by those ports." He then recommended that this should be made clear to the

---

[42] FO 84/1277/245–6, W. H. Wylde, 23.8.67 (quoted); FO 84/1305/271–82, Raby to Clarendon, 10.12.69.

Egyptian government. But in December 1869 the British consul in Jidda observed that no serious effort was made by either the Egyptian or the Ottoman authorities to suppress the slave trade in the Red Sea.

During the late 1860s and early 1870s reports on the traffic in the region made increasingly frequent mention of the trade to and from the port of Ḥudayda in the Yemen. It was said that Ḥudayda was supplied primarily from Zaylaʿ—then under the rule of Abū Bakr, a local potentate often implicated in the slave trade. Abū Bakr recognized Ottoman suzerainty and paid an annual tribute to the Sultan through the provincial administration of the Yemen. The yearly volume of the traffic was estimated at 3,500 to 4,000 slaves, about half of whom were taken from Ḥudayda to Jidda and then to the various Ottoman and Egyptian markets. A British naval officer serving on board an Ottoman cruiser in the Red Sea reported in December 1874 that Ḥudayda was then the principal slave trading port in the region. It was mainly supplied from Zaylaʿ and Massawa, he wrote. Later reports from the Red Sea also mentioned the role of Ḥudayda as being central to the Arabian slave trade.[43]

There were several reasons for the emergence of Ḥudayda as yet another important link in the Ottoman slave trade. The importation of slaves from the Eritrean and Somali coasts into Ḥudayda was not a new phenomenon,[44] but it was largely confined to supplying the Yemeni market. A small number of Ethiopian slaves were, at times, shipped from Ḥudayda and Mukhā to northern markets, such as Jidda, or to the Persian Gulf and Indian ones. However, the Hijaz was usually supplied directly from Massawa and Sawākin, whereas the Gulf area normally got its Ethiopian slaves from Berbera. Thus, the change we witness in the early 1870s in the pattern

---

[43] The naval officer's report is in FO 84/1412/179-82, Lt. H. F. Woods, R.N., memo to Beyts (consul, Jidda), 12.74; other reports for example: FO 84/1472/160–1, Vivian to Şerif Paşa (Egyptian Foreign Minister), 8.4.77; FO 84/1482/231–6, Beyts to Derby, 29.5.77.

[44] Kelly, pp. 413, 417–8.

of trade lies in the incorporation of Ḥudayda into the north-bound Ottoman slave trade.

The principal reason for that was the opening of the Suez Canal and the subsequent establishment of a direct and regular steamer service between Istanbul and the Yemen. The Ottoman government signed contracts with a number of shipping companies, notably the Austrian Lloyd's Company and the Aziziye, in order to carry men, materiel, and supplies to and from the Ottoman division stationed in the Yemen. This was done to supplement the service provided by the Ottoman steamers of the Mahsuse Company. Reports from the area repeatedly asserted that officers and soldiers carried a private small-scale slave trade on their way home to Istanbul. They would buy a few slaves in Ḥudayda, present them to the authorities as household members and personal servants, and, at a later stage, after arrival in Istanbul, sell them and realize a small profit. It was virtually impossible to devise a method against this practice since a prohibition on the transportation of all servants and domestic slaves was not considered operable even by the British.[45]

Another reason for the convenience of slave trading from Ḥudayda was the fact that there were no European, and especially no British, consular representatives in the town. The activity of the consuls in Jidda and of the vice-consuls in Massawa—though it could not bring about an effective suppression—caused the slave dealers inconvenience and, at times, embarrassment. Without a consul in town, compli-

---

[45] For examples of contracts with shipping companies, see Irade/Meclis-ı Mahsus/1892, the Council for Military Affairs, Department of Provisions to the *Serasker*, 29 Şevval 1289/30.12.72; *ibid.*/1945, enclosures 12 and 14, Minutes of the Council of Military Affairs, 22 Muharrem 1290/22 3 73 For reports on private trafficking, see FO 84/1427/82-4, Stanton to Elliot, 29.9.72, *ibid.*/88, F. W Cuming (British commander of an Ottoman steamer) to West (consul, Suez), 16.9.72, BFASS/Mss. Brit. Emp./S18/C43/16-16a, E. B. Evans (Jidda) to Rev. B. Millard, 12.8 74; FO 84/1412/179-82, Lieutenant Woods to Beyts, 12.74; FO 84/1482/231-6, Beyts to Derby, 29.5.77. The British position is expressed in FO 84/1324/130-2, Clarendon to Stanton, 21.2.70; in this case the Foreign Secretary modified the draft dispatch, which included a demand from the Khedive to this effect

ance with instructions from the remote capital could not be verified. Nor could violations of the prohibition be regularly reported so as to generate action by the Central Government. A British attempt in 1875 to extend the jurisdiction of the Consulate in Jidda to Ḥudayda and to other Red Sea ports did not bear fruit,[46] and it was not until 1880 that a French vice-consul took up residence in Ḥudayda.

The British consul-general in Istanbul observed in November 1872 that a powerful combination favored the continuation of the slave trade in the Red Sea. In this he referred mainly to the traffic on board steamers from Ḥudayda via Jidda to Istanbul. There was, he wrote, a general acquiescence in the system, public officers were interested in it, private persons profitted from it, the government was indifferent to it, the crews and the agents of the ships participated in it, and the Metropolis was supplied by it. Indeed, this pessimistic mood was echoed in other British reports as well, though some officials were still advocating that more pressure be brought to bear on the Ottoman and Egyptian governments.[47]

During 1874–1877 a number of European officers were appointed by the Khedive to various positions which enabled them to promote the suppression of the slave trade.[48] They were the Swiss Munzinger in Massawa and Qallābāt, the British McKillop and Morice in the Red Sea, and Gordon in

[46] FO 84/1412/190-1, Beyts to Derby, 30.12.75.

[47] FO 84/1427/235-7, Francis to Elliot, 7.11.72; FO 84/1397/284-6, Stanton to Derby, 9.9.74.

[48] FO 84/1397/253-5, Rev. F. M. Flad (Matamma) to Stanton, 9.2.74; BFASS/*loc.cit.*; FO 84/1397/257-8, Stanton to Derby, 12.6.74; *ibid.*/211-2, Stanton to Derby, 4.12.75; FO/84/1450/340, Vivian to Şerif Paşa, 16.11.76; *ibid.*/342-3, Vivian to Derby, 30.11.76. (On Egyptian policies, see also Baer, pp. 176 ff.); *ibid.*/350-2, Vivian to Derby, 27.12.76; FO 84/1472/86-7, Vivian to Derby, 13.1.77; *ibid.*/89-92, Minute by W. H. Wylde, n.d.; *ibid.*/93-5, the Khedive's instruction to McKillop Paşa; *ibid.*/107-11, Vivian to Derby, 18.2.77; *ibid.*/324-5, Vivian to W. H. Wylde, private, 9.6.77; *ibid.*/326, Vivian to Derby, 7.6.77; *ibid.*/225-6, Gordon to Vivian, 9.4.77; *ibid.*/117-8, Vivian to Derby 2.3.77. For his reports, see *ibid.*/243-51, Commander Morice Bey to Hayri Paşa (Egyptian Interior Minister), 9.3-4.4.77.

the Sudan and the Red Sea littoral. This policy of appointing British, among other, officers to positions of direct responsibility for the suppression of the slave trade probably had a number of goals. It certainly aimed at heading off British pressure concerning the Red Sea traffic by allowing their officers to share the responsibility and consequently, the blame. Such an act of good will was also calculated to produce a positive response to the Khedive's request—at the time under negotiations with Britain—to recognize his jurisdiction over a large part of the Somali coast. Negotiations bearing on this question were conducted during 1877, and finally resulted in an agreement, mentioned above, extending to the Khedive the recognition he sought. What the British called a more "cooperative" approach was also helpful to İsmail in his ongoing, long-drawn-out negotiations with Britain—reaching a crucial stage in the second half of the same year—on an anti-slave trade convention.

With this we turn now to the final, if somewhat protracted, stage of the attempts to suppress the African slave trade within and into the Ottoman Empire. Effective means were needed to deal the last blow to the traffic, and Britain strongly felt that bilateral conventions would provide her with such means. She was prepared to go to great lengths in order to persuade her potential partners—the Khedive of Egypt and the Ottoman Sultan—to climb the top rung of the suppression ladder together.

CHAPTER VII

Anti-Slave Trade Conventions and the Decline of the African Traffic, 1877-1890

IF THE 1840s and much of the 1850s were marked by British attempts to restrict the Ottoman slave trade, the late 1850s ushered in a period in which the traffic in Africans was legally prohibited, but—winked or connived at—was still being actively pursued. Weary of never-ending remonstrances, which in the final analysis failed to stop the trade, the British came to believe that they had to take upon themselves direct enforcement. However, this could be done only through consent, and the legal mechanism to obtain consent was the bilateral convention. Such bilateral conventions had been tried before against the trans-atlantic slave trade, and Britain was eager to obtain similar concessions from the Khedive and the Sultan. The present chapter deals with the conclusion of two anti-slave trade conventions and the results which they produced.

THE ANGLO-EGYPTIAN CONVENTION FOR THE SUPPRESSION OF THE SLAVE TRADE, 1877

On 8 June 1873 the Khedive secured a *ferman* which increased his autonomy and strengthened his position vis-à-vis the Ottoman Porte, almost to the point of being an independent ruler. He was given, among other privileges, the authority to conclude non-political treaties and loan agreements with foreign powers, and the ports of Massawa and Sawākin were included in his hereditary governorship. Sir Henry Elliot observed that the Khedive would want closer ties with Britain and that, therefore, he would be amenable to giving the British satisfaction in matters relating to the slave trade. The moment was "unusually propitious," the ambassador wrote. When he met Nubar Paşa, who was visiting Istanbul with the Khedive, Sir Henry was told by the Egyptian minister that the Khedive was willing to conclude a convention with Britain for the suppression of the slave trade. His idea of suppression, however, was somewhat different from what the British had in mind. Nubar was willing to discuss mainly the exportation of slaves from Egypt, especially from the Egyptian ports in the Red Sea, but not slavery or the importation of slaves into Egypt.[1]

London's reaction was nevertheless positive and Foreign Secretary Lord Granville instructed Elliot in July 1873 to enter negotiations with the Khedive's representatives. But the talks were soon suspended when agreement could not be reached on the right of search and seizure. It also became clear that the Porte's participation was essential if the convention was to be at all effective, since the Egyptian and Ottoman colors were undistinguishable. Elliot felt that in the wake of the July 1873 incident, in which Ottoman fishing boats had been mistaken for slavers and sunk by H.M.S. "Thetis," the Porte would refuse, at least for some time, to grant Britain any rights of search or seizure.[2]

Negotiations resumed in January of 1876 with the same issues dominating the scene. However, British policy now

---

[1] FO 84/1370/67-70, Elliot to Granville, Confidential, 8.7.73; *ibid.*/55, Elliot to the Foreign Office (telegram), 8.7.73; *ibid.*/61-6, Elliot to Granville, 8.7.73.

[2] For the negotiations between 1873-1876, see *ibid.*/13, 15, Granville to Elliot (telegram and dispatch), 11.7.73; *ibid.*/71-101, correspondence—Elliot, Foreign Office, 12-20.7.73; FO 84/1397/173-5, Elliot to Granville, 4.1.74; FO 84/1412/186-9. Foreign Office consultation—W. H. Wylde, Tentenden, Derby, 21-24.6.75; FO 84/1450/231-6, Derby to Stanton, 14.1.76; *ibid.*/104-6, Derby to Elliot, 14.1.76. For the discussion at the Foreign Office, see *ibid.*/143-7, 247-50, Foreign Office consultation—Tentenden, W. H. Wylde, Bourke, Lister, Derby, 3-26.2.76, and *ibid.*/358-63, Foreign Office consultation—W. H. Wylde, Pauncifote, 1.77. On the "Thetis" incident see: FO 195/1020, Slave Trade, No. 9, Granville to Elliot, 23.8.73; FO 84/1370/114, Elliot to Granville, 6.9.73; and below, p. 259.

favored the conclusion of a convention with Egypt alone, for the time being; the approval and cooperation of the Porte, it was decided, would be sought at a later stage. There was a feeling of urgency among British officials about the Egyptian convention, stemming partly from public criticism which was being levelled at the government for its handling of slavery and the slave trade in the East. This feeling was perhaps best expressed in Lord Tentenden's comment entered in the Foreign Office minutes: "This is not a matter to go to sleep over."

But more time elapsed, and the negotiations—bogged down by technical and legal details—dragged on into the second half of 1877.

The convention was finally signed on 4 August of the same year.[3] It appears that both sides achieved what they wanted, at least on paper; the future would tell how effective the convention would be. Both importation and exportation of slaves were forbidden by the convention. "Negroes and Abyssinians"—the convention applied only to them—would not be allowed to leave Egypt unless it was proved "indubitably" that they were either free or manumitted. Regarding the issue of eunuch-"making" the Khedive vowed "to pursue as murderers all persons who may be found engaged in the mutilation of or traffic in children." All domestic trading, that is from one family to another, was to be prohibited after seven years, this time including male and female white slaves. This was declared in a separate ordinance which was attached to the convention. The right of search and seizure granted to British cruisers obtained specifically in the Red Sea, the Gulf of Aden, the coast of Arabia, the East African coast, and in Egyptian waters.

The Porte's reaction was critical though restrained. The Foreign Minister instructed the Ottoman ambassador in London to deliver a statement to the Foreign Office, in which the Ottomans presented three objections:[4]

[3] Text is in Hertslet, vol. XIV (London, 1880), pp. 321-6.
[4] FO 84/1482/34–48, Sir Austin Henry Layard (ambassador, Istanbul) to Derby, including Safvet Paşa's instruction to Musurus Paşa, 24.9-3.10.77.

(1) The Khedive exceeded his authority by concluding what was in fact a political, not merely commercial or financial, treaty.

(2) The Khedive had the right to police Egyptian soil and waters, but he could not confer this right upon a third party, i.e., Britain, for he held it only by delegation.

(3) The Khedive had no right to allow search and seizure of Egyptian vessels in Ottoman waters, i.e., the coasts of Arabia, where he had no authority whatsoever.

The British hastened to allay the Porte's concerns, saying that they had no intention of infringing Ottoman sovereignty rights over Egypt, and that they would not search Egyptian vessels in Ottoman waters.[5] Britain had never intended the Khedive to grant her any rights in Ottoman waters, they added. But the Foreign Secretary urged the Porte to help apply the convention in the Red Sea, stressing the importance of the matter to the British public.

The Khedive, apparently anxious to see the conflict resolved through the conclusion of a similar convention between Britain and the Porte, offered—most confidentially—to try to induce the Ottoman government to begin negotiating with the British on the matter.[6] His representative in Istanbul reportedly approached the Sultan in this regard in December 1877, but Abdülhamit promised only to consider it. These were no times for exerting pressure on the already distressed Ottoman government. With the internal bickering not quite over and the war with Russia well underway, pressure in the cause of abolition was obviously impolitic. For its part, the Porte did not pursue its criticism of the Anglo-Egyptian convention any further. In retrospect, however, its note to the British government meant that no cooperation could be expected from the Ottoman side in helping to enforce the convention, not even to the extent of refraining from abusing its tempting loopholes.

[5] FO 84/1437/290, Foreign Office consultation—Wylde, Pauncifote, Derby, 1.77; FO 84/1510/5-12, Derby to Layard, 3.1.78.

[6] FO 84/1473/287-8, Vivian to Derby, Most Confidential, 14.12.77; *ibid.*/291, Vivian to Derby, Most Confidential, 20.12.77.

PRELUDE TO THE ANGLO-OTTOMAN CONVENTION OF 1880

It soon became clear that the Anglo-Egyptian convention had only a marginal effect on the Red Sea slave trade. The legal complications stemming from the fact that there was no Egyptian flag distinct from the Ottoman one, and Britain's reluctance to offend the Porte by unauthorized searches rendered the convention almost useless. Many dispatches reached the Foreign Office during 1878-1880 reporting an actual increase in the slave trade to Jidda.[7] Charges of connivance by both Egyptian and Ottoman officials followed It was alleged that slaves were the only item exempted from the Egyptian blockade of the ports of Zayla' and Tajūra, imposed in late 1878 as part of the drive against the Kingdom of Showa. In May 1879, 320 slaves were said to have been landed near Jidda. Spotted by the police, 56 of them were captured and detained for two days, during which time 18 slaves were returned to the dealers, reportedly for a bribe.

The British consul intervened and demanded the manumission of the remaining slaves, as well as the retrieval of the 18. The ensuing agitation brought to Jidda the *Vâli* of the Hijaz, who ordered 4 companies into the city in an effort to implement a plan he had designed to suppress the traffic.[8] The governor offered rewards of $M T 3-4 to policemen and others who would report cases of slave trading; liberated

[7] For example FO/1510/303-4, annual report by Consul Beyts, 31 3 78, *ibid* /81-6, correspondence—Layard to Salisbury, 24 6-5 8 78, *ibid* /280-1, Beyts to Salisbury, 15 5 78, FO 84/1544/139-40, Zohrab (consul, Jidda) to Salisbury, 24 3 79, FO 84/1571/94-102, W P Burrell (acting consul, Jidda) to G J Goschen (ambassador, Istanbul), 25 9 80, BFASS/Mss Brit Emp /S22/G23, Menelek (King of Showa) to the Anti-Slavery Society, 14 12 78, *ibid* , Johann Mayer (Ankobar, Showa), to the Anti-Slavery Society, 20 12 78, FO 84/1544/217-20, Zohrab to Salisbury, 14 5 79

[8] *Ibid* /243-7, Zohrab to Salisbury, 30 5 79, *ibid* /355-7, Zohrab to Salisbury, 4 6 79, FO 84/1543/190-1, translation of a telegram from the *Vâli* of the Hijaz to the Porte, 27 5 79, FO 84/1544/249, Zohrab to Salisbury, 2 6 79, FO 84/1571/81-2, Zohrab to Salisbury, 13 3 80, BA/Irade/Meclis-i Mahsus/3012, the *Vâli* of the Hijaz to the Interior Ministry (telegram), 7 Ramazan 1296/25 8 78 *ibid* , the Grand Vezir to the Sultan, 23 Ramazan 1296/11 9 79, and the *Irade*, 24 Ramazan 1296/12 9 79

slaves were to be placed as servants for monthly wages. Through the *Vâli*'s efforts, 13 out of the 18 slaves who had been returned to the dealers were retrieved and manumitted. Other measures included the banishing of 5 slave dealers, the liberation of dozens of slaves, and the dismissal of Jidda's chief of police. Though not explicitly in connection with the slave trade, the *Kaymakam* of Jidda was removed from office, on the *Vâli*'s request, for his "old age and quick temper" caused the deterioration of his relations with the people and the foreign officials. The consequent disturbed situation of the city and the approaching pilgrimage season were cited as factors in the timing of his dismissal.

All these steps did not affect the volume of the trade, but simply diverted it from Jidda itself to the coast outside the city, where slaves were landed and then marched to Mecca. The higher risk now attached to the trade drove prices up but did not reduce supply and demand. Both naval and consular sources continued to report active trading, encouraged by the restoration to power of the old *Şerif* 'Abd al-Muṭṭalib, who was noted for his long-time support of the slave trade.[9] The measures taken by Gordon in the Sudan, and the greater accessibility of the Ethiopian sources as a result of the Egyptian campaigns there, brought more Ethiopians and fewer Sudanese slaves to the Arabian markets. This and the inconveniences experienced by the dealers in Jidda only increased the importance of Ḥudayda in the Red Sea slave trade.

One branch of the Hijaz traffic did decline, nevertheless. This was the overland pilgrim route to Syria and beyond.[10] The major blow to the centuries-old tradition was dealt by the opening of the Suez Canal, which connected Jidda with the main ports of the eastern Mediterranean. But the caravan was not abolished, and in 1879 the British vice-consul re-

---

[9] FO 84/1579/127-56, Admiral William Gore Jones, Annual Report on the Slave Trade (East Indies Station), 24.9.80; FO 84/1571/94-102, Burrell to Goschen, 25.9.80; *ibid.*/153-4, Zohrab to Granville, 9.12.80.

[10] FO 195/1262, Jago to Salisbury, 15.2.79; FO 84/1543/37, Salisbury to Layard, 5.5.79; *ibid.*/202, Karatodori Paşa to Layard, 4.6.79; FO 84/1571/218-21, Jago to Layard, 10.2.80.

ported from Damascus that it brought to Syria 200 slaves per annum. The *Vâli* of Syria, Midhat Paşa, suggested then that the caravan be abolished as a means to prevent the importation of slaves, a suggestion which quickly gained Lord Salisbury's support. Though the Porte reportedly agreed to the idea, it was not carried out. But, through measures adopted in Syria, the number of slaves imported via land declined sharply, with only 16 slaves reaching Damascus in 1880.

As we have seen, the trade from Tripoli decreased considerably as a result of the 1857 prohibition. Egypt and the Hijaz replaced Tripoli as the main source of black slaves for the Ottoman markets. However, with some difficulties experienced during Sir Samuel Baker and General Gordon's governorships in Equatoria, a certain revival of the caravan slave trade to Tripoli occurred in the 1870s. Sir Henry Elliot complained to the Porte in May 1869 about the resumption of the traffic and obtained from Âli Paşa an instruction to the *Vâli* of Tripoli enjoining him to check the trade. But throughout the following decade it was persistently reported from both Tripoli and Benghazi that slaves were being imported to the province, sold there, and exported to Egypt, the Balkans, and Instanbul.[11]

A temporary decline in the Tripoli traffic was recorded in the second half of the decade. Measures taken both at Tripoli and Benghazi combined with other circumstances in the region, such as the Egyptian operations in the Sudan and Ethiopia, to reduce significantly the number of slaves reaching the Mediterranean coast.[12] The vice-consul in Benghazi

[11] For Âli's instruction, see FO 84/1305/46-8, Drummond-Hay to Elliot, 17.5.69; and *ibid.*/44, Elliot to Clarendon, 30.5.69. Some examples of reports concerning importation into Tripoli and Benghazi are BFASS/Mss. Brit. Emp./S22/G96, "Mémoire de M. Cosson sur la traite en Afrique," Private, 16.6.74 (28-page diary) FO 84/1428/76-9, Henderson to W. H. Wylde, 22.6.74; FO 84/1412/41-3, Henderson to Derby, 12.6.75; *ibid.*/47-58, Henderson to Derby, 24.12.75; FO 84/1450/76-7, Foreign Office consultation—Wylde, Lister, Derby, 24.23.75-1.2.76.

[12] FO 84/1450/64-7, Drummond-Hay to Derby, 22.2.76; *ibid.*/84-5, Henderson (vice-consul, Benghazi), to Derby, 20.6.76 (quoted); FO 84/1510/71-2, Layard to Derby, 23.3.78; FO 84/1543/270-2, Dupuis (consul, Benghazi), to Layard, 21.8.79; *ibid.*/234, *Note Verbale* from Layard to Safvet Paşa, 23.8.79.

wrote in June 1876: "I think I can assure Your Lordship that, as regards Benghazi, the exportation of slaves to the Levant by sea is at an end." In March 1878 it was reported that the *Vâli* of Tripoli had been replaced because of his unsatisfactory actions regarding the suppression of the slave trade. However, by 1879 we hear again of violations and connivance in Benghazi, which in the 1880s would become the most active North African slave-exporting port.

In the meantime, measures against smuggling became routine in the major importing city—Istanbul. Their efficacy was perhaps debatable, but standing orders and procedures did exist from the 1870s onward.[13] In November 1871 Elliot praised the vigilance of the authorities saying that ". . . the persons charged with preventing evasions of the law . . . for some time past have shown an exemplary activity in the performance of their duty." But he conceded two years later that consistency was somewhat lacking: "The manner in which this question is treated depends mainly upon the disposition of the Minister of Police, who executes, or neglects, the orders of the Porte very much according to his own inclination, and as it is now seldom that a Minister remains 3 months in office, there is no steady rule of proceeding."

The abolition of slavery and the slave trade came up during the struggle for the Constitution in 1876. It was not mentioned in Abdülhamit II's *hat* (edict) of accession, which was read on 10 September. However, in the discussions which preceded the reading, Midhat Paşa presented a draft *hat*, including, among other reforms, the abolition of the slave trade throughout the Empire and the manumission of all palace slaves.[14] The Sultan refrained from such a drastic measure and omitted the subject from his declaration. But, shortly after, he did take action to back the existing prohibition of 1857.

In January 1877 the Council of State submitted to the Sul-

---

[13] FO 84/1341/60-1, Elliot to Granville, 20.11.71; FO 84/1370/103-4, Elliot to Granville, 26.8.73.

[14] Roderic H. Davison, *Reform in the Ottoman Empire 1856-76* (Princeton, 1963), p. 356.

tan a report on the African slave trade to the Empire.[15] The Council noted that, despite the many reiterations of orders currently in effect, violations continued to occur. Having reviewed the situation in the provinces, the Council recommended that a new *ferman* be issued to prohibit all slave trading in the Empire. The new elements mentioned in this report were few, but some are worth noting. To the three *Vilâyets* most commonly referred to in regard to the traffic—Egypt, Tripoli, and Baghdad—were quite conspicuously added the Hijaz and the Yemen, clearly in recognition of their important role in the trade. There was also the admission that in various parts of the Empire previously abolished slave markets were reopened; markets in Fatih and other Istanbul quarters were specifically mentioned. Orders were to be issued to close them immediately. Another problem was that of the black eunuchs of the Imperial Harem who retired, as was their custom, to the Holy Cities in the Hijaz. They were required to obtain permits to travel to the capital so as to avoid interference with their movement, which might result from the inspection procedures related to the prohibition.

All these new elements were incorporated into the text of the *ferman*, which was promulgated on 25 February 1877. The British were not informed of this action, and the Foreign Office learned about it only ten months later, when fresh and strongly worded instructions were issued, at Layard's request, to the *Vâli* of Tripoli to enforce the prohibition.[16] This was in full agreement with Abdülhamit II's attitude to the question of the slave trade, an attitude which manifested itself later on several occasions. Considering the subject a domestic issue, the Sultan was reluctant to discuss it with foreign representatives. As we shall see, this was the under-

---

[15] BA/İrade/Şura-yı Devlet/1602, enclosure 1, *Mazbata* of the Council of State, 2 Muharrem 1294/17.1.77.

[16] On the *ferman*, see *ibid.*, the Grand Vezir to the Sultan, 13 Muharrem 1294/28.1.77, and the *İrade*, 4 Sefer 1294/18.2.77; *ibid.*, enclosures 2 and 3, Text of the *ferman*, copies here dated 2 Rebiülevvel 1294/17.3.77; FO 84/1482/66–8, French translation of the *ferman*. *Ferman* first mentioned to British, FO 84/1482/62–8, Layard to Derby, and enclosures, 10.12.77.

lying principle of his treatment of Britain's attempt to conclude an anti-slave trade convention with the Ottoman Empire.

THE ANGLO-OTTOMAN CONVENTION FOR THE SUPPRESSION OF THE SLAVE TRADE, 1880

British efforts to obtain Ottoman consent to a bilateral convention for the suppression of the slave trade date back from January 1857, a short while after the promulgation of the *ferman* of prohibition. At the time, Lord Stratford de Redcliffe asked the Foreign Secretary to supply him with a draft treaty so that he might try to induce the Porte to consider it. A draft was sent to Istanbul with Prime Minister Palmerston's blessings, and a while later another text was supplied by the Anti-Slavery Society, but no progress was reported thereafter. The idea was brought up again only in August 1869, when Lord Clarendon asked for a draft treaty to be prepared at the Foreign Office. One official commented that such a treaty would not be enforceable in the Mediterranean, for it was almost impossible to distinguish between free blacks and black slaves. There was also little chance, he added, that the Porte would allow more facilities for suppression at the moment. Another official thought that it was still worth trying, but Clarendon decided to drop the idea. Sir Henry Elliot remarked at the time that it was undesirable to suggest a treaty which was sure to be rejected.[17]

In January 1876 Foreign Secretary Lord Derby asked Elliot to evaluate the chances of wresting an anti-slave trade convention from the Porte. The ambassador replied in unequivocal terms: "I regret to have to state my belief that the repugnance of the Porte to enter into any general Convention would be found insuperable." The capitulations were considered a grievance in the Empire, he wrote, and any demand

[17] For details regarding British attempts to negotiate a convention, see FO 84/1028/90-1, Stratford to Clarendon, 31.1.57; FO 84/1000/35-48, draft treaty of the Anti-Slavery Society, 3.3.57; FO 84/1305/14-7, Foreign Office consultation, 24-27.8.69; *ibid.*/96, Elliot to Clarendon, 19.9.69.

for extended privileges, such as those of search and seizure of Ottoman vessels by British cruisers, would be quite unpopular.[18] Thus, the matter was laid to rest for two more years. During those years Britain recognized full well that its convention with the Khedive of Egypt, concluded in 1877, was virtually useless without a similar engagement by the Porte. However, in view of the internal and external difficulties experienced by the Empire at the time, the British were reluctant to press the matter too strongly. This policy notwithstanding, Sir Henry Layard still continued to pursue quiet contacts with the Ottoman government, asking that the idea of a mutual convention be considered.

The Grand Vezir agreed in August 1878 to address the question to the Sultan and recommend the establishment of a committee headed by the Minister of Justice to study the draft treaty put forward by Britain.[19] Abdülhamit replied that he had studied the document carefully and was himself very much in support of the prohibition imposed by his predecessor on the slave trade. Nevertheless, the Sultan added, sufficient orders had been issued by him, and all that was needed was strict enforcement of these orders. It was therefore unnecessary to set up a committee or to consider a treaty, he concluded. Under growing British pressure—the time of crisis had passed, the Foreign Office perceived—another attempt was made by the Grand Vezir, with the backing of the Council of Ministers, to change the Sultan's mind about a treaty. This time, Abdülhamit demanded clarifications from the British Embassy, but once again rejected the proposal to establish a committee. This was sufficient for the hard-pressed Grand Vezir, who told Layard that negotiations for the con-

[18] For Elliot's report and the British position, see FO 84/1450/139–42, Elliot to Derby, 12.2.76; FO 84/1510/263, Foreign Office consultation—Wylde to Derby, 26.2.78.

[19] Documents regarding this stage of the contacts are in: BA/İrade/Dahiliye/62927, the Grand Vezir to the Sultan, 7 Şâban 1295/6.8.78; *ibid.*, the *Baş Kâtip* to the Grand Vezir, 8 Şâban 1295/7.8.78; *ibid.*, *Mazbata* of the Council of Ministers, 13 Sefer 1296/6.2.79; *ibid.*, the *Baş Kâtip* to the Grand Vezir, 14 Sefer 1296/7.2.79; *ibid.*, the *Baş Kâtip* to the Grand Vezir, 20 Recep 1296/10.7.79; FO 84/1543/122–6, Layard to Salisbury, 3.2.79.

clusion of a convention could now be started in earnest. Following further contacts with the British, the Sultan officially consented to the negotiations, stating that the matter had Şerî implications and should be settled in full conformity with the Şeriat.

We have detailed British and Ottoman accounts of the negotiations conducted between the parties during 1879 and early 1880.[20] However, our concern here is only with the major points brought up by each side in the course of the negotiations. Britain's aim was to obtain the right to search and seize Ottoman vessels suspected of slave trading, especially those operating in the Red Sea. It was clear from the beginning that this was *sine qua non* for the British, and the main reason for the pressure they exerted on the Porte. On the Ottoman side, the Council of Ministers listed three reasons for its support of a convention:

(1) All other countries had already concluded similar treaties with Britain, and the Ottoman Empire was thus singled out as standing against progress.

(2) A convention was an essential means for the suppression of the slave trade, a goal the Sultan declared to enjoy his full support.

(3) The Empire might benefit from the positive reaction a convention would produce towards her in European public opinion.

The Sultan's main concerns were:

(1) To avoid condemnation, even by implication, of past Ottoman performance regarding the suppression of the slave trade. This he accomplished by giving the convention the appearance of a reiteration of an already existing prohibition.

(2) To avoid damaging his image as the head of the greatest Islamic power and hence the protector of all Muslims. That he did by insisting on a face-saving device in the form of a provision which stated that slaves captured by British cruisers would be turned over to the nearest Ottoman au-

---

[20] See Layard's dispatches for 1879-80 in FO 84/1543 and FO 84/1570. The relevant Ottoman reports are in BA/*loc.cit.*, and *ibid.*, *Mazbata* of the Council of Ministers, 5 Sefer 1297/18.1.80.

thorities; only in the absence of such authorities would the slaves be handed over to British authorities. This was done because the slaves—having been converted to Islam by the dealers upon capture—could not be turned over to a Christian power. In addition, reference to land routes was struck out to avoid any implication of the pilgrim routes to the Hijaz.

The British government—pressed by public opinion at home—pushed as hard as possible for the conclusion of the treaty. It was finally signed on 25 January 1880, giving Britain the right of search and seizure and satisfying the basic Ottoman demands. As summed up by a Foreign Office official a year and a half later: "However that may be, the difficulties attending the Ratification of the Anglo-Turkish Convention sufficiently shew that no concessions beyond those which are therein contained could have been well wrung from the Porte by any Diplomatic efforts."[21]

There was immediate criticism from various sources in Britain led by the Anti-Slavery Society.[22] The *Anti-Slavery Reporter* published the text of the convention and blamed Disraeli's government for its hurried and miscalculated signing of the treaty, which they did since they "would not dare to return to their constituencies with the Turkish Treaty still unsigned." The Society charged that the convention failed to guarantee the freedom of captured slaves, for they would be delivered to the Ottoman authorities rather than to especially established mixed courts. Also, the registration of black crews could be abused and slaves presented as crew members, the Society argued. The Secretary of the Society wrote to Prime Minister Gladstone in September 1881 that the convention was "worthless for the suppression of the Slave Trade as the paper on which it was written." Gladstone was reminded that before the elections he had shared that view himself, but

---

[21] Viscount Gladstone Papers, vol. LXV, BM/Add. Mss./46094, p. 34, Foreign Office Memo, 19.9.81. For the text of the Convention, see Hertslet, vol. XV, pp. 417-21.

[22] For the following reactions, see: ASR, 3rd series, vol. XXII (1880), pp. 5-8; BM/*loc.cit.*, pp. 19-23, C. H. Allen to Herbert Gladstone, 6.9.81.

when in office his government was the one which ratified the very same treaty.

Some formalities still remained to be tended to in connection with the convention. Trivial verbal changes were introduced in 1882-1883, and late in 1883 the Council of State finally formulated the regulations needed to put the convention into effect.[23] The courts in Jidda and Ḥudayda were to be reorganized so that they could deal with captured slaves and dealers; and papers were to be issued to vessels which had African crew members in order to avoid mistaking them for slaves. It was now expected that a final blow would be dealt to the Red Sea slave trade—the most active branch of the Ottoman traffic. But it was not to be so. Though the following decade would witness a significant decline in the trade, the end would come gradually and in the face of strong resistance.

THE FINAL DECLINE OF THE AFRICAN SLAVE TRADE TO THE OTTOMAN EMPIRE

The first signs of Ottoman intentions regarding the application of the treaty were encouraging. Following the signing of the convention, the Sultan—initially reluctant to undertake such a commitment—seemed to have adopted a more positive stance toward cooperation with Britain. At the time, the Porte was engaged in negotiations with European powers regarding sanitary regulations during the pilgrimage. On his own initiative, the Sultan instructed his representative to add to the regulations four articles concerning the slave trade.[24] According to these articles, captains of transport vessels were

[23] For verbal changes, see: BA/*loc.cit.*, Correspondence, 26 Recep 1299—2 Rebiülevvel 1300/13.6.82-11.1.83; FO 84/1658/259-61, Granville to Dufferin, 31.12.81; *ibid.*/278-81, Dufferin to Granville, 25.3.82; *ibid.*/306-8, Wyndham (chargé d'affaires, Istanbul) to Granville, 6.3.83. Regulations issued: FO 84/1658/296, the Porte to Dufferin, 23.5.82; FO 84/1642/26, Wyndham to Granville, 25.1.83; *ibid.*/54, Dufferin to Granville, 24.11.83.

[24] FO 195/1295, Layard to Salisbury, 21.8.80; FO 541/48/304-7, Réglement applicable aux Navires faisant le Transport de Pélèrins (Articles 30-33).

made liable to fines of ten to two hundred Ottoman *liras* if they failed to verify that all passengers aboard were either freemen or freedmen carrying manumission papers. Despite French opposition, the Sultan insisted that this was necessary in order to enforce the newly concluded Anglo-Ottoman convention.

However, the situation in the slave-trading provinces remained much the same well into the 1880s. Little changed in the already familiar pattern of detected violations, British remonstrances, Central Government renewed instructions. Again, the areas most prone to the practice were the Red Sea and Benghazi, the latter replacing Tripoli as the main outlet of the North African traffic to the Ottoman markets. There was, nevertheless, a reduction in the volume of the slave trade, which resulted to a large extent from local circumstances. Let us now look into the situation on the most active slaving routes of the Empire during the decade which followed the signing of the Anglo-Ottoman convention.

The renewed predominance of the *Şerif* 'Abd al-Muṭṭalib in the Hijaz, until his removal from office in September 1882 on charges of conspiracy, made things fairly comfortable for the Hijaz dealers. Even in later years, not much was done to curb the Red Sea traffic. Ultimately, it was an interesting combination of external factors which dealt the heaviest blow to that traffic, sharply reducing its volume between the years 1883–1886.[25] The wars in the Sudan and Ethiopia disrupted the trade and limited the flow of slaves to the western coasts of the Red Sea. 'Uthmān Diqna's operations in the Sawākin area during 1883–1885 and the Mahdist-Ethiopian campaigns around the great market town of Qallābāt in 1885–1887 brought the traffic to a standstill. The British presence in Sawākin since 1884 and the Italian occupation of Massawa in 1885 denied the exporters access to their most important ports. Early in 1887 the *Khalīfa* forbade the exportation of male slaves from the Sudan. This was done out of both religious—

[25] On the following developments, see Holt, *The Mahdist State*, pp. 73–9, 150–5, 177; FO 84/1849/275–83, Jago to the Foreign Secretary, 9.7.87; *ibid.*/288–90, Jago to the Foreign Secretary, 2.11.87.

fear of losing *Mahdiyya* members—and military considerations. The British occupation of Egypt in 1882 made the Suez Canal a less than safe waterway for the slave traders, and the careful checks in Port Sa'īd discouraged pilgrims from carrying on their small-scale, private traffic.

Some revival in the slave trade was reported from Jidda in 1887. The traffic was attributed to a relaxation of the *Khalīfa*'s prohibition in exchange for much-needed supplies of lead and war materials imported from the Hijaz. But this slave trade, in Holt's estimation, was on a very limited scale. Still, we have reports from British sources in Jidda, Aden, and Cairo which indicate that active trade—though not on the same level as during the period before 1883—was being pursued in the region in the late 1880s. In spite of the efforts by the British, the Egyptians, and the Italians to check the Red Sea traffic, they could not effectively put a stop to it.[26]

The Ottomans were also active in attempts to suppress the slave trade. For some of their efforts in Jidda we have an interesting source. The lieutenant-governor of the city, Ârifi Paşa, kept a register of the official correspondence which he conducted during the period 1880-1890.[27] Most of the documents in the collection pertain to the years 1887-1890. The importance of this collection is in the fact that, unlike most of the archival material of the Central Government in Istanbul, it contains correspondence on the local provincial level, e.g., letters exchanged between the governor's office and the various bureaus and departments of the city. Ârifi Paşa's reg-

[26] For the situation during that period, see FO 84/1849/154-7, Abdur Razzak to Wyndham (ambassador, Istanbul), 25.7.87; BFASS/Mss. Brit. Emp./S18/C160/191, Rev. Waldmeier to Dr. Kingston Fox, 13.6.87; Holt, *The Mahdist State*, p. 177; FO 84/1903/202-4, Cecil G. Wood (consul, Jidda) to Salisbury, 27.10.88; *ibid.*/398-409, Sir Evelyn Baring (consul-general, Cairo) to Salisbury, 5.12.88; *ibid.*/410-4, Baring to Salisbury, 6.16.88; BFASS/Mss./Brit. Emp./S22/G2, Report by Charles Gissing, Senior Officer and Commander of the Aden Division, 1.7-31.12.88.

[27] İstanbul Üniversitesi Kütüphanesi/Mss. T 1072, Ârifi Bey'in Cidde Vâli Kaymakamlığında bulunduğu zamana ait muhâberat-ı resmiye mecmuası; *ibid.*/Mss. T 1075, Ârifi Pasa'nın 1297'den 1307 tarihine kadar zaman-ı memuriyetine ait muhâberat-ı resmiye mecmuası.

ısters ınclude a number of references to the suppressıon of
the slave trade ın Jıdda and the Red Sea

From these references[28] ıt appears that Ârıfı Paşa hımself
was opposed to the slave trade—whıch he descrıbed as *mek-
ruh* (here not ın the *Şerî* sense, but sımply repugnant)—and
wıshed to see ıt extınct. But regulatıons were not always
clear and, owıng to the sensıtıve nature of the ıssue, cautıon
had to be exercısed. Consequently, the *Kaymakam* often consulted hıs superıors on matters related to the slave trade. Ârıfı Paşa's records also bear wıtness to Brıtısh actıvıtıes ın the
Red Sea; that ıs, both search and seızure of suspected slavers
and consular efforts to verıfy the authentıcıty of manumıs-
sıon papers. On the whole, these few but sıgnıficant documents ındıcate that the traffıc was stıll beıng pursued ın the
area ın the late 1880s, though one does not get the ımpres-
sıon that many slaves were ınvolved.

We thus leave the Red Sea slave trade ın the 1890s, for ıt
then fell ınto an already famılıar pattern whıch ıt would follow ın future decades Open tradıng was forbıdden and
whatever traffıc that was stıll carrıed on was consıdered con-
traband. It could be pursued only clandestınely. Brıtısh consuls, accordıng to ınterest and ınıtıatıve, would occasıonally
report vıolatıons of the conventıon, and the Ottoman au-
thorıtıes would, at tımes, capture and manumıt freshly run
slaves. The sıtuatıon stıll gave rıse to querıes from the Antı-
Slavery Socıety, but wıth ıts numerıcal declıne the Red Sea
slave trade also lost much of ıts appeal as a *cause célèbre* for
abolıtıonısts.

The other slave route whıch was actıve ın the 1880s was
the one from Benghazı to the Ottoman ports of the eastern
Medıterranean Throughout the decade consular reports con-
tınuously accused Ottoman offıcıals, wıth some exceptıons,

---

[28] The followıng ıs based on *ıbıd* /Mss T 1072, pp 55a-55b (no 399),
Ârıfı Paşa to the presıdent of the Court of Appeals, 22 Sefer 1306/28 10 88,
ıbıd /pp 7a-7b (no 303), Ârıfı Paşa to the *Vılâyet* of the Hıjaz, 16 Revıulâ-
hır, 1305/1 1 88, *ıbıd* , p 39a (no 408), Ârıfı Paşa to the *Vılâyet* of the Hıjaz,
1 Sefer 1306/7 10 88, *ıbıd* , p 516, cırcular by Ârıfı Paşa to seven bureaus
and departments ın Jıdda, 26 Rebıulâhır 1305/11 1 88

of connivance at the slave trade.[29] These reports resulted in British remonstrances, which in turn led to renewed Ottoman instructions to the provincial authorities to suppress the traffic. The governors of Benghazi during that period consistently denied any wrongdoing and pointed out the fact that slaves were often manumitted in the province and cared for at government expense. Though this was true, there were persistent reports that manumitted slaves were often re-enslaved. In 1883, the British consul estimated that approximately 1,000 slaves had reached Jālō in the preceding year; of these slaves 680 were disposed of within the city of Benghazi itself. Though governors of Crete were said to oppose the trade, measures on the island were generally considered to be lax and insufficient to deter the slave dealers.

From letters exchanged in 1884 between the Benghazi authorities and the Central Government we can learn that questions relating to the slave trade in the province did occupy the attention of Ottoman officials. The problem was rightly identified as the need to care for the manumitted slaves by providing food and temporary shelter until suitable employment could be found for them.[30] Thus, it was maintained, the slaves would not be an easy prey for dealers and former owners who might wish to re-enslave them. Liberated slaves were housed and fed at the expense of the Treasury under the supervision of a special official, and strict registration was kept of their situation. The local treasury, however, did not have sufficient means to cover the cost of the operation and duly applied to Istanbul for additional funds amounting to

[29] For details, see the relevant correspondence from Benghazi and Istanbul in FO 84/1570, 1618, 1641, 1642, 1849. Quoted below is FO 84/1641/81-93. Wood to Granville, 14.3.83, and enclosures. Sincere efforts by governors noted in FO 84/1903/66-7, Wood to White, 29.1.88; *ibid.*/108-9, Barnham (acting consul, Izmir) to White, 30.5.88; FO 198/82, the Istanbul police to Marinitch (dragoman, Istanbul Embassy), 5.4.89.

[30] BA/İrade/Dahiliye/62927, *Mazbata* of the Council of State, Department of the Interior, 11 Zilkâde 1301/3.9.84; *ibid.*, the Interior Minister to the Grand Vezir, 24 Zilkâde 1301/15.10.84; *ibid.*, the Grand Vezir to the Sultan, 1 Muharrem 1302/21.10.84; *ibid.*, the Baş Kâtip to the Grand Vezir, 5 Muharrem 1302/25.10.84.

5,000 *kuruş*. The Council of State recommended that the funds
be provided and the Interior Minister endorsed the Council's
recommendations. Sultan Abdülhamit II, nevertheless, took
a different view of the matter.

In his reply to the application of the Benghazi authorities,
the Sultan ruled that a more drastic solution was needed. All
freed blacks, he wrote, should be transported to Istanbul or
Izmir, where the men would be drafted to the army and
placed either in military bands or in units teaching naval skills,[31]
and the women would be given manumission papers and
placed as domestic servants on suitable monthly wages. The
cautious and experienced sovereign then raised the amount
intended for the freed slaves from 5,000 to 10,000 *kuruş*, but
stipulated that it be spent in Istanbul and Izmir and not remitted to Benghazi. This was probably an indication of the
Sultan's mistrust of the provincial authorities; it clearly points
out the awareness of the Central Government that it lacked
the means and ability to maintain effective control over certain aspects of local government.

In 1890 the Porte reduced the funds previously allocated
to the Benghazi treasury for the maintenance of freed slaves,
and the local authorities had to apply for more funding.[32] It
appears that the Porte suspected irregularities in Benghazi
and demanded tighter supervision over the program A charge
was made that a number of slaves remained jobless, prefer-
ring the life of vagabonds (*serseri*). They would present
themselves to the authorities as newly imported slaves and
ask, once again, to be manumitted and maintained by the
government. The Council of State recommended that the
matter be carefully investigated. Reacting to the accusations,

---

[31] On the recruitment of freedmen to the army, see above, pp 8, 173-7
The naval crafts unit (*Sanayı Alayı*) was established to train and employ
young men, mainly in the service of the Imperial Navy (Pakalın, vol III,
p 113)

[32] BA/Irade/Dahılıye/62927, *Mazbata* of the Council of State, Department
of the Interior, 28 Rebıulevvel 1308/11 11 90, ibid , the Grand Vezır to the
Sultan, 27 Cemazıyulevvel 1308/9 1 91, ibid , the *Baş Kâtıp* to the Grand
Vezır, 28 Cemazıyulevvel 1308/10 1 91

the Sultan reiterated, albeit in a somewhat modified way, his earlier instructions demanding that all manumitted slaves be sent to Istanbul and drafted in the army. Abdülhamit then asked to be notified of the arrival of such slaves so that he could instruct the officers what to do with them. Thus we learn that orders which had been issued by the Sultan more than six years previously were not carried out by the provincial government of Benghazi and had to be restated.

It has been argued, quite convincingly, that the Porte's policy regarding the slave trade from Tripoli and Benghazi during the 1880s was, in fact, a political compromise.[33] According to this explanation, the Ottomans became concerned about the French advances in the Sahara, aimed at luring caravans away from Tripoli to Algerian markets, as well as about the growing strength of the Mahdist movement in the Sudan. The loss of Egypt to Britain only increased the isolation of their North African possessions. Thus, the Ottomans became uncomfortably dependent upon the cooperation of the nomad tribes in the hinterland of Benghazi and Tripoli; these tribes were by then already under the strong influence of the *Sanūsiyya*. Vigorous actions against the slave trade would have alienated the still loyal tribesmen, for many of them relied on slave work and were involved in the slave trade. On the other hand, no action at all against the traffic might have given France and Italy the pretext they were looking for—according to the Ottoman view of the situation—to meddle in the affairs of, or perhaps even occupy, the *Vilâyet* of Tripoli. Thus, the Porte chose to act in a way which would offend neither side. This it did by allowing the trade to go on while still opposing it on record and urging the provincial authorities to comply with the prohibition.

The available Ottoman sources neither confirm nor deny this argument. There is no explicit or implicit reference in the documents to such high-level international considerations. It is, however, feasible to assume that both the Porte and the Sultan were aware of the precarious Ottoman posi-

[33] Miers, pp. 72-3.

tion in North Africa during the last quarter of the nineteenth century. What the documents do reveal—and they are perhaps too few to enable any broader generalization—is the existence of a discrepancy between the orders of the Central Government and the situation in the province. Moreover, they show a mistrust on the part of the Sultan and his government of the ability of the provincial authorities to implement the Porte's orders. Abdülhamit's desire to have the slaves transported to Istanbul and Izmir, his refusal to remit funds to Benghazi for maintenance of freed slaves there, and the doubts raised by the Council of State with regard to manumission procedures in Benghazi are examples of such mistrust.

As far as the *Vilâyet* of Tripoli was concerned, the Sultan's attitude is somewhat surprising. Between the years 1881-1898, the province was governed by a highly experienced and able *Vâli*, Râsim Ahmet Paşa (sometimes Ahmet Râsim Paşa).[34] The biographer Mehmet Süreyya describes the *Vâli* as "honest, virtuous, intelligent, prudent and efficient administrator" (*müstekim afif zeki müdebbir müdür idi*). His long tenure as governor of Tripoli was quite unusual and indicates that he enjoyed the Porte's trust. However, his control over Benghazi might have been weak, or this could support the above-mentioned argument of Miers.

In the spring of 1889 steps were taken by the major European powers to convene an anti-slave trade conference with a view to suppressing the East African traffic.[35] Though ostensibly motivated by humanitarian reasons alone, the idea was, in fact, inextricably linked to the colonial ventures of Britain, France, Germany, Italy, and Belgium in Central and Eastern Africa. The Ottomans were asked to participate in the conference since it had been realized that much of the slave trade from those regions went to the Empire, mainly through North Africa and the Red Sea.

[34] For his biography, see Mehmet Süreyya, *Sicill-i Osmani*, vol. IV (Istanbul, 1308), pp. 856-7.

[35] For a detailed account of the background to the Brussels conference of 1889-1890, see Miers's comprehensive study, pp. 190-235.

In anticipation of the conference and the possible criticism which might be directed at the Porte, the Sultan enacted on 16 December 1889 a code (*kanunname*) against the slave trade in Africans.[36] The code consisted of ten articles which in essence summed up earlier *fermans* and instructions on the subject. An important addition, however, was a procedure established in the code for search and seizure. According to Article IX, a slaver was made liable to a fine of five Ottoman *liras* per slave, which was payable to the capturing vessel. Property belonging to the slaver, and even the vessel itself, could be sold to pay the fine. The code also stipulated that if masters failed to have their slaves registered in their passports, the slaves would be manumitted and the master could face charges of slave dealing.

The international conference was convened in Brussels, holding sessions during the winter of 1889-1890. The Ottomans consistently rejected even the slightest insinuations of any negligence or wrong-doing on their part with regard to the suppression of the slave trade. In his speech, the chief Ottoman delegate mentioned the various *fermans* and instructions which had been issued by the Porte against the trade and strongly asserted that blame for the continuation of the traffic should not be put on the "Eastern Countries."[37] He concluded with the following statement:

"I desire to declare in the most formal possible manner that, conscious of the duties incumbent on it, the Sublime Porte fulfils scrupulously, and in every detail, and in so far as lies in its power, the international obligations it has assumed. . . . But should the regulations be, nevertheless, sometimes infringed in isolated cases in a manner which the most active precautions unceasingly

[36] Text of the code is in *Kavanin*, vol. I, pp. 463-4; English translation can be found in Hertslet, vol. XVIII, pp. 1154-6.

[37] A detailed account of the proceedings of the conference is provided by Miers, pp. 23-91. The protocols were published in an English translation in Accounts and Papers, 1890, vol. L, pp. 657-849. For the Ottoman delegates' speech, see Accounts and Papers, 1890, vol. L., pp. 673-4 (Karatodori Paşa in the sitting of 23.11.89).

taken are unable to prevent, I need hardly add that the Imperial Government will always be the first, after having ascertained the correctness and exactitude of the alleged facts, to put down and to punish, with all the severity allowed by law, as it has always done in similar circumstances, such criminal offences, which it emphatically condemns."

The chief British delegate, Lord Vivian, stated then that the Porte had indeed lived up to its commitments according to the Anglo-Ottoman Convention of 1880 and added that the Ottoman government had acted scrupulously on every British complaint regarding violations of the convention.[38] However, when the British proposed that an auxiliary international bureau for information on suppression be set in the Red Sea, the Ottomans objected. A Russo-Ottoman rapprochement and a deterioration in Anglo-German relations— both connected to issues other than the traffic—combined to defeat the British proposal. The Ottoman argument was that there was no justification for such a bureau since the Porte disputed the European reports about an increase in the Red Sea trade.

On 2 July 1890, the participants signed the Brussels Act, which laid down procedures for the suppression of the African slave trade. Recommending that the Sultan ratify the act, the Council of Ministers asserted that it contained nothing that could harm the interests of the Empire. All changes proposed by the Ottoman delegation to the conference, the Council stated, were accepted and incorporated into the text of the act. In June 1891 Abdülhamit agreed to ratify the act.[39] Earlier that year the Ottoman government initiated a program to speed up the manumission of African slaves and to care for their needs.

[38] Accounts and Papers, 1890, vol. L, p. 674.

[39] For an English translation of the Act, see Miers, pp. 346-63 (Appendix I); Ottoman translation in BA/İrade/Dahiliye/62927, enclosed with the Grand Vezir's report to the Sultan, 25 Şevval 1308/3.6.91. Ottoman ratification is discussed in BA/*loc.cit.*/*Mazbata* of the Council of Ministers, 25 Şevval 1308/3.6.91; *ibid.*, the *Baş Kâtip* to the Grand Vezir, 30 Şevval 1308/8.6.91.

The program was prompted by continuous British complaints about the plight of manumitted slaves.[40] The idea was to establish public guest-houses (*misafirhanes*) for freed slaves in Istanbul, Izmir, Tripoli, Benghazi, Jidda, and Hudayda. In these guest-houses, slaves would be housed, fed, and protected to prevent them from being re-enslaved. The main guest-house was to be built in Izmir, and manumitted slaves were to be sent there from the other guest-houses. From Izmir they would be gradually moved to various parts of the *Vilâyet* of Aydın, where they would be given land for cultivation and settlement. No estimation of the actual number of freed slaves who were to be cared for in this way is to be found in the Istanbul archives, but the Izmir guest-house was planned for 200 occupants in transit.

In a detailed report to the Minister of the Interior, the *Vâli* of Aydın added some of his ideas to the general program, ideas which he said were already being implemented in the *Vilâyet*.[41] Freedmen were sent to primary schools, to units teaching naval skills, or to military bands. Freedwomen were placed as servants in Muslim households and paid monthly wages. The African newcomers were encouraged to marry and establish their own homes on the land granted them by the provincial government. The *Vâli* estimated that expenses for building small houses for these people and for providing one ox per family and some agricultural tools would amount to approximately 3,000 *kuruş* for each household. He expected that the Imperial Treasury would defray the cost of this program. The Sultan, however, asserted that the same could be done for much less and that the cost should be borne by the local inhabitants. It was the *Vâli*'s duty, Abdülhamit continued, to mobilize the people for this purpose. In 1892 it was reported that the program had been revised so that only married Africans were to be transported to Izmir for settlement, whereas the unmarried freedmen were to be set-

---

[40] *Ibid.*, *Mazbata* of the Council of Ministers, 13 Recep 1308/22.2.91.

[41] *Ibid.*, Halil Rifat Paşa (*Vâli* of Aydın) to the Interior Minister, 14 Cemaziyülâhir 1308/25.1.91; *ibid.*, the Baş Kâtip to the Grand Vezir, 14 Recep 1308/23.2.91; FO 84/2227/214-9, Ford to Salisbury, 13.7.92.

tled in the places of their manumission. All we know at present is that the guest-houses were indeed established, but we do not know how successful the program was or how many freed slaves were settled and cared for through it.

In February 1893 the Foreign Office replied to a letter from the British and Foreign Anti-Slavery Society which charged that the Porte was not living up to its commitments in regard to the suppression of the slave trade.[42] Disputing the Society's allegations, the Foreign Office listed the steps taken by the Ottomans since 1889, including the establishment of the above-mentioned guest-houses, and asserted that the traffic into Tripoli and Benghazi had ceased entirely. The measures resorted to by the Porte, the Foreign Office said, were quite effective. They added: "In the face of all these measures taken with a view to the suppression of the Slave Trade, Lord Rosebery [the Foreign Secretary] is of opinion that a general charge of indifference to the obligations of the Porte under the Brussels Act cannot be sustained."

Thus, the late 1880s and early 1890s saw a significant decline in the slave trade to the Ottoman Empire. Though still carried on to a limited extent, the traffic certainly lost much of its force. External pressures and the internal actions which these pressures generated made the trade too hazardous within the Empire. European advances in Africa sharply reduced slave trading on the continent and, in the last decade of the nineteenth century, the sources of supply were severely curtailed. We shall now examine some aspects of Britain's pressure policy and the reactions it produced among the Ottomans.

[42] BFASS/Mss. Brit. Emp./S18/C162/161, (for) the Earl of Rosebery (Foreign Secretary) to the secretary of the Anti-Slavery Society, 21.2.93.

CHAPTER VIII

Some General Aspects
of British Pressure
and Ottoman Reaction

AT THE TURN of the century the African slave trade to the Ottoman Empire no longer was what it used to be. Although a small number of slaves continued to be imported into Ottoman territories until the disintegration of the Empire—and later into some of the successor states, especially in Arabia—the traffic as described in this book ceased to exist. Once a steady stream, at times even a torrent, it turned into a mere trickle. Without renewed supplies, Ottoman slavery itself was destined to disappear as time passed. The last generation of slaves would be gradually manumitted or die off. When official declarations abolishing slavery came, they generally confirmed an already existing reality rather than introduced a major social change.

Looking back on the suppression of the African traffic, one can hardly fail to recognize the dominant role which Britain played in it. But what were the mechanisms through which the British intervened in the Ottoman slave trade? When there is pressure, it is always applied on someone, some party. And there are, of course, various ways in which reactions to pressure can find expression. Thus, although we shall deal in this chapter with the political-diplomatic axis of Anglo-Ottoman relations regarding the slave trade, we shall also venture beyond that to examine some attitudes within British and Ottoman societies.

MODES OF INTERVENTION

Influence and pressure were exerted by Britain on the Ottomans in various ways, nearly all of them on what may be termed the government-to-government level. The most common form which British abolitionist efforts took was the use of diplomatic channels in order to influence the policy of the Porte. The strategy was to induce the Ottoman government to issue orders, first restricting and later prohibiting the slave trade, and then—through the network of consulates—to monitor compliance with these orders. Violations were reported to the Embassy and to the Foreign Office, in consequence of which remonstrances were made to the Porte demanding that measures be taken to enforce existing orders. Presentations to the Ottoman authorities were made on two levels, according to the severity of the infraction: the Foreign Office—Istanbul Embassy—Foreign Minister or Grand Vezir level in severe cases; the Consul—*Vâli* or *Kaymakam* level, with notification to the Foreign Office and the Embassy, in mild cases.

The degree of pressure applied varied from case to case, again according to severity and often also according to the susceptibility (as perceived by the British) of the Ottoman government to pressure at a particular time. For example,[1] when large-scale violations of the prohibition against the slave trade were reported from Benghazi and other parts of the Empire in 1873, Sir Henry Elliot told the Ottoman Foreign Minister in strong words that the *fermans* regarding the slave trade had been obtained through British presentations and for the sake of Ottoman interests, and Britain would not accept a backward trend in this regard. In June 1879 the Marquis of Salisbury, dismayed at reports of Ottoman connivance at the slave trade in Jidda, instructed Ambassador Layard to tell the Porte that Britain would have to find a way to enforce the Sultan's orders with her own means if nothing was done by the Ottoman government. Layard told the Ottoman Foreign Minister that Britain would consider invoking the repealed Aberdeen Act—an 1845 Act of Parliament which unilaterally empowered British cruisers to search and

[1] Documents on which examples are based: FO 84/1370/47-9, Elliot to Safvet Paşa, 14.4.73; FO 84/1543/51-3, Salisbury to Layard, 23.6.79; *ibid*./218-20, Layard to Salisbury, 6.7.79 (quoted).

seize Brazilian vessels suspected of slave trading—"for she could not permit Turkey alone to stand in the way of the suppression of an odious and inhuman traffic, which the English people were determined should cease."

But the use of such harsh language was indeed rare. More characteristic was the quiet diplomatic style of the head of the Slave Trade Department and the under-secretaries at the Foreign Office, which, though firm, was realistic, and not overtly offensive. Between 1877-1879 Britain refrained from pressing the Porte to conclude an anti-slave trade convention similar to the Anglo-Egyptian one, because of the delicate political situation in Istanbul during those years. This remained the policy, despite the fact that in the absence of such a convention it was almost impossible to reap any benefits in the Red Sea from the convention already signed with Egypt.

However, intervention of any kind tends, at times, to bring forth offensive demands, and British intervention was no exception. In mid-1859 Britain demanded the dismissal of the governor of Massawa for threatening the British vice-consul there in a dispute concerning slave trade matters. After lengthy negotiations, the Porte agreed to recall the governor to Istanbul for an investigation, but refused to dismiss him without proper and fair procedure. In April 1879 the British demanded the removal from office of the *Kaymakam* of Jidda for similar reasons. This time the Porte put up little resistance and the man was dismissed. In June of the same year the British ambassador demanded an increase in the penalty of a man convicted in Mecca for abducting six children from Haydarabad in order to sell them as slaves; the man had been initially sentenced to six months' imprisonment. These demands reflected Britain's growing frustration with its inability to put an end to the Red Sea slave trade.[2]

---

[2] Dismissal of Massawa governor demanded in FO 84/1090/1-10, 23-7, correspondence—Malmesbury, Russell, Bulwer, 4.8.59 Removal of *Kaymakam* of Jidda in: FO 8411543/29-30, Salisbury to Layard, 24.4 79; *ibid.*/242, Layard to Salisbury, 30.8.79; *ibid.*/264, Malet to Salisbury, 29.9.79. Increase of penalty demanded in *ibid.*/200, Layard to Salisbury, 17.6 79; *ibid* /226, Layard to Savvas Paşa, 3.8.79.

Still within the realm of diplomacy, Britain resorted also to indirect measures, that is, by not dealing directly with the Porte, in order to advance her policy of complete suppression of the Ottoman slave trade. As we have seen, the British realized that the Central Government could not, or would not, act decisively against the Red Sea traffic. They then tried to induce the Khedive of Egypt to undertake some anti-slave trade measures in that region in exchange for recognition of his rule over most of the African coast of the Red Sea and the Gulf of Aden. These British moves, crowned by the conclusion of the Anglo–Egyptian convention in 1877, were taken in effect behind the Porte's back. The Ottomans were left out of the whole process, though they were officially asked to approve the procedures, which they grudgingly did. In yet another case, the British tried (in 1878-1879) to enlist the support of the moderate *Şerif* of Mecca Ḥusayn ibn Muḥammad for the suppression of the Ḥijaz slave trade.[3] Here, too, the Porte was not apprised of these contacts until their positive conclusion.

At times, the Foreign Office had to restrain its own consuls, whose zeal caused disruption in the relations with local authorities, which ultimately hurt more than helped the efforts to suppress the slave trade. They were only a handful,[4] and one example will suffice here During his service in the important port city of Izmir between 1869-1876, Consul

---

[3] On the *Şerif* and his negotiations with the British, see Ismail Hakkı Uzunçarşılı, *Mekke-ı Mukerreme Emırlerı* (Istanbul, 1972), p 138, FO 84/1510/274, Yūsuf Qudsī (Consulate dragoman, Jidda) to A J Powlett (commander of "Wild Swan," Jidda), 26 3 78, *ibid* /272-3, Powlett to 'Umar Nasīf (Agent of the *Şerif* in Jidda), 27 3 78, FO 84/1548/128-31, Layard to Salisbury, 5 2 79, *ibid* /132-4, Foreign Office consultation—Wylde et al , 5 2 79, FO 84/1544/160-5, Zohrab to Salisbury, 26 4 79, FO 84/1543/204-5, Layard to Salisbury, 11 6 79

[4] The most noteworthy "zealots" were Consul Cumberbatch of Izmir (see below) and Consul Drummond-Hay of Tripoli [FO 84/1324/62-4, Barron (Chargé d'Affaires, Istanbul) to Clarendon, 18 1 70, *ibid* /66-7, Barron to Drummond-Hay, 1 1 70] For Cumberbatch's dispatches, see FO 84/1341/117-94, Cumberbatch to Granville, 5 1-16 12 71, FO 84/1354/206-73, Cumberbatch to Granville, 19 1-19 12 72

Cumberbatch was especially interested in the slave trade. In those years he closely followed the traffic on board the Egyptian, Ottoman, and European steamers from Ḥudayda, Jidda, and Alexandria to Izmir, often reporting the most minute details concerning the transportation of persons suspected of being slaves. In 1871 he sent the Foreign Office thirty dispatches on the slave trade, and in 1872 thirty-one. His interference and probing drew sharp complaints from the *Vâli* of Aydın in July 1870, to which Elliot remarked: "I am of opinion that the interference of our consular agents would . . . be more likely to retard than to advance the progress of the views which we must wish to see gain ground."[5]

At this point we should perhaps let the dispatches speak for themsleves:[6]

Elliot to Cumberbatch, 24 September 1871:

"I have to inform you with reference to your Telegram of the 20th Instant that there is no reason why African Slaves should not be conveyed in the Steamers from Smyrna to Constantinople when travelling with their masters.

"It has previously been explained to you that Slavery in this country is not an illegal institution."

Elliot to the Foreign Secretary Lord Granville, 13 August 1872:

"The traffic is not however carried on at all to the extent that Your Lordship has probably gathered from Mr. Cumberbatch's despatches, a large proportion of the Blacks whom he imagines to be sent up here for sale proving on investigation to be slaves belonging to some private household, or free Blacks brought for domestic service."

[5] FO 84/1324/80–4, Elliot to Granville, 17.7.70.
[6] Quotations, in order of appearance, are from: FO 84/1341/168; FO 84/1354/151; *ibid.*/155; FO 84/1427/64; FO 84/1354/200-1.

Elliot to Granville, 18 August 1872:

"It was, therefore, possible that slaves for sale were occasionally brought in the Lloyd Steamers, but certainly not with the frequency to be inferred from Mr. Cumberbatch's reports, which bear the mark of manifest exaggeration."

Elliot to Granville, 28 September 1872:

"Mr. Cumberbatch, whose zeal in the cause frequently outruns his discretion, is apt to see a slave dealer in every person who passes with a Black belonging to him."

The Under-Secretary of State (for Granville) to Cumberbatch, 27 September, 1872:

". . . while giving you full credit for the zeal which you display in this matter, His Lordship suggests that you should make as minute enquiries as possible into the condition of the negroes passing Smyrna [before you jump into conclusions, E.R.T.]."

Again, Consul Cumberbatch's case was the exception rather than the rule. Over-zealousness occurred more often—though by no means always—in other branches of the British government dealing with the suppression of the Ottoman slave trade. Those, notably the Royal Navy, lay outside the immediate control of the Foreign Office, and will be discussed later in this part. Still within political and diplomatic circles, however, we find that different views were voiced with regard to the extent of intervention and pressure which were likely to produce compliance with Britain's desire to suppress the traffic. Throughout the second half of the nineteenth century, there was no serious challenge within the Foreign Office—and among the main political figures of the time—to the notion that Britain was justified in bringing pressure to bear on the Ottoman government in order to put an end to the slave trade. There were humanitarian and moral reasons for this policy, and it enjoyed broad support in British public opinion. And there were also political and economic reasons shaped by the British perception of what were the British interests in that part of the world. As put in 1881, with regard to Egypt, by a British professor of International Law:[7]

> "The resistance to Egyptian slavery and to the Abyssinian slave trade—though that resistance has its foundation in genuine humanitarian feeling—is undoubtedly deriving strong political support from the apprehension that the best interests of England and France in Egypt are incompatible with the continued existence of an institution fatal to Egyptian progress and to Egyptian concert with Europeans."

The question was, therefore, of degree rather than of principle. With public opinion, led by the Anti-Slavery Society, pushing for more intervention, and many of the ambassadors and consuls expressing the opposite view, the Foreign Office tried to take the middle of the road. In most cases, a realistic and level-headed approach prevailed among the top policymakers in Whitehall.[8] To be sure, interventionists like Palmerston and Stratford de Redcliffe had their day, but so did non-interventionists like Aberdeen, Clarendon, and Elliot. The day-to-day, middle-level decision-making, however, was left to professionals like W. H. Wylde, Sir Julian Pauncifote, and T. V. Lister, whose expertise and diplomatic approach normally prevailed. Since the suppression of the Ottoman slave trade was not—during most of the time—an issue of the highest priority in British foreign policy, it was usually handled by the under-secretaries of state and the heads of department at the Foreign Office in consultation with the

[7] ASR, 4th series, vol. L (1881), pp. 207-9, a paper by Professor Sheldon Amos on "What are the Limits of the Right of Intervention for the Suppression of Slavery and the Slave Trade," delivered at the Congress of the Social Science Association.

[8] For some examples of moderation and restraint, see Aberdeen Papers, vol. C, BM/Add. Ms. 43138/319-21, Canning to Aberdeen, Private, 1.3.44; *ibid.*/323, Aberdeen to Canning, Private, 5.3.44; FO 84/1324/130-2, Clarendon to Stanton, 21.2.70; FO 84/1370/165-6, Foreign Office consultation, 26-28.2.73; FO 84/1641/127-8, Minute by Lister, 26.10.83.

ambassador to Turkey. The foreign secretaries were always kept well informed of the developments in the area—mainly because of its extensive exposure to public opinion—but the depth of their involvement varied according to their individual interests and to the seriousness of the situation.

Perhaps the most striking example of the exchange of views inside the Foreign Office is the following episode.[9] It is cited here in greater detail for it may throw light on the decision-making process in regard to the suppression of the Ottoman slave trade and the problems involved in it. In a confidential dispatch from the British consul in Jidda to Granville, dated 9 November 1884, Consul Jago reported that information had reached him that the private steamer of the Sultan of Zanzibar, the "Malika," was anchored at Jidda. It had on board 6 Ethiopian boys, 4 of whom were eunuchs, and 2 Circassian girls brought from Istanbul. All had been purchased from the Sultan and were about to sail for Zanzibar. The consul expected that he would soon be asked to endorse their manumission papers as a precaution against interference by British cruisers.

Upon receipt of the Consul's dispatch at the Foreign Office, Clement Hill wrote the following minute:

"This is a very *mal à propos* piece of information. We can't afford just at this moment to fall foul of the Sultan of Zanzibar. We should not object to the Circassians and have not done so on a previous occasion, but the Abyssinian Eunuchs are different. However, I think that for the moment we had better say nothing about it, and tell the Admiralty, very confidentially, not to interfere sending them copy of this Despatch. Kirk [the British consul-general and agent in Zanzibar] will have got the information and will know what to do, which I fancy will be nothing. Later on we can tell the Sultan he must give up such practices."[10]

[9] FO 84/1674/125.
[10] *Ibid.*, Minute dated 3.12.84.

Hill also enclosed a draft instruction with his minute. Reading this, Under-Secretary Lord Edmund Fitzmaurice commented in a note to Sir Julian Pauncifote:

"I do not like this Draft. It is to say the least dangerous. Suppose this was to get out, there would be an uproar . . . and we should be accused of conniving at the Slave Trade for political reasons. Would not the best course be to instruct Consul Jago to pursue the usual course in regard to the letters of manumission, i.e., to grant or refuse them according as he is satisfied with the evidence, and let the "Malacca" take its chance with our cruisers. The Sultan of Zanzibar will respect us all the more if he sees we intend to stand no nonsense: in other words he is an Oriental."[11]

Sir Julian then wrote to Lord Granville:

"This is the Draft to Admiralty to which Fitzmaurice takes exception and I think you are disposed to agree with him—as I do. If so shall we cancel this Draft and telegraph to Consul Jago to take all the measures he properly can to ensure the manumission of the slaves before they embark."[12]

Lord Granville accepted Fitzmaurice and Pauncifote's view and ordered the draft to be destroyed. On his instructions, the following telegram—in cypher—was sent to Consul Jago on 13 December 1884:

"Your Despatch no. 3 Africa. Take all measures you properly can to ensure the manumission of the slaves before they embark."[13]

It all turned out to be much ado about nothing. The papers of manumission were not submitted to the consul for endorsement, possibly because, as he himself suggested, it was not expected that British cruisers would apprehend the Sul-

[11] *Ibid./128–9*, dated 9.12.84.
[12] *Ibid./130*, dated 12.12.84.
[13] *Ibid./106.*

tan's private steamer, and the "Malika" was not searched by the Royal Navy.[14] Calm returned to the Foreign Office; an embarrassment had been avoided. But other embarrassments could not be avoided and had to be dealt with. Most of those occurred at sea and involved miscalculated use of force by Her Majesty's cruisers.

In July 1861 it was reported that an Ottoman vessel on its way from Zanzibar to Jidda was searched by the British frigate "Sidon." The boat was suspected of slave trading. The Ottomans charged that the British crew mocked the sailors; debased the Ottoman pavillion; beat one sailor, who died later; seized merchandize worth £5,000; and then sank the vessel. Over two years later, the matter was finally settled, and the British paid over £5,750 in damages. In November 1866 the Ottoman ambassador in London remonstrated to the Foreign Office against the behavior of the officers of H.M.S. "Pantaloon" during an incident which took place off the Arabian coast in the Red Sea. According to the remonstrance, the British cruiser stopped the Ottoman corvette "Lûtifiye," boarded it, and humiliated the crew—among whom were forty Yemenis suspected by the British of being slaves—by drilling them for some time on the deck. Following investigation, the Foreign Secretary extended an official apology to the Porte.[15]

These incidents were not isolated as far as the Royal Navy was concerned, though it appears that Ottoman vessels were more fortunate than others in that some restraint was shown toward them. On 24 January 1870 the Committee on the East African Slave Trade submitted its report to the Earl of Clarendon. The committee criticized the Navy's policy on

[14] *Ibid.*/136-7, Jago to Granville, 14.12.84.
[15] For the details of the "Sidon" case see FO 84/1144/196-205, correspondence—Russell, Musurus Paşa (Ottoman ambassador, London), Rostand (Ottomand consul, Mauritius), 6.7-22.8.61; FO 84/1131/33-53, correspondence—Russell, Musurs Paşa, Rostand, 3-10.62; FO 84/1204/198-204, correspondence—Russell, Musurus Paşa, 30.6-7.8.63. For the "Pantaloon," see FO 84/1260/21-33, correspondence—Musurus Paşa, Lord Stanley, 1.11-7.12.66.

prize and booty and its performance in cases of seizure.[16] Destroying suspected slaving vessels before condemnation, landing their crews in remote places, and obtaining condemnation *ex parte* were called unacceptable practices. Since the East African trade—unlike the West African—was carried on in dhows engaged in both legitimate commerce and slave trading, the committee argued, there was no justification for the destruction of vessels even upon condemnation.

Other incidents involving Ottoman subjects and vessels occurred in the 1870s:[17] In July 1873 H.M.S. "Thetis," cruising at Assab Bay in the Red Sea, encountered ten dhows which the captain suspected of slave trading. The boats were destroyed and 30 black crew members—thought to be slaves—were carried off to Aden. Four persons were killed in the skirmish and 216 sailors were abandoned on an island, later to be rescued by a British ship when the error was discovered. After proceedings lasting three years, Britain apologized to the Ottomans and agreed to pay large indemnities of over £10,000. In May 1877 the commander of H.M.S. "Wild Swan" admitted in a private letter to the British consul-general in Egypt that he had captured an Ottoman slaver with 49 slaves aboard, in spite of the fact that he was not allowed by law to search and seize Ottoman vessels. The Admiralty ordered the boat to be returned to the Ottoman

---

[16] Accounts and Papers, 1870, vol. XVI, pp. 899-915, report addressed to the Earl of Clarendon by the Committee on the East African Slave Trade, 24.1.70 (for criticism of the Royal Navy referred to here, see pp. 909, 911, 913, 925).

[17] For the details of the "Thetis" case, see FO 195/1020, Slave Trade No. 9, Granville to Elliot, 23.8.73; FO 84/1370/114, Elliot to Granville, 6.9.73; FO 84/1412/114, Elliot to Derby, 26.10.75; FO 84/1460/192-213, Sir Louis Mallet (Permanent Under-Secretary, India Office) to the Under-Secretary of State (Foreign Office) and enclosures, 23.8.76; BFASS/Mss. Brit. Emp./S22/G113, Major-General Robert Shaw to the Anti-Slavery Society, 23.2.75. (For impact of case on the Ottoman government, see above, p. 225.) For case of "Wild Swan," see FO 84/1511/177-9, Vivian to Salisbury, 12.5.77. For "Ready," see FO 84/1510/308-11, N. H. Beyts (acting consul, Jidda) to A. Beyts (consul, Jidda) and enclosures, 18.12.78; FO 84/1543/137, memo from Porte to the British ambassador in Istanbul, 24.2.79; *ibid.*, Malet to Karatodori Paşa (Foreign Minister), 29.4.79.

authorities in Jidda. In December 1878 H.M.S. "Ready" seized three dhows near Jidda on suspicion of slave trading. When the Bedouins on board refused to yield, a chase developed, during which one of the Bedouins was shot and killed. The consequent agitation among the Bedouin population caused great concern to both the Ottoman and British authorities. The issue was finally settled following a British pledge to pay blood-money, which a mixed committee in Jidda put at £550.

Though the Navy's actions were supposed to emanate from and support the general policies of the government, these excesses caused the Foreign Office great embarrassment, and in some cases actually impeded Britain's efforts. Whereas naval activity was quite successful in suppressing the slave trade in the Atlantic and Indian oceans and in the Persian Gulf, it had little positive effect on the Red Sea traffic. The reasons for that were at once legal, political, and technical. Until 1880 British cruisers had no right to search or seize Ottoman vessels, and, owing to the delicate and special relations between Britain and the Porte, there was no desire in London to offend the Ottomans by acting against their vessels without a convention. The technical reasons consisted of the geographic conditions in the region which favored the trade— such as the short distance between the two coasts of the Red Sea—and the difficulties of dealing with small-scale traffic mixed with legitimate trade and carried on in regular boats.

Within our discussion of non-diplomatic activity, we should take note of an action which, though it comes under this category, was nevertheless taken in full cooperation with the Foreign Office. This was the British occupation in 1857 of Perim Island in the straits of Bāb al-Mandab. Perim had been previously occupied by Britain in May 1799 as a precaution against a possible French attempt to extend Napoleon's expedition to Egypt via the Red Sea to India. The island was later evacuated when the French threat vanished. However, with plans to dig the Suez Canal in the offing—under French auspices—Britain reassessed her strategic position in the Red

Sea and deciced to "re-occupy" Perim. The reasons for that were three:[18]

(1) To control the sea route to India if the canal was dug.

(2) To be in a better position to check the slave trade from Zayla', Tajūra, and the Zanzibar coast to the Yemen.

(3) To erect a lighthouse on the island, which would greatly facilitate the passage of steamers engaged in commerce.

"It is I think difficult to overrate the importance of this small island," wrote the governor of Bombay.

For fear of obstructive French intervention in Istanbul, no application was made to the Porte to cede the territory to Britain, and on 29 December 1856 a small expeditionary force from Aden was ordered to occupy Perim. The mission was accomplished with no resistance—the island was uninhabited, though it was regularly frequented by fishing boats—and the results were reported to the government of Bombay in February 1857. The occupation of Perim caused some consternation among the slave dealers in Jidda, who expected a British drive to suppress the slave trade in the Red Sea.[19]

HOW THE BRITISH WERE DECEIVED

The ingenuity of the slave dealers, as well as that of those engaged in slave trading on a small scale and not as a vocation, was hard, if not impossible, to defeat. With or without the connivance of the Ottoman authorities, it still went on. The British themselves, it will be shown, fell victim to deception and could not, for a variety of reasons, prevent the traffic in their own backyard.

In 1873 several reports reached the Foreign Office of slave

[18] On the occupation of Perim, see FO 78/1333/3–6a, Brigadier Coghlan (Political Resident, Aden) to Lt. Col. Melville (Secretary to the Bombay government), 27.8.56; *ibid.*/78–9, Coghlan to the Secretary of the Secret Committee of the East India Company (London), 27.10.56 (quoted); *ibid.*/19–21, memo by the governor of Bombay, n.d. (ca. October 1856); *ibid.*/94b–98, Coghlan to Lt. Creig, 29.12.56; *ibid.*/103–6, Coghlan to the Secretary of the Bombay government, 4.2.57.

[19] MAE/Corr. Cons./Turquie/Djedda/vol. I, pp. 395–7, Gérant Emerat (Jidda) to the Foreign Minister, 16.9.57.

trading carried on board *British* steamers from the Red Sea and Egypt to Izmir and Istanbul.[20] But not until 1876 was the British government alerted to the proportions of the problem. During that year the practice of slave trading by pilgrims transported from Jidda on board British steamers was detailed in several reports from the area. Tickets for British carriers from Jidda had no names on them, and no passenger lists could be produced by owners and captains upon inquiry. Thus, pilgrims who had purchased slaves in Mecca and Jidda could easily present them as household members whom they had brought to the Hijaz from their countries of origin. They would later sell these slaves, either on the way after debarkation or on arrival at their home towns. Sir Henry Elliot observed in April 1876 that "the practice of passing slaves as members of Turkish families is one which it is not possible to control."

The problem was discussed at the Foreign Office, and measures were considered to curb the practice.[21] Whereas it was held that slaves accompanying their masters should not be interfered with, it was decided that fresh purchases, whether for domestic use or for trading, should be prevented. The only measure possible was to demand that the number of slaves, their sex, and their description be recorded in the master's passport. But when the British consul in Jidda tried to verify the passengers' identity, it was reported, the Ottoman authorities threw obstacles in his way. Sir Henry Layard strongly protested against such actions in a remonstrance presented to the Ottoman Foreign Minister. During that year it became clear that no form of registration could be applied

[20] FO 84/1370/171-2, Cumberbatch to Elliot, 13.3.73; FO 84/1482/100-3, Nixon to Derby, 26.3.77; *ibid.*/4, Commander Francis S. Clayton to Vice-Admiral Sir R. MacDonald, 21.8.77; FO 84/1450/158-9, Elliot to Derby, 14.4.76.

[21] FO 84/1482/108, 109, Foreign Office Consultation—Wylde, Derby et al., 5.77; *ibid.*/80, Derby to Nixon, 5.6.77. Documents regarding this problem are: *ibid.*/23-5, Layard to Safvet Paşa, 25.6.77; *ibid.*/223-8, Foreign Office consultation—Wylde, Derby et al., 4-12.77; *ibid.*/197-8, Derby to Beyts, 14.12.66; FO 84/1570/281, the Porte to the British Embassy, 31.10.80; FO 84/1596/122-3, Lord Dufferin (ambassador, Istanbul) to Granville, 26.7.81.

without the full cooperation of the Ottoman passport authorities; alone, the consuls, the ship owners, and the captains could do little. In order to lend more authority to the British efforts to check the slave trade aboard their own vessels, a man-of-war was temporarily stationed at Jidda in December 1877 with instructions to assist the consul in this regard. But the practice did not completely disappear, for further—though less frequent—incidents were still being reported from Istanbul.

Another mode of deception was reported in 1877 from Jidda. Slave dealers and owners, in order to avoid loss and inconvenience when searched by British cruisers, would apply to the British Consulate, asking to certify, upon presentation of slaves and certificates of manumission, that their companions were either their own domestic slaves or freedmen.[22] This became so common that in one case it was reported that an Iranian colonel bought three slaves while in Jidda on the pilgrimage, and, before transporting them to Iran, asked the British consul to confirm that they had been properly manumitted. It was then discovered that two of the slaves were eunuchs, obviously intended for harem service or for resale. How much of a routine this procedure came to be was revealed by an exchange of letters between two slave dealers from Jidda; the letters fell into the hands of the captain of a British cruiser operating in the area. A list including the names of newly imported slaves sold to pilgrims, who later took them to Iran and Istanbul, bore the seal of the British Consulate, attesting to the fact that the slaves had been properly manumitted.

Again, little could be done to prevent the small-scale, almost private, slave trade carried on by the pilgrims. The confirmation of the authenticity of the manumission papers—considered by Britain as giving them a more permanent character and militating against abuse by the slave dealers—became in fact a procedure which granted immunity from

[22] FO 84/1510/238-8, A. B. Wylde (vice-consul, Jidda), to Derby, 16.2.77; *ibid.*/259-60, Deposition by A. B. Wylde, 25.2.77; FO 84/1594/357, list of slaves registered at the Consulate on 6.1.81.

search and trouble and legitimized a clandestine traffic. The truth of the matter was that there was nothing anybody could do to prevent sales once the (port of purchase—to carrier—to port of debarkation) line could not be made "smuggle-proof." And with the crowded conditions on board the steamers during the pilgrimage season, and the lack of strict passport registration and inspection procedures in Jidda, checking this form of slave trading was virtually hopeless. However, the pilgrims' traffic was not the most annoying thorn in Britain's side.

Far more embarrassing was the slave trade via Malta, a Crown Colony. The location of Malta made it a natural entrepôt on the sea route from Tunis and Tripoli to Istanbul, Izmir, and ports in the Balkans and the Levant—often via Crete and the Aegean Islands. The need to replenish water and food supplies made Malta an almost essential touching point for small and middle-sized sailboats. An alternative route would be from Tripoli to Benghazi and then, via Crete, to the ports of destination in the eastern Mediterranean. Until late in the nineteenth century, all steamer lines operating between Tripoli and Istanbul used to touch at Malta.

In the early 1870s a growing number of reports about the use of Malta in the slave trade focused the attention of the British government on the problem. In August 1872 Elliot wrote that the traffic between Tripoli and Istanbul via Malta was considerable. Both he and the consul-general in Istanbul put the blame on the Maltese government for not conducting proper investigations to verify the status of transit passengers. They said that the government of Malta had more means and was in a better position than the consulates in the Ottoman Empire to deal with the problem and to manumit the slaves.[23]

---

[23] For earlier reports of slave trading through Malta, see BFASS/Mss. Brit. Emp./S20/E2/20/54, John Scoble (Anti-Slavery Society) to Aberdeen, 13.1.44; FO 84/774/20-1, Canning to Palmerston, 19.7.49; FO 84/1120/153-4, Herman to Victor Houlton (Chief Secretary to the government of Malta), 30.4.60. Increase in number of reports perceived in FO 84/1341/241-2, Drummond-Hay to Granville, 9.5.71; FO 84/1427/1-3, Cumberbatch to

Between 1872-1875 the governor of Malta ordered a number of investigations into allegations that officials in his administration were conniving at the slave trade, following which he adamantly denied any laxity or wrongdoing by the Maltese authorities.[24] The main difficulty was that the slaves themselves wanted to leave Tripoli and go to Istanbul, where they hoped—and rightly so in many cases—to find a better life. Therefore, they would obey the dealers' instructions and state that they accompanied them as members of their households and out of their own free will. Still, some measures were attempted by the British government in order to cope with the situation. The first step was to ask the ship owners—through the Board of Trade—to ensure that they were not carrying persons suspected of being slaves. When this proved futile, the Secretary for the Colonies suggested that the governor of Malta enact an ordinance to find captains and owners who would carry blacks without manumission papers signed by a British consular authority on the North African coast.

However, owing to legal complications, the enactment was postponed, the idea was then temporarily shelved, and finally it was brought back in August 1876.[25] In the meantime, efforts were being made to intensify the searches and, without violating the law, to prevent the passage of slaves through

Granville, 12.1.72; *ibid.*/224-7, Stevens (consul, Nicolaieff—on leave in Malta) to Granville, 13.12.72; ASR, 3rd series, vol. XVIII (1870-1), p. 225, excerpt from a letter to the editor of the *Times*, 29.9.71 (signed—A Barrister). Other relevant documents: FO 84/1427/43-43A, Elliot to Granville, 30.8.72; *ibid.*/218-9, Francis to Elliot, 29.11.72; FO 84/1412/83-4, Elliot to Derby, 12.2.75; FO 84/1570/259-62, Francis to Granville, 11.10.80.

[24] FO 84/1427/116-31, Sir C. Van Stanbenzee to Lord Kimberley (Colonial Secretary), 8.11.72; FO 84/1428/198-213, Van Stanbenzee to Lord Carnarvon (Colonial Secretary), 21.7.74; FO 84/1427/265-90, the Board of Trade to the Under-Secretary of State (Foreign Office), 17.3.73; *ibid.*/183-95, the Crown Advocate to the governor of Malta, 1.7.74; FO 84/1428/160-2, R. Herbert (Colonial Office) to the Under-Secretary of State (Foreign Office), 5.8.74.

[25] FO 84/1429/234-7, Herbert to W. H. Wylde, 3.5.76; *ibid.*/396-7, W. H. Wylde to Herbert, 31.8.76; FO 84/1428/360-1, Francis to Houlton, 20.1.75 (quoted below); FO 84/1429/117-8, Colonial Office to Foreign Office, 9.10.75.

Malta. All these failed, observed the consul-general in Istanbul early in 1875, and added: "All that can legitimately be effected by us is the use of ordinary vigilance in watching the so-called "Slave Trade" and protesting against the forced or involuntary transport of slaves by sea and in preventing British subjects participating in an illegal trade."

The thorough searches by the Maltese authorities brought a protest from the Porte. The reason was that, during the investigation, women were made to remove their veils so as to enable the police to identify them.[26] The Ottoman consul in Malta made on two occasions strong and angry presentations to the governor, criticizing the harsh methods used by the police. Hands, he wrote, should suffice to determine the color of a woman, and there was no need to offend Muslim religious feelings by demanding that women uncover their faces in front of strangers. Following an inquiry, it was suggested that women would be asked to unveil only by women agents, and some other changes were also introduced into the proceedings. The Ottoman Foreign Minister expressed to Elliot his satisfaction with the steps taken at Malta to redress this grievance.

The United States of America—often criticized before 1865 by Britain and others for slave holding and trading—used the Malta situation in order to embarrass the British, who were doing their best to keep the matter out of the public eye.[27] The American consul in Tripoli conducted several in-

[26] Ibid /146-52, Nahum Duhany (consul, Malta) to Houlton, 16 7 74 FO 84/1429/142-5, Duhany to Van Stanbenzee, 9 9 75, see also ibid /69-77, Musurus Paşa to Derby, 20 11-7 12 75, FO 84/1428/144-5, Van Stanbenzee to Carnarvon, 21 7 74, ibid /156-7 The police adjutant to the superintendent of the police, 20 7 74, FO 84/1429/146-66, the police adjutant to the governor of Malta 17 9 75, ibid /289-92, correspondence—Foreign Office, Colonial Office, 29 5-3 6 76 FO 84/1450/166, Safvet Paşa (Foreign Minister) to Elliot, 31 7 76

[27] FO 84/1427/309-10, Consul Vidal to Granville, 1 1 73, ibid /313-5, Sir E Thornton (Minister, Washington, D C) to Granville, 27 10 73, ibid /332-3, Thornton to Granville, 15 12 73, FO 84/1428/26-39, Benjamin Moran (Chargé d'Affaires, London), to Derby, 17 3 74, ibid /270-2, Foreign Office consultation, 1 75, FO 84/1427/316-21, Foreign Office consultation, 27 10 73

vestigations into the slave trade via Malta and presented his conclusions to both the State Department and the Foreign Office. The Secretary of State brought up the question with the British Minister in Washington, and so did the American Chargé d'Affaires in London with the Foreign Secretary. The Americans offered to help through their consulates in the Ottoman Empire, in a way somewhat reminiscent of British presentations to the Porte, which only annoyed the British more. One Foreign Office official called the American presentations "troublesome," and another remarked that the Americans were "rather fond of throwing at our teeth" the Malta "scandal."

But the Americans were not the only ones who seized the opportunity to criticize the Foreign Office. Sir Henry Elliot and the consul-general in Instanbul used the Malta situation to illustrate the difficulties which both they and the Ottoman authorities had to deal with in regard to the suppression of the slave trade.[28] Wrote Sir Phillip Francis: "Whilst Malta is made a Slave Dépôt and the English ships carry slaves to Constantinople, it does not become us to reflect severely on other Governments."

And Elliot added: "I may perhaps be permitted to remark that if the Malta Government, which cannot be ever suspected of connivance, is unable to defeat the shifts that are adopted to evade the law, it is the less to be wondered at if some blacks, although in much smaller numbers, are smuggled in the steamers from Egypt to Smyrna and Constantinople, where there is no strong feeling against the abominable traffic."

The acting consul in Izmir observed in September 1875 that the transporation of slaves on board British vessels via Malta produced a very bad effect on the Ottoman authorities, who were constantly being urged by the British to suppress the traffic.

[28] *Ibid.*/235-7, Francis to Elliot, 7.11.72. *ibid.*/212-3, Elliot to Granville, 6.12.72; FO 84/1429/77-8, Joly to Elliot, 18.9.75.

THE ROLE OF PUBLIC OPINION IN BRITAIN

We have so far discussed British intervention through official channels, both diplomatic and non-diplomatic. Although these were by far the most important and most regularly used channels, they were not the only ones. The Anti-Slavery Society, at times dismayed by the way in which the government handled Ottoman slavery and slave trade, tried to take its message directly to the Ottomans.[29] In July 1867 the Society addressed the Sultan through his Foreign Minister, Fuat Paşa presenting its case against slavery, to which Fuat replied in a very positive and encouraging note. In 1872 the Bureau of the International Anti-Slavery Society sent a memorial to the Sultan, urging the abolition of slavery and the slave trade. A similar memorial was sent to the Khedive of Egypt a year later, to which he reportedly answered favorably and promised to introduce measures to that effect. These attempts had little impact on the course of events or the views of the Ottomans. Anxious not to antagonize British public opinion, the Ottomans were careful to express views which they knew the British public considered as progressive. These did not necessarily reflect their own thinking on the issue of slavery and the slave trade. It does, however, bring us to the role which public opinion played, or tried to play, in shaping the policy and actions of the British government with regard to the Ottoman slave trade.

We are not concerned here with the general anti-slavery campaign in Britain—a subject inextricably linked to other questions of domestic and foreign British policies, and one which has been treated in detail by a number of studies, some of them recent.[30] What concerns us in this work are the ma-

[29] For the following, see ASR, 3rd series, vol. XV (1867), pp. 182-3 (including text); FO 84/1324/94-105, correspondence—Elliot, Francis, Cumberbatch, 8-14.8.70 (Fuat's reply was considered by officials to be deceptive and calculated to produce a favorable impression on British public opinion); ASR, 3rd series, vol. XVIII (1872-1873), p 190 (including text); BFASS/Mss Brit. Emp /S18/C161/182, Lord Enfield (Foreign Office) to the secretary of the Anti-Slavery Society, 19.5.73

[30] See, for example, Howard Temperley, *British Antislavery 1833-1870*

jor attempts, led by the Anti-Slavery Society, to bring public pressure to bear on the British government to act rigorously in regard to Ottoman slavery and slave trade. In fact, the Society never gave up the struggle for the abolition of slavery in the Empire, though, as we have seen, the British government had relinquished that idea quite early on and concentrated instead on the more attainable goal—the suppression of the Ottoman slave trade.

During the second half of the nineteenth century, the Society addressed numerous memorials and petitions to the various ministries, primarily to the Foreign Office, and from time to time its supporters in Parliament directed questions to the concerned cabinet members and made speeches on the subject. With the gradual decline of the Atlantic slave trade and following the abolition of slavery in the United States in 1865, much of the attention of abolitionists shifted to the Near Eastern traffic to focus on the last of the great Muslim powers—the Ottoman Empire. The fact that throughout most of that period Britain was a close ally of the Ottomans—in the eyes of many Britons protecting and preserving their Empire—justified putting pressure on the Porte to accede to British demands.

One of the Society's continuous efforts was to induce the British government to bring up the abolition of Ottoman slavery and slave trade in international conferences which had a bearing on the future of the Ottoman Empire. The strategy was to exact a concession from the Porte in this regard as a part of a general pact, which on many such occasions entailed some combination of territorial arrangements and commitments to implement reforms. Thus, in March 1856, the Society addressed a memorial to Palmerston in the hope of having the subject treated at the Peace Conference in Paris following the Crimean War. And again in June 1874, the Society asked the Foreign Secretary to instruct the British

(London, 1972); Edith F. Huruwitz, *Politics and the Public Conscience* (London, 1973); Suzanne Miers, *Britain and the Ending of the Slave Trade* (New York, 1975); M. Craton, J. Walvin, and D. Wright, *Slavery Abolition and Emancipation—Black Slaves and the British Empire* (London, 1976).

representatives to the Brussels conference on the conduct of belligerents in war to bring up for discussion the abolition of slavery in "Egypt, Turkey, and other Muslim countries." In December 1876 the Society tried once more. This time they asked that the subject be discussed at the international conference convened in Istanbul to deal with the crisis over Serbia, Montenegro, Bulgaria, and Bosnia-Herzegovina. All of these requests were rejected by the government as being outside the scope of the above-mentioned conferences.[31]

The Society did not give up. When the Congress of Berlin was convened in 1878, it sent a special delegation to Berlin in order to persuade the powers to pass a resolution against slavery and the slave trade, most notably in the Ottoman Empire.[32] This was done after the British government had once again refused to sponsor a resolution in compliance with the Society's wishes. The rest of the powers, the delegation reported, were reluctant to take the initiative in a matter seen by them as lying within Britain's traditional domain. Disappointed and bitter, the delegation returned to London and to the renewed attacks on the "pro-Ottoman" policies of Disraeli's cabinet.

Disraeli's government—in office since 1874—did not have the best record in the eyes of the Society. It was too closely aligned with the Ottomans' sacrificing moral principles, such as the abolitionist cause, for reasons of *realpolitik*. The Foreign Office was attacked for playing down Ottoman vices, and the Embassy and the consulates for relying solely on information provided by Ottoman sources and for rejecting reports critical of Ottoman performance in regard to the slave

[31] For details of all these cases, see ASR, 3rd series, vol. IV (1856), pp. 81-5 (text pp. 83-5, memorial dated 7.3.56); *ibid.*, vol. VI (1857), p. 13; BFASS/Mss. Brit. Emp./S18/C162/7, (for) Derby to the secretary of the Anti-Slavery Society, 24.6.74; FO 84/1450/62-70, the Anti-Slavery Society to Derby, 29.12.76; *ibid.*/71, Foreign Office consultation, n.d.; BFASS/Mss. Brit. Emp./S18/C161/217, Pauncifote to the Secretary of the Anti-Slavery Society, 13.1.77; ASR, 3rd series, vol. XX (1876-1877), pp. 167-8.

[32] ASR, 3rd series, vol. XXI (1878-1879), pp. 57-61, report of the delegation to the Congress of Berlin, 15.7.78. Attack on the government is in *ibid.*, p. 98.

trade.[33] The attack was joined by members of Parliament friendly to the Society and, at times, became vicious. A speech delivered at Croydon in September 1877 by the Rt Hon Robert Lowe included the following statement

> "What, then, shall we say of ourselves when, for the petty miserable object of setting up the decrepit Turk as a means of fighting Russia, we are content to keep alive, mainly by our influence in Europe, the slave trade in its most odious form? . . . While we cannot tolerate a Brazilian running a cargo on the coast of Brazil, we are doing all that is in our power to keep up the slave trade in the heart of Europe, and in the seat of ancient civilization. Therefore, I do feel with a strength which I can hardly express, that we are in the last degree degraded and disgraced by our union with the Turk."

Not surprisingly, in the elections of 1880, the Society issued an "Address to the Electors of Great Britain," which was highly critical of Disraeli's policies regarding Ottoman slavery and the slave trade.[34] Its concluding sentence said "We commend these facts to the most serious consideration of the electors and trust that on the day of polling they will bear them steadily in mind." Gladstone, in a speech to the electors of Mid-Lothian, quoted the Society's address in *extenso* When in office, however, he too was not always willing to lend his ear to the Society's representations In May 1880 he turned down a request to meet with a delegation to discuss the slave trade in Egypt, citing "pressure of business." And in March 1881 he answered a memo of the Society on slavery in Egypt and the Sudan by promising to receive a delegation "when the more immediate pressing public

---

[33] BFASS/Mss Brit Emp /S22/G96, "Considerations as to what could most effectively be done at the present crisis (of a meeting of a European Conference) to get slavery done away with in Turkey once and for all " 5 6 78, ASR, *loc cit* , pp 67-9, Dr Humphrey Sandwitch to the secretary of the Anti-Slavery Society, 22 7 78, *ibid* , pp 140-2, an editorial Quoted below is ASR, 3rd series, vol XX (1876-7), pp 172-3

[34] ASR, 3rd series, vol XXII (1880), pp 39-40, address dated 18 3 80

questions have been disposed of by Her Majesty's Government."[35]

Thus, the role of public opinion must not be exaggerated. Although any British government had to take into account public sentiment and the well-organized, vociferous anti-slavery "lobby," no government, in fact, let the issue interfere with the conduct of its foreign policy in the East Yet, most governments in Britain genuinely shared the wish of the public to see the Ottoman slave trade at an end. Moreover, during most of the period under discussion, there was no conflict between this attitude and the major goals of British foreign policy, which sought to reform the Empire according to Western concepts Britain did not hesitate, therefore, to interfere in Ottoman affairs—in various ways and by different means, as we have seen—in order to induce the Porte to suppress the slave trade.

OTTOMAN ATTITUDES TO SLAVERY AND THE SLAVE TRADE

Accepted by custom, perpetuated by tradition, and sanctioned by religion, slavery was an integral part of Ottoman society. As practiced in the Empire during the nineteenth century, it was mild and—excepting the case of agricultural slavery among the Circassians—did not give rise to any tension within Ottoman socio-political culture. The suffering and mortality which accompanied the slave trade were little known to the majority of slave holders in the urban centers of the Empire. When information did filter in, mostly through British reports and remonstrances, it was deemed tendentious and exaggerated In any case, except for those involved in the trade, most Ottomans had only a vague idea of the nature of the traffic, which they associated with faraway places and unfamiliar countries. It is, therefore, not surprising that

---

[35] Use of the Address by Gladstone is in *ibid*, pp 40-1 Gladstone's treatment of the Society when Prime Minister BFASS/Mss Brit Emp /S18/C162/1, J A Godley (for Gladstone) to C Allen (secretary of the Anti-Slavery Society), 24 5 80, *ibid* /2, E W Hamilton (for Gladstone) to Allen, 21 3 81

no effective abolitionist movement ever emerged in the Empire.

However, one issue in the context of slavery did disturb the harmony of social order in the Ottoman Empire.[36] This was the type of agricultural slavery practiced by the Circassian immigrants and imported into the Empire in the 1860s. The friction between Circassian slave holders and their slaves was seen as threatening law and order, and the traffic in freeborn Circassian Muslim children was rejected as contrary to the *Şeriat*. Consequently, the Porte moved to redress these grievances by gradual abolition.

No similar tension arose with regard to African slaves, for they were converted to Islam upon purchase and rarely used in agriculture. Yet it was precisely in the area of trading in Africans that Britain followed her most aggressive interventionist policy. This policy elicited two types of reaction from the Ottoman side: political and, to a lesser extent, intellectual.

Ottoman political reaction can be characterized as continuous resistance—both passive and active, and in varying degrees of intensity—to British abolitionist pressures. Here we have a number of statements from and about Ottoman officials who were dealing with British policy and its repercussions. The British attributed the prohibition of 1857 to Mustafa Reşit Paşa's efforts, and Sultan Abdülmecit himself made a strong anti-slave trade comment to a British representative. Addressing the Council of Ministers in 1854, the Grand Vezir Kıbrıslı Mehmet Emin Paşa forcefully argued that the Circassian and Georgian slave trade should be restricted.[37]

Mustafa Paşa, Commander of the Batum Army, praised Kıbrıslı's policy in a letter to the British and French vice-

---

[36] Slavery agreed with the Ottoman value-system, hence it did not disturb social harmony. However, that harmony was being seriously threatened by Western intrusion throughout the nineteenth century. It finally gave way to a new social order.

[37] For Sultan Abdülmecit's views and the British assessment of Mustafa Reşit Paşa's role, see above pp. 144-6. Kıbrıslı's position on the Circassian slave trade is on pp. 117-20, above.

admirals in the Black Sea. The great reformer Mıdhat Paşa reportedly proposed strong language against the slave trade for inclusion in Abdülhamıt II's accession proclamation, but the text was deleted. The same Paşa later suggested the drastic measure of abolishing the pilgrimage caravan between Damascus and the Hıjaz to prevent slave importation into Syria. In reports to their superiors, both the *Kaymakam* of Massawa, in 1860, and the *Kaymakam* of Jidda, in the late 1880s, condemned the slave trade.[38] Regretably, this evidence is still insufficient to allow any general observations as to the prevailing views in government circles about either the suppression of the traffic or the abolition of slavery

Attitudes among Ottoman intellectuals are even harder to pin down. For one thing, we still lack enough evidence to determine what was the extent of public interest in the issue of slavery and the slave trade. It seems certain, however, that they were not highly debated matters and did not figure prominently on the agenda of the educated classes. Most of our evidence comes from literary sources and is primarily concerned with white, not black, slaves, it contains little about the slave trade. Still, it may be of interest to cite here the most telling expressions we have come across

The most explicit anti-slavery statement encountered in the material appears in Ahmet Mıdhat's short story "Slavery" (*Esaret*), published in 1874.[39] The story is about two young Circassian slaves, a boy and a girl, raised in an upper-class Istanbul household. It is told in the first person by the master of the house, has a tragic ending, and amounts to a strong indictment of the institution of slavery. Clear expressions of the writer's disapproval of the practice appear in several places An intimate conversation between the two slaves is cited in

[38] Mustafa Paşa's praise for Kıbrıslı is on p 121, the views of Mıdhat Paşa are cited above, pp 229-31, the report of the *Kaymakam* of Massawa is on p 206, above, and that of the *Kaymakam* of Jidda is on p 240, above

[39] Ahmet Mıdhat, *Letâif-ı Rıvâyât*, vol I (Istanbul, 1290), pp 45-104 References in this paragraph are to the following pages 49-51, 56-7, 75, 103, 68-73, the quotation is from pp 73-4 ("*Ah dilerim Allah'dan bızı satanların gozlerı kor olsun*"), 103

detail, in which they bemoan the loss of their freedom, though not condemning their living conditions. At one point in the conversation the girl exclaims: "Please God, may the eyes of those who sold us be blinded." At the end, following the slaves' tragic death, the author intimates: "I vowed never to buy a slave again. I began cursing the sellers and buyers [of slaves] for thus separating the poor children from their mothers and fathers and for causing this and thousands of similar painful tragedies."

In a novel entitled *Intibah* (Awakening) published in 1876, the well-known poet, thinker, and public figure Namık Kemal voiced his rejection of female slavery. A similar attitude was later expressed in Samipaşazade Sezai's *Sergüzeşt* (Adventure), a novel about a slave girl published in 1888. Şerif Mardin compares the novel with *Uncle Tom's Cabin* and claims it had the same effect on Ottoman intellectuals as did Stowe's book in America. Sezai's book was banned by Sultan Abdülhamit II's censors.[40]

Mardin also suggests that the critique of slavery in the Empire was closely associated with, if not derived from, the broader debate about the position of women. The emancipation of women and the Westernization of upper-class men, he argues, were the two dominant issues in nineteenth-century Ottoman novels. Namık Kemal, Sezai, and others had a strong aversion to slave love, since the woman in the relationship was not free to act as she wished.

Yet, even these writers dealt only with white female slavery and not with black slavery or the slave trade. Their attitude to slavery may have been self-evolved, or a result of internalized Western views, but they did not react directly to the British thrust which sought to suppress the African slave trade to the Ottoman Empire. Were they aware of the mood which prevailed in Britain and in other Western European countries concerning Ottoman slavery and slave trading? Did

[40] Şerif Mardin, "Super Westernization in Urban Life in the Ottoman Empire in the Last Quarter of the Nineteenth Century," in Peter Benedict et al. (ed.), *Turkey, Geographic and Social Perspectives* (Leiden, 1974), pp. 403-46.

they read what the British and Foreign Anti-Slavery Society published about these subjects? Clearly, more work is required on such questions before we can offer satisfactory answers.

The Istanbul *élite* was by no means the only Ottoman group which was exposed to Western ideas and ways. In Cairo and Alexandria, the upper and middle classes were as much in contact with Europeans, if not more so. On 1 July 1888 Cardinal Lavijerie, one of France's most active abolitionists, gave a speech in the church of St. Sulpice in Paris. The Cardinal condemned Islam for the evils of slavery and the slave trade in Central Africa. In the audience sat a French-educated Egyptian, Aḥmad Shafîq Bey, who took great offense at the Cardinal's words. In a reaction to the speech, he wrote in French a short book entitled *L'Esclavage au point de vue musulman*.[41]

Shafîq's book is a defense of Islam and its humane view of slavery. The author claims that Islam wished to abolish slavery, but since it could not do so without causing much damage to the social fabric, it chose at least to mitigate the institution. He goes on to state that the slaves found in Egypt at the time were not in fact slaves in the legal, Şer'î sense, but abductees who should be set free immediately. In this book we have a clear reference to African slavery and to the slave trade in a direct response to Western criticism. Appropriately enough, it comes from Egypt, where African slavery was widespread.

The book was debated in the foreign and Egyptian press and was translated into Arabic. It also elicited an interesting response from a former Ottoman Foreign Minister, Karatodori Paşa, then the Ottoman ambassador to Belgium and the Porte's representative at the Brussels Conference of 1889-1890.[42] In his letter to Shafîq, this high-ranking non-Muslim

---

[41] Ahmed Chefik, *L'Esclavage au point de vue musulman* (Cairo, 1819), and the Arabic translation by Aḥmad Zakī, *al-Riqq fī'l-Islām* (Cairo, 1892); references are to the Arabic translation. This work is discussed by Gabriel Baer (Baer, pp. 187-8).

[42] Shafîq, pp. 130-3.

official reveals his frustrations in trying to convey to the Europeans the humane Muslim position on slavery and the traffic. Karatodori Paşa goes on to charge the Europeans with ignorance and thanks Shafiq for providing him with useful ammunition to counter their arguments.

Two more examples may fit in this context. They come from Tunis and Morocco, which, though not part of the Ottoman Empire, can still be considered as belonging to the same *milieu*—the Islamic-Mediterranean culture. Tunis, only nominally an Ottoman regency, tried to restrict the slave trade as early as 1841, in the time of Ahmet Bey. On 31 October 1863 Ḥusayn Paşa, the mayor of Tunis, addressed a letter to Amos Perry, the American consul-general in that city, as a response to Perry's query regarding the Tunisian law on slavery.[43] In it, the obviously very Westernized Paşa explains the Islamic concept of slavery and Ahmet Bey's policy to phase out the practice in Tunis. He then provides economic justification for abolition and argues that a free person is more productive than a slave, which accounts for the greater prosperity of countries where slavery no longer exists. The mayor concludes by urging the Americans—in the name of "human mercy and compassion"—to reconsider their attitude toward slavery.[44]

The last example takes us to the Kingdom of Morocco.

[43] For details of attempts to restrict the slave trade in Tunisia see L. Carl Brown, *The Tunisia of Ahmad Bey, 1837-1855* (Princeton, 1974), pp. 321-5. Ḥusayn Paşa's letter is cited in Salīm Fāris al-Shidyāq (ed.), *Kanz al-Raghā'ib fī Muntakhab al-Jawā'ib*, vol. VI (Istanbul, 1295), pp. 46-51. This text is also quoted in Ra'īf Khūrī, *al-Fikr al-'Arabī 'l-Ḥadīth* (Beirut, 1973), pp. 278-84. I could not locate the original text in the American archives, which may raise a question about the authenticity of the Arabic text. If the response is a forgery, we can ask who might have written it and for what purpose. Nonetheless, its very appearance in the *Kanz* in the late 1870s is in itself indicative of the changing views among certain literary circles in Istanbul. See also USNA/Record Group No. 84, Tunis Consulate, Amos Perry to General Hussein (Ḥusayn Paşa), 12.11.63 (pp. 178-80).

[44] This was ten months after the Emancipation Proclamation, while the Civil War was still being fought and before the thirteenth amendment was passed by Congress on 1 February 1865 and ratified by two-thirds of the states at the end of the same year.

What is probably the strongest criticism of slavery and the slave trade in nineteenth-century Islamdom was written in 1881 by the Moroccan historian Aḥmad al-Nāṣirī in his history of the Maghrib—*Kitāb al-Istiqṣā'*.[45] Al-Nāṣirī condemns the slave raids carried on in Africa against the blacks as being contrary to humanity and to Islam. The importance of his argument lies in his attempt to show that the law of Islam prohibits enslavement and slave trading. Like Shafiq eight years later, al-Nāṣirī too asserts that the Şerî permission to enslave the heathen who are defeated in Holy War no longer applies. The majority of blacks in the regions bordering on the Abode of Islam, he adds, have already accepted Islam and it is, therefore, illegal to enslave them.

In sum, it thus seems that for the Ottoman writers we cited here, the harmony which had existed in their sociocultural view of slavery as part of life in the Empire was disturbed. A kind of moral tension, absent before, began to grow around the age-old practice. In some, the feeling was a byproduct of their evolving views on the emancipation of women; in others, it emerged as a result of the assimilation of Western ideas; and, for yet another group, this was a defensive reaction against Europe's political and intellectual assault. But the uneasiness regarding slavery and the traffic was there. For those who experienced it, this feeling was joined to the already difficult predicament of many thinking Ottomans in the nineteenth century. They would find it increasingly harder to maintain the traditional posture that Westernization did not apply to the ideational-moral sphere, where Ottoman culture was superior. Some would turn to Western ideas; others would find refuge in Islam.

[45] Aḥmad al-Nāṣirī, *Kitāb al-Istiqṣā' li-Akhbār Duwal al-Maghrib al-Aqṣā'*, vol. V (Casablanca, 1955), pp. 131 ff.

EPILOGUE

WHEN WE BEGAN to follow the Ottoman slave trade, in the 1840s, over 10,000 slaves per annum were being *legally* and *openly* imported into the Empire. Slave markets existed in all major cities, and domestic slavery was widespread in many of the Sultan's domains. All that was to change within fifty years. By the last decade of the nineteenth century, only few slaves were still being smuggled, against the law, and the slave population was sharply reduced. How and why it came to be is the subject of this book. In closing, a last reflection on the disappearance of such an ingrained social phenomenon may be opportune.

The interdependence of slavery and the slave trade is self-evident. It was clear to British statesmen, diplomats, and abolitionists throughout the nineteenth century. But there was no agreement among them as to the precise nature of that interdependence and the ways to deal with it. It was often debated whether the abolition of slavery or the suppression of the slave trade should come first in the attempts to eradicate the practice.

Some thought that the traffic would continue as long as the status of slavery remained legal. Others argued that if the traffic was checked, slavery would gradually disappear as a consequence. However, only the few observers familiar with Ottoman society recognized the fundamental differences which existed between Islamic and Western socio-cultural patterns; only they realized that both roads to the end of slavery were paved with enormous difficulties.

We have seen that agricultural slavery was not practiced in the Ottoman Empire until the Circassian immigration of the 1860s. It then presented the Ottomans with problems that were subsequently solved internally by gradual abolition. In social terms, however, the center of gravity of nineteenth-century Ottoman slavery was domestic servitude, which was part and parcel of the highly important harem system.

The late Marshall Hodgson rightly emphasized the centrality of the household organization in Islamic society.[1] Monogamy and the strict hierarchical relationships within the Western family, he argued, ensured the supreme status of the "legitimate" wife, both inside the house, as hostess to her husband's guests, and outside. Domestic slaves were replaced by free servants early on in the Occident. In Islam, however, rigid female segregation was necessary to assert the inaccessibility of women to outside male company in what was a society of greater mingling and more relaxed class structure. The need to maintain within the household separate establishments for several wives and concubines was best met by domestic slavery.

The harem section housed all the wives, concubines, slave attendants, children of both sexes, and female dependents. The social network of harems, all secluded from the male world, extended over the urban centers of Islam and was an active, powerful world unto itself. In it, women ruled over women, maneuvered to manipulate the men's world outside, determined the quality and nature of the upbringing of male offspring, and not infrequently influenced the affairs of state.

As Hodgson points out, the harem system was fully developed only among the wealthy families of the upper classes. But, much as those classes spared no effort to imitate the Imperial harem structure and life-style, so did the rest of society try its best to emulate the upper classes. Veiling and seclusion of women were the norm, and one would own as many slaves as he could afford to buy and support. Status and prestige were often measured by the size of one's household and by the number of slaves who belonged to the family.

Indeed, slaves in Ottoman society did actually *belong* to the family and were not merely owned and employed by its members. Master-slave relations were socially and legally far more binding and entailed greater commitment on both sides

[1] Marshall G. S. Hodgson, *The Venture of Islam*, vol. II (Chicago, 1974), pp. 140-5, 354-5.

than master-free servant relations. Even after manumission and marriage, these ties were often maintained, to the benefit of all involved. In fact, one may argue that the mild nature of Ottoman slavery conduced master and slave alike to oppose the abolition of the institution. Interference with slavery was thus considered an intrusion on family life and a violation of its strongly protected privacy.

The absence of slave-breeding practices and the encouragement of manumission by the Şeriat made the continued existence of slavery totally dependent on slave importation. Any attempt, therefore, to obstruct the traffic was seen by the Ottomans as a threat to the traditional character of social and family life in the Empire. Many would have probably objected to the iniquities of the slave trade, had they been aware of them, but they would in all likelihood still insist on having a continued supply of slaves for their harems. Ottoman resistance to the suppression of the slave trade was, then, mainly socio-cultural and stemmed from the unwillingness to give up a deeply ingrained, highly intimate institution.

Although the Şeriat does not recognize color distinctions within the status of slavery, there were essentially two classes of Ottoman domestic slaves:[2] white and African. Almost all African slaves were engaged in menial work and could not aspire to much upward social mobility. Many white slaves were also employed as servants and attendants, but had prospects of betterment, mostly through marriage to upper-class males. Marriage across racial lines seems to have been rare, especially among the upper echelons of Ottoman society. The attitude of this predominantly white *élite* toward white slaves was psychologically determined by a pervasive sense of "sameness." Even though not all white slaves were in fact better off than all African slaves, the hope and chance of improvement were clearly color-bound.

The traffic in Circassians and Georgians was less complicated than the African traffic, for the routes were shorter,

[2] Agricultural slavery among the Circassian immigrants formed a different category and is discussed in detail in Chapter V, above.

easier to traverse, and not so exposed to foreign, mainly British, observation. This, in addition to the status distinction between slaves of different races, accounts for dissimilarities in the suppression of the African versus the Caucasian traffic. Much greater resistance was put up against the attempts to interfere with the Caucasian slave trade, while ostensible accommodation of British demands was the policy on the African scene.

As a result of measures taken to suppress the slave trade, it became more difficult in the 1880s to obtain slaves in the Empire. Slaves were gradually replaced by free domestic labor. Gabriel Baer has shown that in Egypt, during the last decade of the nineteenth century, this was facilitated by the emergence of a free labor market.[3] Through its manumission bureaus, the Egyptian government freed in those years many slaves, who joined the urban work force, by then no longer controlled and directed by the guild *shaykhs*. At the same time, Baer concludes, anti-slavery ideas began to take root in the Westernized segments of the Egyptian public.

Some of these developments had their parallels also in the Istanbul-influenced urban centers of the Ottoman Empire in the 1880s and 1890s. But, in the absence of a government-initiated and enforced mass manumission of slaves—such as took place in Egypt under the British occupation—the disappearance of Ottoman slavery was a quieter and more gradual process. At no times, it appears, were large numbers of liberated slaves "dumped" on the labor market. Nor does it seem that a shortage of domestic servants was suddenly created.

Rather, the worsening economic conditions gradually reduced the size of upper-class households and the number of slaves required to maintain them. The surplus manpower was manumitted and, conversely, old slaves often chose to remain with their masters even after manumission. When new help was needed, poor families—white and black—would willingly link themselves to wealthier patron families by giv-

---

[3] Baer, pp. 186-7.

ing their free children as servants to these families. The nature of that free patronage resembled slavery in all but the legal aspect.

Thus, a smooth transition from household slavery to free domestic service took place with minimal damage to the traditional structure of the Ottoman family in all classes. The more drastic social change of the old ways would be left to later years and to more violent times, until the emergence of a new Turkey from the ashes of the Ottoman Empire.

This book opened with a reference to cross-cultural perceptions and the difficulties tending the study of socio-culturally bound institutions, such as slavery. It seems appropriate that we should end on a similar note. A thoroughly Westernized upper-class Turkish woman, writing in 1963 an excellent family diary, was obviously uneasy when she touched on the subject of Ottoman slavery. Emine Foat Tugay found it necessary to devote a special appendix to "Slaves Under Ottoman Rule in the Nineteenth Century."[4] At the beginning she wrote: "During Ottoman rule, slaves were so much a part of family life that I am giving the subject full treatment, since any description of this period would be incomplete without it. So many false reports and inaccurate statements have been published regarding slaves and harem life that a brief description of the actual facts may not be out of place here."

Her statement thus reflects the dual problem of many contemporary Turks and other Muslims, a problem which was also shared by their nineteenth-century predecessors: namely, the awareness of the centrality of slavery in their society and the frustration with what is seen as the West's total misapprehension, and consequent condemnation, of the Ottoman-Muslim version of the institution. While the reaction is often defensive and apologetic, it reflects a genuine sentiment.

But Western culture—sometimes surprisingly tolerant of various forms of abuse and violation of human rights—is

---

[4] Emine Foat Tugay, *Three Centuries, Family Chronicles of Turkey and Egypt* (London, 1963), pp. 303-12.

unlikely to show any sympathy or understanding toward even the mildest version of servitude coming under the rubric of "slavery." The zeal of abolitionism, often imbued with religious fervor, absolved the West of the heavy guilt incurred as a result of European and American slavery. It became a symbol and the cause of a world-wide crusade spearheaded by Britain. The word "slavery" acquired a spell and turned into a powerful weapon against what were considered inferior, backward cultures.

In this book I have tried to avoid the pitfalls of crude cultural value-judgment without, however, hiding my own convictions. Thus, while rejecting the self-righteousness of much of the writings in the West on Ottoman slavery, this book—in organization, emphasis, language, and even metaphor—was written with the belief that the abolition of *legal* bondage, regardless of mildness or severity, was a positive step toward the still distant goal of true human freedom.

BIBLIOGRAPHICAL NOTE

THE FOLLOWING are remarks concerning the various types of sources used in the present work. They include some general observations on the quality and usefulness of these sources.

(A) ARCHIVAL SOURCES

(1) *State Archives*

(a) *Başbakanlık Arşivi*, Istanbul (BA)

This is the most important source for the history of the Ottoman Empire. Since only about 10 percent of the material is at present catalogued, we should assume that more relevant documents will become available as the process of cataloguing continues. However, the records that are already available constitute a firm basis on which we can reconstruct the history of the suppression of the slave trade. For information concerning the institution of slavery in the Empire from its rise to its demise, scholars should turn to the Ottoman archives, both the administrative and judicial sections. The cataloguing system does not provide the researcher with a special classification on slavery or the slave trade.

A general description of the material contained in the Istanbul archives can be found in Atillâ Çetin, *Başbakanlık Arşivi Kilavuzu* (Istanbul, 1979); Midhat Sertoğlu, *Muhteva Bakımından Başvekâlet Arşivi* (Ankara, 1955); Stanford Shaw, "Ottoman Archival Materials for the Nineteenth and Early Twentieth Centuries: the Archives of Istanbul," *International Journal of Middle East Studies*, vol. VI (1975), pp. 94–114. The most valuable series for information regarding the slave trade is the *İrade* collection. This series contains correspondence between the various departments of the government which normally culminates in a report from the Grand Vezir to the Sultan. Related documents are assembled in one file.

(b) The Public Record Office, London

The bulk of the PRO material used in this work consists of
official reports of British consuls and agents residing in many
of the important cities and commercial ports of the Ottoman
Empire. These representatives were expected to watch for
any manifestation of the slave trade, as well as actively to
seek and gather information, and report it to their superiors
or directly to the Foreign Office in London. In this respect
some consulates were more important than others, normally
those located on major slave routes or in major slaving ports.
During the second half of the nineteenth century, the most
active consulates, in addition to the Istanbul Embassy and
Consulate-General, were those of Izmir, Alexandria, Cairo,
Tripoli, Benghazi, Crete, Jidda, and Trabzon. They all employed dragomans, who were also the main tool of infor-
mation-gathering for their contacts with the local population
and their familiarity with its customs and language. Some
consuls had in their service paid informants, who helped them
to gain access to sources of information, such as ports and
bazars, without identifying the consulate as the interested
party, which would be the case if the dragoman or the consul
himself were involved in the questioning.

Consular reports were discussed at the Foreign Office and
served as the basis for British policy-making. Though by far
the most reliable source available to the British on the slave
trade in the Ottoman Empire—along with reports from naval officers, which were somewhat less important in the Ottoman case—these reports in many instances lacked the authenticity that stems from intimate knowledge of the local
language and culture. Many of the consuls, though not all,
lived in cultural isolation, if not alienation, from the society
surrounding them, and made little effort to learn and understand what they considered to be an inferior civilization.

Most of the relevant material is found in the general slave
trade series of the Foreign Office (FO 84, the files concerning
Turkey, Tripoli, and Egypt). Additional information is provided by the general Foreign Office series on Turkey (FO 78

and FO 195). Important parts of many of the documents included in these series have been laid before Parliament and published in the Sessional Papers (*Accounts and Papers*). But the published material gives only a partial picture and does not, of course, contain the minutes, which are often more important than the official correspondence. The British documents are mainly ambassadorial and consular reports from Istanbul and various parts of the Ottoman Empire, and instructions from the Foreign Office to the Embassy and consulates. This PRO material is very useful for studying the position of the British government regarding the slave trade and the decision-making process inside the Foreign Office.

(c) Ministère des Affaires Étrangères, Paris (MAE)

The French were considerably less interested in the suppression of the slave trade in the Ottoman Empire than were the British. This is reflected in the limited amount of relevant material available at the archives of the French Foreign Ministry. The Ministry did not require French consuls in the Empire to report regularly on matters relating to the slave trade. Individual consuls, however, provided from time to time, on their own initiative, useful information on the subject. The French reports are especially important when they come from places where there were no British representatives. For lists of available material, see Archives du Ministère des Affaires Étrangères, *État numerique des fonds de la correspondance politique de l'origine à 1871* (Paris, 1936), pp. 483-485, 504-510, and Basile G. Spiridonakis, *Empire Ottoman: inventaire des mémoires et documents aux Archives du Ministère des affaires étrangères de France* (Thessaloniki, 1973).

(d) United States National Archives (USNA)

Ambassadorial and consular reports from the Ottoman Empire can be found in the files of the Department of State, which are catalogued in the *Catalog of National Archives Microfilm Publicatoins* (Washington, 1974).

(2) *Private Papers*

The archives of the British and Foreign Anti-Slavery Society (BFASS/Mss. Brit. Emp.), Rhodes House, Oxford.

The archives contain a large number of reports and letters from correspondents of the Anti-Slavery Society who resided in the Empire. These people, in most cases missionaries and merchants, acted out of philanthropic motivation, occasionally reporting to the Society what they considered as slave trade. Their report served as the basis of the Society's actions, and often appeared in the *Anti-Slavery Reporter*. In many cases, direct political action followed, either by addressing the Foreign Office and demanding investigation and remonstration, or by raising the issue in Parliament through members who supported the Society's views. The quality of the correspondents' reports was generally poor. They stemmed more from evangelical abolitionist zeal than from any real understanding of the institutions of Ottoman society and of the complexity of the slave trade. Sir Austin Henry Layrd, when ambassador to Spain, was fiercely attacked by the Society for his actions regarding the abolition of slavery in Spain. In his response he commented on the Society's information and methods of operation:

> "The exaggerations and unscrupulous misstatements of those gentlemen have had a most serious and lamentable effect upon public opinion in Spain, and have greatly strengthened the hands of the already too-powerful pro-slavery party. . . . Although I do not yield to Mr. Cooper and his friends in detestation of slavery, and in the earnest hope and desire that this horrible and inhuman institution may speedily cease to exist in every part of the world, I have a profounder conviction that the great cause of abolition is better promoted by a regard for truth and by a wise, prudent, and statesmanlike policy than by reckless assertion and by misrepresenting the actions, motives, and opinions of other men." (*The Rt. Hon. A. H. Layard and the Anti-Slavery Society*, London, 1877, pp. 9-10.)

Defending the Egyptian governor-general of the Sudan against accusations of the Anti-Slavery Society, the British consul-general in Egypt wrote in 1880: "If the Society is to wield the influence here which I desire to see it wield, it must show that it is animated by fairness as well as by zeal" [FO 84/1597/153-9, Malet to Granville, 2.4.81.]

However, some of the reports which reached the Society came from experienced people and were quite reliable. Both General Gordon and Sir Samuel Baker wrote to the Society several times and offered their own observations about slavery and the slave trade. In the present work, I used only the correspondents' reports and letters exchanged between the Society and the government; the minutes of the Society's committees and conventions are not relevant to the study of Ottoman slavery and slave trade. The archives are generally useful for an assessment of the Society's often exaggerated impact on British foreign policy regarding the Ottoman Empire.

(B) TRAVEL ACCOUNTS

Slavery and the slave trade—and particularly slave markets—attracted the travellers' attention and, too often, set their imagination in motion. Most travellers were denied access to harems and slave dealers' houses, where they could learn much about the subject. This, however, did not discourage them from trying to provide their readers with vivid descriptions of slavery in the East. Therefore, one should approach this type of literature with caution. Nevertheless, there were some important observers who spent long periods of time in the Empire, who knew the language and culture, and whose accounts should be taken seriously. For the purpose of this work, I relied mainly on White, Colomb, Blunt, Brown, Keane, and Kıbrıslı, though I have used a larger sample of travel accounts (listed in the "Selected Bibliography").

SELECTED BIBLIOGRAPHY

(A) Manuscript Sources:

(1) *Başbakanlık Arşivi*, Istanbul (BA):
    İrade Collection
    Bab-ı Asafi/Ayniyat
    Bab-ı Âli Evrak Odası
    Meclis-i Vükelâ Mazbata ve İrade Dosyaları
    Kepeci Collection
    Yıldız Collection

(2) Public Record Office, London:
    Foreign Office 84—Slave Trade (FO 84)
    Foreign Office 78—Turkey (FO 78)
    Foreign Office 195—Turkey, Consular (FO 195)

(3) Ministère des Affaires Étrangères, Paris (MAE):
    Correspondance Politique, Turquie (Corr. Pol. Turquie)
    Correspondance Consulaire, Turquie (Corr. Cons. Turquie)

(4) United States National Archives (USNA):
    Department of State—Despatches from U.S. Ministers to Turkey, 1818–1906 (M46)
    Despatches from U.S. Consuls to Tripoli, Libya, 1796–1885 (T40)

(5) Archives of the British and Foreign Anti-Slavery Society, Rhodes House, Oxford (BFASS/Mss. Brit. Emp.)

(6) African Collection, Rhodes House, Oxford: Mss. Afr. s. 1091/Box 1/Item 1, C. J. Barker, *Memorandums of a Route Overland from Ceylon to England, by Bombay and the Red Sea* (commenced in December 1822)

(7) British Museum (BM):
    BM/Add. Ms. 42565, Brant Papers
    BM/Add. Ms. 39028, Layard Papers
    BM/Add. Ms. 43138, Aberdeen Papers

BM/Add. Ms. 46094, Gladstone Papers

BM/Add. Ms. 39300, John Parsons, *Travels in Persia and Asiatic Turkey* (ca. 1874-1876)

(8) University of Istanbul Library (*İstanbul Üniversitesi Kütüphanesi*):

T 1972, *Ârifi Bey'in Cidde Vâli Kaymakamlığında bulunduğu zamana ait muhâberat-i resmiye mecmuası*

T 1075, *Ârifi Pasa'nın 1297'den 1307 tarihine kadar zaman-ı memuriyetine ait muhâberat-i resmiye mecmuası*

(B) PUBLISHED DOCUMENTS AND OFFICIAL CORRESPONDENCE:

Aristarchi, Gregoire. *Législation Ottomane*, vol. II (Istanbul, 1873) (Aristarchi)

Atmar, H. "Zenci ticaretinin yasaklanması," *Belgelerle Türk Tarih Dergisi*, 3 (1967), pp. 23-9

Cevdet, Ahmet. *Tezâkir* (Cavid Baysun, ed., Ankara, 1953-1967), 4 vols. (Cevdet, *Tezâkir*)

Düstûr, first edition, 5 vols. (Istanbul, 1289-1302) (*Düstûr*)

Great Britain. House of Commons. *Sessional Papers* (Accounts and Papers)

Hakkı, Abdürrahman. *Kavanin ve Nizamat Mecmuası* (Istanbul, 1312)

Hertslet, Edward. *A Complete Collection of the Treaties etc.* (Hertslet)

Tükay, "Esircilerle ilgili bir belge," *Belgelerle Türk Tarih Dergissi*, 11 (1968), p. 60

Young, George. *Corps de droit ottoman*, vol. II (Oxford, 1905), s.v.

(C) NEWSPAPERS:

Anti-Slavery Reporter (ASR)
Takvim-i Vekayı

(D) TRAVEL ACCOUNTS:

Albemarle, Earl of (Major George Keppel). *Narrative of a Journey Across the Balcan* (London, 1831)

Bell, James Stanislans. *Journal of a Residence in Circassia during the Years 1837, 1838 and 1839* (London, 1840), 2 vols.

Blunt, Lady Fanny Janet (A Consul's Daughter and Wife). *The People of Turkey* (London, 1878), 2 vols. (Blunt)

Boulden, James E. *An American among the Orientals* (Philadelphia, 1855)

Brown, Demetra. *Haremlik* (Boston and New York, 1909) (Brown)

Burton, Richard. *Personal Narrative of a Pilgrimage to al-Madinah and Meccah* (London, 1913; first edition 1855), 2 vols.

Colomb, Captain P. *Slave Catching in the Indian Ocean* (London, 1873) (Colomb)

Cosson, E. A. de. *The Cradle of the Blue Nile* (London, 1873), 2 vols.

Cox, Samuel S. *Diversions of a Diplomat in Turkey* (New York, 1887)

Davey, Richard. *The Sultan and His Subjects* (New York, 1897), 2 vols.

Davis, Rev. E. G. *Life in Asiatic Turkey* (London, 1879)

De Koy, James E. *Sketches of Turkey in 1831 and 1832* (New York, 1833)

Ellison, Grace. *An Englishwoman in a Turkish Harem* (London, 1915)

Ferriman, Z. Duckett. *Turkey and the Turks* (London, 1911)

Fontmagne, La Baronne Durand de. *Un séjour a l'Ambassade de France à Constantinople sous le second empire* (Paris, 1902)

Garnett, Lucy, M. J. *The Women of Turkey and their Folk-Lore* (London, 1891)

———. *Home Life in Turkey* (New York, 1909) [Published in London under the title *The People of Turkey*]

Grenville, Murray, E. C. *Les Turcs chez les Turcs* (Paris, 1878)

Keane, T. F. *Six Months in Mecca* (London, 1881) (Keane)

Longworth, J. A. *A Year Among the Circassians* (London, 1840) 2 vols. (Longworth)

Mac Farlane, Charles, *Turkey and its Destiny* (London, 1850), 2 vols. (Mac Farlane)

Marigny, Chev. Taitbont de. *Three Voyages in the Black Sea to the Coast of Circassia* (London, 1837)

Melek-Hanum Wife of H. H. Kıbrızlı Mehemet-Pasha. *Thirty Years in the Harem* (Berlin, 1872), 2 vols. (Kibrisli)

Oscanyan, C. *The Sultan and his People* (New York, 1857)

Pears, Sir Edwin. *Turkey and its People* (London, 1912)

Slade, Adolphus, *Records of Travels in Turkey, Greece, etc.* (London, 1854) (Slade)

Smith, Albert. *Customs and Habits of the Turks* (Boston, 1857)

Spencer, Edmond. *Travels in Circassia, Krım Tartary, etc.* (London, 1837), 2 vols.

Tugay, Emine Foat. *Three Centuries, Family Chronicles of Turkey and Egypt* (London, 1963)

White, Charles. *Three Years in Constantinople*, vols. II, III (London, 1845) (White)

(E) MODERN SCHOLARSHIP (BOOKS AND ARTICLES):

Abir, Mordechai. *Ethiopia: The Era of the Princes* (New York, 1968) (Abir)

Allen, W.E.D. and Muratoff, Paul. *Caucassian Battlefields* (Cambridge, 1853)

Altunsu, Abdülkadir. *Osmanlı Şeyhülislamları* (Ankara, 1972) (Altunsu)

Baer, G. *Studies in the Social History of Modern Egypt* (Chicago, 1969) (Baer)

————. *Egyptian Guilds in Modern Times* (Jerusalem 1964) (Baer, *Guilds*)

Beachey, R. W. *The Slave Trade of Eastern Africa* (New York, 1976)

Berkes, Niyazi. *The Development of Secularism in Turkey* (Montreal, 1964)

Brunschvig, R. "'Abd," *Encyclopedia of Islam*, New Edition (*EI²*) vol. I (Leiden, 1960), pp. 24 ff. (Brunschvig)

Cevdet, Ahmet, *Tarih* (Istanbul, 1301-1303), 12 vols. (Cevdet, *Tarih*)

Curtin, Phillip D. *The Atlantic Slave Trade—A Census* (Madison, 1969)

Çayci, Abdurrahman. *Büyük Sahra'da Türk-Fransız Rekabeti, 1858-1911* (Erzurum, 1970)

Danişmend, İ. H. *İzahlı Osmanlı tarihi kronolojisi*, vol. IV (Istanbul, 1955)

Davison, Roderic. *Reform in the Ottoman Empire 1856-76* (Princeton, 1963)

Doresse, Jean. *Histoire sommaire de la Corne Orientale de l'Afrique* (Paris, 1971)

Durukan, Zeynep M. *The Harem of the Topkapı Palace* (Istanbul, 1973) (Durukan)

Eren, Ahmet Cevat. *Türkiye'de göç ve göçmen meseleleri Tanzimat devri, ilk kurulan Göcmen Komisyonu, çıkarılan tüzükler* (Istanbul, 1966)

Fisher, Alan. "The Sale of Slaves in the Ottoman Empire: Markets and State Taxes on Slave Sales," *Boğaziçi Üniversitesi Dergisi*, vol. VI (1978), pp. 149-174 (Fisher)

Fisher, Allan G. B., and Humphrey J. *Slavery and Muslim Society in Africa* (London, 1970) (Fisher and Fisher)

Hill, R. *Egypt in the Sudan, 1820-81* (Oxford, 1959)

Holt, P. M. *Modern History of the Sudan* (London, 1963) (Holt, *Modern History*)

————. *The Mahdist State in the Sudan, 1881-1898* (Oxford, 1958) (Holt, *Mahdist State*)

Hurgronje, C. Snouck. *Mekka in the Latter Part of the Nineteenth Century* (London, 1931) (Snouck Hurgronje, *Mekka*)

İnalcık, Halil. "Čerkes," iii (Ottoman period), *EI²*, vol. II (Leiden, 1960), pp. 24-5.

Issawi, Charles, *The Economic History of the Middle East, 1800-1914* (Chicago, 1966) (Issawi, *Economic History*)

————. *The Economic History of Iran 1800-1914* (Chicago, 1971) (Issawi, *Iran*)

Kelly, J. B. *Britain and the Persian Gulf 1795-1880* (Oxford, 1968) (Kelly)

Kopytoff, I., and Miers, S. *Slavery in Africa* (Madison, 1977) (Kopytoff and Miers)

LeVeen, Phillip E. *British Slave Trade Suppression Policies, 1821-1865* (New York, 1977)

Lewis, Bernard. *The Emergence of Modern Turkey* (Oxford, 1968) (Lewis, *Emergence*)

Lewis, Bernard. *Race and Color in Islam* (New York, 1971) (Lewis, *Race and Color*)

Mardin, Şerif. *The Genesis of Young Ottoman Thought* (Princeton, 1962)

————. "Super Westernization in Urban Life in the Ottoman Empire in the Last Quarter of the Nineteenth Century," in Peter Benedict *et al.* (ed.), *Turkey, Geographic and Social Perspectives* (Leiden, 1974)

Marston, Thomas, *Britain's Imperial Role in the Red Sea Area, 1800-1875* (Hamden, Conn., 1961)

Midhat, Ahmet. "Esaret," *Letâif-i rivâyât*, vol. I (Istanbul, 1290), pp. 45-104.

Miers, Suzanne. *Britain and the Ending of the Slave Trade* (London, 1975) (Miers)

Millant, R. *L'ésclavage en Turquie* (Paris, 1912)

Nwulia, Moses D. E. *Britain and Slavery in East Africa* (Washington, D.C., 1912)

Ochsenwald, William. "Muslim European Conflict in the Hijaz: The Slave Trade Controversy, 1840-1859," *Middle Eastern Studies*, vol. 16, no. 1 (January, 1980), pp. 115-26 (Ochsenwald)

O'Fahey, R. S. "Slavery and the Slave Trader in Darfur," *Journal of African History*, vol. XIV (1973), pp. 29-43.

Orhonlu, Cengiz. "Osmanlı-Bornu münasebetine âid belgeler," *Tarih Dergisi*, 23 (1969), pp. 111-130.

Pakalın, M. Z. *Osmanlı tarih deyimleri ve terimleri sözlüğü* (Istanbul, 1946-1956), 5 vols. (Pakalın)

Pankhurst, R. "The Ethiopian Slave Trade in the Nineteenth and Early Twentieth Centuries: A Statistical Inquiry," *Journal of Semitic Studies*, vol. IX (1964), pp. 220-228

Penzer, Norman H. *The ḥarēm* (Philadelphia, 1937) (Penzer)

Pinson, Mark. "Ottoman Colonization of the Circassians in Rumili after the Crimean War," *Études Balkaniques* (Sofia), 1972 (3), pp. 71-85 (Pinson)

Shafîq, Aḥmad. *al-Riqq fî 'l-Islām* (trans. from French by Aḥmad Zakī, Cairo, 1892) (Shafîq)

Shaw, Stanford and Ezel Kural. *History of the Ottoman Empire and Modern Turkey* (Cambridge, 1976-1977), 2 vols. (Shaw, *History*)

Süreyya, Mehmet. *Sicill-i Osmanı* (Istanbul, 1308-1315), 4 vols.

Temperley, Howard. *British Antislavery 1833-1870* (London, 1972)

Uluçay, Çağatay. *Harem* (Ankara, 1971) (Uluçay)

Uzunçarsılı İ. H. *Mekke-i mükerreme emirleri* (Ankara, 1972) (Uzunçarsılı, *Mekke*)

———. *Osmanlı devletinin merkez ve bahriye teşkilatı* (Ankara, 1948)

———. *Osmanli devletinin saray teşkilati* (Ankara, 1945)

Vatikiotis, P. J. *The Modern History of Egypt* (London, 1969) (Vatikiotis)

Walz, Terrance. *Trade between Egypt and Bilād as-Sūdān 1700-1820* (Cairo, I.F.A.O., 1978) (Walz)

INDEX

(Prepared by Gabriel Peterberg)

This index should be used together with the detailed Table of Contents, pp. *vii-ix* above, for full coverage of subject matters. Some necessary definitions and explanations are provided in parentheses. Muslim names are alphabetized according to first name with cross–references, when needed.

Milton Keynes UK
Ingram Content Group UK Ltd.
UKHW030442211024
449933UK00006B/129